W0114963

Ethnic Life-Worlds in North-East India

Ethnic Life-Worlds in North-East India

An Analysis

PRASENJIT BISWAS
CHANDAN SUKLABAIDYA

SAGE Studies on India's North East

Los Angeles | London | New Delhi
Singapore | Washington DC | Melbourne

Copyright © Prasenjit Biswas and Chandan Suklabaidya, 2008

All rights reserved. No part of this book may be reproduced or utilized in any form or by any means, electronic or mechanical, including photocopying, recording or by any information storage or retrieval system, without permission in writing from the publisher.

First published in 2008 by

SAGE Publications India Pvt Ltd
B1/I-1 Mohan Cooperative Industrial Area
Mathura Road, New Delhi 110 044, India
www.sagepub.in

SAGE Publications Inc
2455 Teller Road
Thousand Oaks, California 91320, USA

SAGE Publications Ltd
1 Oliver's Yard, 55 City Road
London EC1Y 1SP, United Kingdom

SAGE Publications Asia-Pacific Pte Ltd
18 Cross Street #10-10/11/12
China Square Central
Singapore 048423

Published by Vivek Mehra for SAGE Publications India Pvt Ltd, typeset in 10.5/12.5 Times New Roman by Inosoft Systems, Delhi.

Library of Congress Cataloging-in-Publication Data

Biswas, Prasenjit 1969–
    Ethnic life-worlds in north-east India: an analysis/ Prasenjit Biswas, Chandan Suklabaidya.
        p. cm.
    Includes bibliographical references and index.
    1. Ethnology—India, Northeastern. 2. Community life—India, Northeastern. 3. Politics and culture—India, Northeastern. 4. Ethnic conflict—India, Northeastern. 5. India, Northeastern—Politics and government. 6. India, Northeastern—Ethnic relations. 7. India, Northeastern—Social conditions. I. Suklabaidya, Chandan, 1966– II. Title.

GN635.I4B593   305.800954'1—dc22   2007   2007045917

ISBN: 978-07-619-3613-8 (HB)

SAGE Team: Sugata Ghosh, Neha Kohli, Vijaya Ramachandran and Trinankur Banerjee

To
Father Rawlson, Alfred Schutz and Nations-From-Below
whose presence is emancipatory

Contents

Acknowledgements

In the course of writing this book, the work of which began in 1992, we were in the midst of the after-effects of our learning of anthropology and philosophy bringing back to our minds all our teachers at Dibrugarh University and North Eastern Hill University respectively. The major part of the work, in a sense, was completed in 1998 as we were able to collate the anthropological observations with our search for an alternative way of philosophizing, guided by a polyphonic insurgency of voices and meeting of critics of such insurgency from the state and the bureaucracy. We owe a lot to them. The course of writing such a book had a fusion of horizons that happened only after a lived experience of dialogue with a number of partners.

We have special words of thanks and appreciation for Sushila and Guddu, who are not only partners in the dialogue but who bind us in gratitude by caring for us in the midst of difficulty. We owe our thanks and gratitude to T. Mapu Jamir, Fr. Rawlson, Suma Trite, Pu Vanlalanghak and others whom we have met during the course of field-work and study, for an enriching experience and their unreserved hospitality of ideas.

Our friend Jishnu is an invaluable gift of ideas and information. A rich source of knowledge with an encyclopaediac knowledge of history, he showed us the way to reach quite a few conclusions pregnant with historical and political correctness.

Both of us owe an immeasurable debt to Ashok Acharya, B.S. Butola, M.M. Agrawal, N.B. Biswas, Sarat Chandra Sarma and others who contributed to our growth and enrichment of ideas.

The intellectual influence of Hiren Gohain and Mrinal Miri, in the course of our writing is far from being appropriated, rather we express our inability to comprehend and fully grapple with these figures of twentieth and twenty-first century North-East. We also owe special thanks to Sugata Ghosh and his team at SAGE India for their help, encouragement and initiatives. Especially, we thank Neha Kohli of SAGE for her editorial assistance without which the book would not have taken its present shape.

Both of us express our infinite debt to Sushi and Sukalpa, Guddu and Pushkin for their patience and tolerance of our esoteric enterprise of writing.

Preface

India's North-East or North-East's India—a coinage in terms of the peculiarity of the relationship between India and its North-East brings out the disjunction and the difference that pervades the balance of power and politics between the centre and its periphery Neither the question of belonging and non-belonging to each other, nor their existence as mere 'disjuncts' exudes any sense of contemporariness either in the context of India or in the territory of the 'North-East'. Contemporary social and cultural history of North-East India has marked a tense and contested terrain of political claims and counterclaims with all its cultural overtones. The claims of peoples belonging to the ethnic and cultural settings of the North-East, and a consequent national identity of their own, posited against the Indian national identity has generated considerable debate and controversy among scholars, intellectuals, social activists and others. There is quite a bit of indecisiveness in finally settling claims of specific ethnic and cultural identities that defy the dominant logic of identity, as propounded by the Indian State. The dominant logic is that of construction of an identity that consents to an inclusion within the Indian national identity and thereby lives in agreement with the territorial and constitutional authority of the Indian State. Most of the identities in India's North-East assume a space of difference for realization of their own aspirations, cultural and political, with all other economic and social ramifications.

The phenomenal rise and growth of various identities in North-East India presents a picture of the possibilities of multiple emergences of identities with many distinct claims. However, the Indian State uses its ideological and repressive organs to simultaneously persuade these identities to join the Indian mainstream and coerce them into submission. In response to such a two-pronged strategy of the Indian State, various identities reciprocate to the persuasion of the former in terms of insurgency and resistance with their strategic alliances with the state. In response to repressive organs of the state, identities from North-East India bring up their own insurgent groups; and such groups take the lead voicing the identity concerns of their respective ethnic communities. As insurgent groups take the decisions of resistance away from the domain of the public, the gulf between insurgence and its popular support widens. There is also no gainsaying the fact that various people's organizations, comprising of civil society members, have also joined the ideological struggle to protect human rights and democratic decision-making procedures in the course of this struggle, in order to stave the monopoly of insurgents. The latter also responded to such initiatives in a politically appropriate manner.

Insurgents and civil society organizations, on the one hand, and and the state comprising of the army, police and other governmental organs, on the other, clash over issues such as citizenship, sovereignty, ethnic and cultural identity and human rights, including the right to development. In all such matters it is not the strength of the group alone which legitimizes and rationalizes, rather a stronger undercurrent of concerns with respect to rights, democracy and security determines the shape of the struggle between the two sides. But such processes of determination often take forms of self-determination and constitutional determinism, thereby bring the open-ended struggles for rights to some kind of resolution.

The book asks a deeper question: how is cultural politics a determinant of ethnic- and identity-oriented struggles as it happens in the North-East? At a particular level, this book examines the instances of life-world moorings and their reflections in constructions of the ideas of nation-state and self-identity. It argues that life-world norms are subordinated to official discourses of anthropology by the state, be it the colonial or post-colonial Indian State, thereby reverting to a subtle discourse of colonial domination. Ethnic insurgencies respond to such colonial discourses by a complex reworking of the history of self-determination, which statist discourses cannot appropriate. In doing so, they give rise to counter-discourses that remains a constant worry for the Indian State in its goal of achieving legitimacy and development in the North-East region. Civil society organizations join issues in terms of hegemony of the state and ruling classes, and its formation at the local and regional levels. As a matter of affirmation of their specific point of view, civil society organizations seek to establish the significance of voicing concerns that affect a specific community and society without being oblivious of larger issues at the national and global level. They simultaneously perform the role of crusader as well as vigilante in matters of conflict and concern between state, insurgency and civil society. While both the state and the insurgent groups carve out their distinct ideological and political agenda, the civil society organizations only require an agenda of empowerment, as opposed to voicelessness, dispossession and disempowerment. In a sense, civil society organizations represent those aspects of culture and ethnicity that are unaddressed in the course of struggle against hegemony and, therefore, allow a free space of articulation of issues of empowerment, by mobilizing key resources of the community. The community operates at the level of articulation, while at the level of struggle it is only an opposition between the state and the community that propels the struggle. Therefore, unwittingly, such struggles against the state gets diverted into a struggle for political and cultural recognition by the state. The engagement in the struggle between the state and non-state actors stipulates the place of an enemy within the struggle, which necessarily comes from the supposed breaches in the relationship with other communities resulting into inter-ethnic and inter-community clashes. It is at this moment of diversion from state to others that such struggles lose the strength of self-determination and fall into the trappings of constitutional determinism.

The key issues involved in two major ongoing struggles—(United Liberation Front of Assam and National Socialist Council of Nagaland, Isak-Muivah) in North-East India are that of sovereign homeland and internal colonization. Both these issues generate a severe conflict and clash with not only the Indian State but also with other sections of people. But the appeal of both the movements lies in their critique of the Indian State and the parliamentary politics of justification for the role of the state. Although the capability of any such insurgent outfit in creating a separate homeland is doubted, their uncompromising struggle for it generates a kind of enthusiasm among the people to fight harder for rights and justice, be it within the Indian union or outside. The strategy of mobilization of this support often meets with severe crackdown by the state nevertheless the struggle goes on, citing instances of excesses done by the state. In effect, counter-insurgency operations by the state help sustain popular critique of the Indian State by the insurgents and develop waves of sympathy for militant outfits. This is a way of using the acts of the state in support of ethnic insurgency. In fact, it is a discursive strategy in garnering support towards insurgencies and the success of the strategy can be understood from how insurgent outfits withstand the onslaught of the state.

Recent happenings in North-East India could be a good point of discussion in our understanding of the situation there. The movement against imposition of Armed Forces Special Powers Act in Manipur, which is led by *Apunba Lup*, the apex body of 27 social organizations of Meitei community, brought out the complex relationship between state, insurgency, human rights and civil society. The demand for withdrawal of the Act is met with resistance from the army engaged in counter-insurgency, while insurgents and civil society groups critique the act for its arbitrary extra-judicial character. Indeed the truth does not lie either with the state or with the other side. The fact of repression of struggles, armed or unarmed, which goes with the domination of the ruling classes, retains its validity amidst such a contentious battle of ideas. What is put to severe test here is the concern for security and a healthy social life as part of a democratic political and moral order, for which both the state and the struggling groups acts as contingent players; and in a sense it is the autonomy of 'good life' in an Aristotlean sense, independent of state and insurgency, that poses a high stake for the political state and the civil society. The fear of losing the very idea of good, which is greater than the cause of the state or insurgency, is what raises the value of democratic self-governance, part of which could be recuperated in a relationship of responsibility, which lies away from insurgency and counter-insurgency. What Apunba Lup, as a civil society body is engaged in, is this reclamation of the right and the good, in its forced entry into a sphere of battle over human rights, legality and constitutional propriety. Nothing could be more neutral, and at the same time, more engaged than a voice like Apunba Lup, which is neither on the side of the insurgents nor on the side of the state, but, which voices the larger common good. Will the parties in conflict pay heed to its voice?

There is a kind of self-pity that emerges at this point. If the Indian State goes ahead with its counter-insurgency and counter-terrorism operations, and if the insurgents carry forward their struggle for sovereign, independent North-East India, how would the people of the region poise themselves? In fact it is a pity that the voices of the silent majority fall on deaf ears and there is a constant erosion of democratic sensibility and commitment to the larger good. Nothing seems to find its rightful place beyond a cause, even if the cause involves the interests of the silent majority. The practice of political and moral majoritarianism, in the drive for legitimacy for social and political action, leading the actors astray to a point of irreconcilable justification for one's own acts, often derives from a counterfactual response to the act of the other. This is an inversion of the moral sense of the self, into a politics of morality that prioritizes the act of the other, in order to overcome one's errors, make-beliefs and dogmas. Insurgency in North-East India has got diverted to this abyss of moral vacuum, in which it emerges only as a respondent of the state and vice-versa, in an uncanny silence about the larger common good.

Given this self-pity and self-criticism, there is a move from larger globalization oriented bodies to take away the burden of critique by the civil society groups *to* some global agenda of removing the borders and trading across the transnational routes.

The apparent challenge to the nation-state by the insurgents is bypassed by these sets of global actors, who, in the name of advancing development and bringing in a global regime of Capital, are now trying to make deep inroads into the ethnically protected and community-owned cultural and natural resource base of the region. The state is becoming party to such propaganda of liberalization of the frontiers and boundaries, beyond the reaches of civil society. Insurgents in their trigger-happy mood are also kowtowing to the idea that the state will lose its sovereign territory, and would possibly wither away in the winds of global market and liberal trade regimes, with the North-East having a taste of free cash, possibly dollars, and luxury goods from East Asia. Both the state and insurgents are jubilant about the cash value of such an idea of removing frontiers and boundaries, and coeval with such dissolution, the rigidly fought barriers of identity and ethnic boundaries shall give way to integration to a larger global community. This is the other face of bypassing the larger common good that organizations like Apunba Lup, Naga Mothers Association, various human rights groups and other civil society bodies are trying to stand up to. It is in this context, one also needs to look at the indigenous debates surrounding matriliny, and its proposed changeover to patriarchy, a distinct possibility that goes into a struggle for redefining identities in North-East. In a much deeper vein than 'Vandemataram', the unrecognized ethnography of matrilineal societies of North-East needs to be pondered over, to really sing the ode to the mother!

The book, in its seven chapters, attempts to knit together this kaleidoscopic land, the culture and human scapes of North-East India. While doing so, the book keeps in view the importance of imaging an inside of thinking and imagination, as against an outside of struggle against the state and hegemony. The bigger picture that the book tries to draw is a 'phenomenological representation' of the North-East Indian articulation against the hegemony of power and self, while the smaller picture that it draws focuses on logic(s) of practice as it obtains in the life-world. The availability of life-world actors makes it also possible to articulate a counterhegemonic ensemble of difference, marginality and dominance in the book. The book further tries to widen the philosophical and political imagination of communities of North-East India, by way of locating a subaltern position of imagination, that of the nation-from-below. Whether such a construction extends the scope of understanding the struggles of various identities, not merely in terms of self-determination but in terms of discursive self-articulation, is an open question that the reader can delve into. The authors refrain from taking sides and discuss issues of increasing relevance to the North-East as well as to India.

November, 2006   **Prasenjit Biswas**
                                                           Chandan Suklabaidya

1

Reconceptualizing an Ethnic Life-World

North-East India, comprising of the seven sister states, presents a wide diversity of almost 400 tribal, ethnic and non-ethnic communities, with their distinct culture, language and economy. Social formations in this part of the country are marked by pre-colonial, colonial and post-colonial transformations. One interesting area of transition is from the pre-colonial royal legitimation to the colonial production of division of cultural and economic labour, to the post-colonial distinctiveness of being 'such and such' in terms of self-definition. Such transitions are grafted on the institutional mechanism of reproduction of imagination of the collective self in the narratives bridging the past and the present. The most significant effect of an already existing specificity came in the two-fold policy orientation towards India's North-East in the continuity between the colonial and the post-colonial: leaving the tribes to adapt to the emergent order without any interference and the practice of a kind of neutrality by the state. Following this, the British for the first time introduced the Inner Line Regulation (restricting the entry of outsiders) and created excluded and partially excluded areas in various states of the region. The purpose of such segmentalism was to allow the tribes to grow in their own style without much outside interference. In time, it has resulted in a form of exclusivism, while at the same time, it also strengthened the cultural and economic bases of these societies.

If one looks into the environmental and cultural niches that traditionally sustained the livelihood practices of the various tribes of the region, one would encounter a conflict between nature and culture. While ethnographers and anthropologists have emphasized on the preservation of ethnic and natural styles of living, politicians and planners have asked for larger public investments. There were clear divergences of goals: whether to pursue the path of model institutional development or strengthen the resource bases of the communities became an either-or question. As the choice of development was not left to the people themselves, but was delivered by the statist and market agencies, it has led to a dichotomy between choice and outcome. The whole region promises to hold indigenous ways of development that are somehow scuttled, and an exogenous model of development came in force. As the resource base of the North-East was gradually weaned away, it produced a displacement of communities from their life-world; at the same time, the introduction of various other ways of life could not involve a sustainable process of balanced growth.

CONCEPTUALIZING THE LIFE-WORLD

The life-world, as a bedrock of any society, presents and preserves a set of values and norms that are self-evidently real. Before anything could be known of such a society, there are unexamined grounds of this reality (Schutz, 1989: 55). This is not only a description of the foundational structure in which a human being is rooted, but this is what constitutes the common, communicative and surrounding world. Is such a foundational structure available in the construction of an ethnic identity? How do we get to know such a foundational structure? We cannot succeed in making sense of an ethnic identity through a process of construction and imposition of an ontological framework. Are we then going to construe a 'possible ontology' by which we mean nothing more than the stipulation of a world made of certain characteristics, the reality of which can be related to the world inhabited by the ethnic identity? Donald Davidson (1984: 227–41) suggests that the determination of ontology does not take place in the world or in concepts or in the interpretation of the identity. David Lewis distinguishes between 'the way[s] the things could have been' and the 'way[s] the things are' with its obvious pointer that the 'ways' are inexhaustibly different and multiple, refusing to be conceptualized within an ontology (Lewis, 1973: 84). Thus, for Davidson and Lewis, the original problem of knowing the 'foundational structure' of an 'ethnic identity' boils down to constructing possible worlds of theory and interpretation.

The interpretations given to the concept of 'life-world' in Schutz, and later in Thomas Luckmann's phenomenological elucidation, termed it primarily as the repository bedrock of knowledge, of the world that includes self-knowledge (see Berger and Luckman, 1966: 70–84). Further, an individuated subject vested with consciousness of the world experiences the world because of a 'universal correlational' a priori of 'I and World' that gives rise to a 'background', which can be conceptualized as a surrounding world, consisting of objective, subjective and social, in the way Habermas (1987) had extended the concept. An 'ontology' calls for a distinction between the 'world' and the identity. The key question becomes, 'is the world itself a being (an identity) like multifarious beings (identities) in the world?' This reconception of 'life-world' as a possible way of world-making and making of possible worlds illuminates the social discourses of identity.

The Cartesian-instrumental idea of development that derives its objective value from reducing the 'observed subject' into a separable, quantifiable and disjointed means for attaining certain rational ends cannot really take into account the non-measurable, invisible and subjective aspects of historically and culturally embedded multitudes of North-East India, specified by their sense of place and belonging. They further give rise to praxis of holistic notion, of human–nature relationship that is irreducible in its wisdom, which remains as an unheard voice in a modern and postmodern nation space of India. Colonial and post-colonial nation-states have simply bypassed these stateless societies from the processes of cultural and political recognition, although they have been made a part of the constitutional and institutional framework of India. Their recognition in terms of scheduled tribes, with attendant cultural and political rights, has certainly made them a part of the system, but not with a sense of belonging. At an anthropological and epistemological plane, the culturally embedded practices of the tribal life-world are still 'un-appropriable' in many ways—in terms of dresses, attires, languages, music and spiritual values, to name a few. Therefore, the question of tribal, ethnic and national identity, with all its attendant political, economic and cultural claims, has remained an unresolved paradox for the mainstream developmental model, adopted throughout the country. The important question is, in what ways can the mainstream models of economic development in terms of liberalization–globalization be adopted in the context of North-East India? Inversely, in what ways can the dominant paradigm of development be enriched by tribal and ethnic specificities of North-East India? This question brings out the mutuality of the developmental processes that has to make a beginning in the life-world itself.

Keeping this perspective in mind, how the value of a complete identification between human-nature-culture as it prevails in the North-East can be accommodated/altered within the instrumental value of human-human, human-nature relationship that dominant models of development construe? An answer is the possibility of sharing of the life-world values between what is known as a culturally-constructed India and the area called 'North-East'. Given the current emphasis on indigenous knowledge systems and rights over intellectual and cultural property with a renewed sense of economic and social justice, a paradigm of recognition and redis-tribution can mitigate the problem of what is being construed out of this region. This makes us look at the very structure of identity claims that emanate from the region.

Producing a Subject

The divergence between an individuated subject and a collective subject arises in such a way that it problematizes the talk about collective subject types, such as ethnic identities. It is the particular mode of politics that arbitrarily determines the process of self-identification of the subject, without any 'universalizable' ways of producing a subject.[1] For example, in the context of North-East India, the description 'North-East' sets up the faultline of our nation-building exercise, in terms of a strategy of exclusion/ inclusion. Such a description is also a representation of the world that is made within the lived frame of social life. Treated as an excluded or partially excluded and scheduled area, the idea of the North-East emerged as a resistance to both exclusion and inclusion. As India's own North-East, it resists exclusion; while as the 'North-East' it resists inclusion in the mainstream pan-national identity. Indeed, it only is connected with the rest of India through a chicken neck between Bhutan, Nepal and North Bengal. So, the production of North-East as the subject resists universality and at the same time it suggests only a particular way of world-making.

There are various possibilities of making the world lie in the semantic representation of a possible world that generates a string of identities. One example of such 'possible worlds' is imagining very briefly the situation in which people live in certain cultural locations, without any deep commitment to it; 'but what matters is their mastery of and acceptability in a culture', something like sharing some characteristics of the world in which they live (Goodman, 1978). The notion of a 'possible world' is important in order to describe the making of an 'identity', in terms of certain determinate designations of characteristics; the presence of these characteristics gives rise to an identity. The furniture of such identities is culturally and contextually constructed by certain social and historical forces. This kind of construction is mediated in language[2] (see Caroll and Whorf, 1964: 36–38), and such expressions are 'artifactual'[3] (see Goodman and Elgin, 1998). Moreover, such language-conferred construction of identity presents itself as a self-subsistent entity with a shared background, which keeps on transmuting itself by some articulated features that ensure the continuance of such an identity.[4] Every time the identity expresses itself, it articulates itself using resources drawn from its specific location. This mode of representation through articulation often gets entwined with concrete interests, and hence the identity becomes a specific social construct with a particular mode of representation.

An attempt to reduce the 'identity' in terms of some characteristics does not capture its entire potential. Even if concrete interests can be enumerated from the representation of an identity, the fact that it has been articulated cannot be reduced to those interests alone (Mrinal Miri, 2003: 62–63). The mode of articulation may as well be categorized, but the task of finding the agency that is involved in the making of the identity remains elusive[5] (see also Williams, 1990). The 'agency' performs several roles: artifactual construction of an ontology, identification, assertion and so on, which creates an identity that can ultimately distinguish itself from others. It performs and manifests itself in different ways; such acts always leave open possibilities of assuming roles in an uncharted terrain, so that the identity is never 'disarticulated' and never completely determined by certain limited roles.[6]

Let us take a contrasting look at the 'realistic' understanding of an identity, in terms of positive and normative necessities, and contingencies of social life that make it just a 'subject of power'.[7] In a way, this can be termed as 'repression of the social' under the imposing network of power.[8] Within such an imposing network of power, the monologue of describing identities as an articulation for rights and opportunities alienates the 'social' character of such identities by disposing off their own world, the specific artifactual elements of their make.[9] The identities are given some negative description, articulating some 'lack' without any 'positive' interior such that the reductionist realism does not stop short of fracturing the positive interior of an identity.[10]

The positive interior of an identity is not only its 'agency' role, but also its narrative potential; through which it does things such as symbolic invocation of social and material relations, and asserts definite positions within those relations. To understand how those definite positions are taken, a few specific cases could be discussed here. In the context of North-East India, the distinction between 'good' and 'evil' is drawn in terms of human qualities, such as righteousness and protection of life. 'Good' is symbolized in terms of such values embodied in human characters. Bad omens and destructive activities are symbolically invoked and attributed to evil. For example, in Khasi culture, *U Blei* becomes symbolic of the righteous, the clean and the good; *U Thlen* gets identified with the unclean, the dangerous and the *sang* (crime/sin) (Sujata Miri, 1998: 28).

Khasis and Centred Subjectivity

Clifford Geertz has commented, in the context of Javanese culture, on the nature of a prudent, wise man who tries to adapt a 'tranquil detachment which frees him for his endless oscillation between gratification and frustration' (1973: Chapter 5). Similarly, in the Khasi context, one can locate a 'tranquil detachment' arising as an effect of equilibrating correspondence between good and evil. 'Good' or 'evil' cannot be radically separated from each other in the psyche of an individual, and so the desired state of tranquility can come by exercising a kind of self-control in everyday life. The Khasi, therefore, creates a 'centred subjectivity' in the moorings of his/her self and never resorts to practices that would wean it out. This aspect of Khasi subjectivity empowers the Khasis to exercise their agency in a specific way to avoid pitfalls of life. This could be seen in the example of nature playing a generic role in Khasi imagination, as they fondly call it 'mother nature'—in their dialect, *Ka meirilung risan*—while the moral order of Khasi life is preserved in *phawars,* or self-regulated stories and norms. Both nature and tales of self-regulation create a 'centered subjectivity' and it is made possible by embedding the word or meanings in various layers of Khasi life.

Consequently, by being cautious about some evil effects, the Khasis pursue the path of good, which takes them to an 'emergent' consciousness of 'identity', in which they describe themselves as the bearers of the spiritual law of *Ka Hok*, meaning 'righteousness'. Identity is constructed through mobilization of one's imagination against the evil, symbolically expressed in terms of what is considered as a bad omen or happening. This sense of 'righteousness' combines the construction of 'nature' and 'culture' with an underlying principle of transference between them. Khasi scholar Morning Lyngdoh explains Ka Hok in its interrelatedness with *Ka Rngiew*—a kind of power bestowed upon man by God—both acting as 'complementary' to each other[11] (Lyngdoh, 1991). The principle of transference goes like this: righteousness is not a given and humans earn it by making use of the god given 'power' of Ka Rngiew within them.[12] Ka Rngiew, the concept of the capacity or power, manifests itself in action, and if the action is 'good', in the sense of not falling into the trap of doing something 'evil' (such as endogamy in Khasi culture), then the person earns Ka Hok. Ka Rngiew remains as a variable power that depends upon whether a person is morally good, and the degree of her goodness determines the strength of Ka Rngiew in her. In other words, Ka Rngiew marks what is imbibed in human nature in the form of an intrinsic spirit; a spirit that is essentially constitutive of the human being and what is good about that human in an intrinsic sense. This is a kind of faculty that not only operates in ordinary human acts, but also in actions that determine the strength of Ka Rngiew in human beings. The circularity of the two concepts, Ka Hok and Ka Rngiew, portrays a fully explored Khasi understanding of 'virtue', while at the same time presenting the lack of a clear borderline between 'nature' and 'culture'. According to Khasi beliefs, Ka Hok is both a cosmic and moral law of order and harmony, with an effect of synthesizing the two in God's scheme of things. There is an indication of synchrony between Ka Rngiew and Ka Hok through which a balanced and good human nature is created.

Therefore, one can see the operation of a sense of 'autonomy' in the Khasi attitude towards morality that harps on being sensitive about what one is doing[13] (Sujata Miri, 1998: 48). Moreover, the creation of a 'self' is also linked with the realization of the conscious capacity of human beings. The creation of the 'self' blends the 'moral law', faculties of the self, and determination of good and evil by a cosmic law. Therefore, the creation of the self does not act upon humans as mere knowledge of what is good and what is not, but can undertake the interpretation of an act through a creative application of laws and principles conceived in the belief of a cosmic order. One can also get a sense of being-in-the-world as a 'human in history'. In the construction of Khasi morality, the 'self' emerges through self-conscious realization of thoughts and deeds that converge into the horizon of Khasi identity.

The horizon of Khasi identity involves the backdrop of the pre-interpreted life-world, but what it envelopes is the construction of the self-identity that draws its resources from the 'world', figured in the interpretative discourse of the community. The move from the pre-interpreted sphere of meaning available in the life-world to the interpreted discourse of meaning and relevance creates various modes of self-construction and self-understanding that go into the making of the world of the Khasis. But this move is not limited within the closure of their life-world as it produces a variety of meanings by the invocation of a 'life-world' concept.[14] For example, the notion of U Blei, as the 'reality of meaning', creates an already present backdrop of the Khasi 'world-view' that operates as the law, the 'given' of meaning (Sujata Miri, 1998: 25). This clearly indicates the possibility of the expression of a variety of meanings that gives rise to a 'world' of possible meaning entities. What is essential here is to draw the distinguishing markers between: (*i*) pre-interpreted meanings; (*ii*) meanings created from the foundational reality of meanings; and (*iii*) meanings derived by application of laws and rules of meaning. For example, one should look for a way to distinguish between the pre-interpreted meaning of Ka Rngiew and the determination of the degree of its presence in a human. The conceptual interpretation of 'Rngiew' in terms of 'self experience of humans in history', takes a foundational route, while U Thlen devouring Ka Rngiew[15] unfolds 'meanings' at an applied level of human experience. While Ka Rngiew remains a pre-interpreted meaning, known as an intrinsic power of the human self, the way it manifests in concrete corporeal and embodied human beings bears a foundational relation with the human being in the world. As an applied concept, it further becomes a functional entity, in terms of the possibility of an alimentary relationship, as U Thlen may devour Ka Rngiew, marking the weakness of the self or its capacity to overcome the evil powers of Thlen. These multiple possibilities of meaning open up the interpretive–discursive realm of meanings that go beyond the pre-interpreted horizon of the life-world and transgresses the limits of the contexts embedded within the horizon. So far as the act of evaluating the nature of an action is performed in terms of 'good' or 'evil' guided by the principle of Ka Hok, these 'values' arise out of the sheer artifactuality of the principle that privileges a particular application of those notions. There is a simultaneous possibility of experiencing mutually-antinomic 'values', given the reality of both 'good' and 'evil'. But the interaction between the person, society and culture creates a particular possibility of 'actually' experienced meaning, and this possibility creates the 'world' for Khasis. Giving a Lewisian twist to such possibilities, one can say that the concepts like Ka Rngiew and Ka Hok operate in an interrelationship that creates the 'possible worlds' for the Khasis. Once again a Davidsonian understanding of such meanings would harp on the capacity of encoding the elements of being a Khasi as 'anchorage points' that hold between the world and the life-world of Khasis. For example, concepts like Ka Rngiew and Ka Hok provide anchorage points to hold the inner potentialities of humans as manifested in their action. In Davidsonian metaphor, one can say that nobody could be 'bolted' to the world of the Khasis without the triangulating markers of concepts such as Ka Rngiew and Ka Hok. Such triangulation assures a 'bond' that loosens up the interrelated concepts by positing such concepts within the 'world' of a culture—here within the world of Khasi culture. In a similar vein, one can also see how the process of 'identification' takes place by interpolation of concrete individuals within such a world.

Apatanis and Life-Cycle Rituals

Symbolic performances link individuals. One very common, popular and universal celebration is the performance of the life-cycle rituals among the Apatanis of Arunachal Pradesh. The relationship between parents and their married daughter is symbolically reproduced in the former's wishes of well-being for the latter. The ritual is held to ensure the realization of the parental wish that their daughter has children after marriage. Apatani scholar Takhe Kani explains:

> The people do not appreciate and respect the wealth and status of the spouse in this society unless the couple has children....Thus barren parents died with a sad ballad, 'Oh! why they don't give us at least a son or daughter to have our wealth and status'(1996: 43).

What is framed here is the ethics of birth that determine the provisions of care and well-being. It further highlights the reflexive agency of parenthood that wishes an institutional realization of childbirth, which, put in the negative, represents an emotional and material marker of wealth and status. The ritual for the purpose of ensuring the birth of children is called *Mida,* which is not only a symbolic exchange of gifts but also a marker of the continuation of the generation. Mida functions to sustain marital relationships and to prevent aberrations. It acts like a normative custom that ensures thwarting of all uncertainties that can crop up in a marital relationship. For example, Mida is performed in the cases of aberrations such as divorce, or the lack of a male child; it is resorted to when there is a challenge to the marital relationship. It reveals both a sense of serious desire to see something fulfilled as well as a jocular response to the need of ensuring the attainment of something that is necessary through its performance, which reflects the swing of such moods and temperaments, the rise and fall of which are related to situations in life.

Mida serves the purpose of bringing together the parents of the bride and the groom as a higher-order 'social intervention', which takes the presence of almost the entire clan and kinship ties into its ambit. Such holistic involvement is described by Takhe Kani (1996: 43) in the case of *datti Mida*, an elaborate ritual that requires the exchange of gifts such as a full grown Mithun ox given from the groom's family. The bride's family may not reciprocate immediately, but pays back as it suits them, when they desire to organize a Mida in order to celebrate the union. Mida coordinates several functions simultaneously—exchange of gifts, bargain between two sides, among others—all of which implicitly relate to larger societal arrangements. It reproduces the norms and rules that bind society and gives it a particular orientation.

The worship of the deity *Murung*, gives the name for a ritual that is celebrated to ensure the well-being of an individual. Takhe Kani quotes an Apatani proverb: '*Gyunyang tiggo mi ralyang mako da miyu sanko nyima*'—there is no way we can live without performing religious rites and ceremonies (Ibid.: 56). This proverb points to the evocation of lived experience, as also to a historic context. Murung bears the palimpsest of the moment of origin, which invokes a series of reversals as the Lacanian 'Real', the signs of danger that prompt its invocation. One should give a full-blooded representation of such signs resulting from certain unexpected happenings. Takhe Kani (Ibid.: 58) catalogues such 'real' signs:

(*i*)   When a couple is childless after many years of their marriage.

(*ii*) When a man has no sons, or a child is mentally or physically handicapped at birth.

(*iii*)   When a man's domestic fowls and animals are handicapped at birth.

(*iv*)   When bees, snakes or other strange insects and reptiles enter the house or granary.

(*v*)   When mushrooms grow in the hearth or in the hind of a pig.

(*vi*)   When any family member is sick for a long period of time and cannot be cured through other ceremonies.

(*vii*)   When a man has dreams of a banana tree or mushroom growing at the house and granary sites.

(*viii*)   When there are enough mature mithun and oxen.

The people believe that the reasons enumerated from (*i*) to (*viii*) above have sent a message to *Gyutii Gigro Wuhi,* the spirit-god, who has already entered the house of the performer of the ceremony. The reading of signs charted out as preconditions of the presence of Murung at someone's house bears both positive and negative characteristics. The catalogue consists of obvious natural events that perplex and yet are not wholly ominous, but rather are something of a mixture. There is ambivalence between apprehension and hope borne out of these events, which seeks its symbolic resolution in the invocation of various Murung gods. As we had already noted, the creation of a centred subjectivity in the Khasi making of the world is quite different from that of the Apatani ritual of Murung. It is a sense of 'lack' that places the Murung deity in the aporias of personal and community history. At some level, there is an entwinement of the personal and the natural, mental states and events, meanings and ritual framing of these meanings, to display a pattern of intermingling between personal and social. The text of Murung remains in an uncanonized form, in which the ritual performance does not bring about already anticipated results; rather it enacts a process of creation and sets up an ecological context. The context is symbolized in the form of judging a set of evidences that are not warranted in the animals, plants and human beings, that together constitute an ecological relationship.

The functional significance of Murung can be traced by reading of the omen by priests in determining the nature and timing of its celebration. The reading of an omen and deciding whether it is favourable or unfavourable establishes a sacral and ritual rule which then can be applied to the human–nature interface. Murung, and its particular type, delimits the physical and symbolic space carved out of the human–nature interface in the rituals, such as the splitting of wood and the taming of the Mithun ox. The physical space is 'delimited' by several performances in spaces within and without. The large amount of firewood necessary for the month-long celebration requires a mode of gathering and collection in which the wood is ritually carried from the grove to the domestic sphere, and Mithuns are also caught from the forest for sacrificial rites. The sense of offence associated with the cutting of wood and the capture of the Mithun is compensated by oblations through hymns and chants that induce a sense of loss. Takhe Kani quotes such a chant recited by the priests: 'O Gods of trees, groves and other Gods of nature, don't harm us for the felling of these trees for this ceremony!'(1996: 57).

What is even more striking, is the 'ritual' associated with taming of the Mithun ox. The observation of the omen, the selection of the ox by a process of 'naming' and then dedicating it to a particular 'Lapang-God' are parts of the ritual of sacrifice. The taming of the ox is, in the first place, a process of domestication that requires the animal to grow to maturity. The process of domestication is fulfilled only when the Mithun lives almost its whole lifespan at the home of the solemnizer, signifying a sense of fulfilment of its own life, as well as that of its 'master'. It is only then that its master qualifies to sacrifice it at the altar of God. Therefore, one sees that the operation of a symbolic law of fulfilment does not allow an infringement on life, and the performance of sacrifice of a fulfilled life ensures the satisfaction of the Gods. In addition, the rite of sacrifice brings in the notion of being 'saved' in various forms. Through such 'forms' of gods and sacred deities, the ritual of Murung secures the well-being of the solemnizer. *Murung Bussi*, a 'text' of the performance, expresses the fulfilment of nature and man, as can be gathered from a song by Takhe Kani:

In this year, we heard that the solemnizers have got plentiful and gracious woods, leaves, cane, rice, rice beer and meat to appease men and deities through this ceremony…In this evening, you invite us into your house to have this gracious meal and beer just as a delicious fruit tree invites birds and a deep river invites fish, and our team is coming into the house like a joyful flock of bird[s] and fish (Ibid.: 88).

This song is an expression of 'deep ecology' involved in the celebration of Murung. The metonymic effect of the song in comparing the solemnizer's gracious offerings, with the sheltering of birds and fishes in trees and in the river comes full circle, when it devolves into how beautifully the guests are entertained by the solemnizers. There is a simultaneous spirit of joy that overcomes the physical and symbolic limits, constituted by Murung norms, to touch the whole of nature. Such expressions of collective participation in the celebration of a common practice of hunting and cultivation are stretched to the extent of recreating the familiar. The only distance that is maintained comes through the belief of the presence of some deities, who are ingrained in the imagination of the solemnizers.

A sense of location and direction also becomes a part of the imagination of Murung, especially in the distribution of meat. The meat is distributed by 'betrothal friends' (Kani, 1996: 94–95) of the solemnizer, signifying not only sharing, but also the socialization of the betrothal. The meat is carried round through the Apatani villages, in a clockwise or anti-clockwise direction, and is welcomed with respect. Thus, the various forms of Murung are associated with agricultural and food-gathering activities. The Apatani concept of nature is one in which nature is recreated through ritual performances in a sequence, thus turning nature into a force of shared communication and participation.

Domesticity among the Ao Nagas

J.P. Mills' (1926) extraordinarily supple description of Ao Naga culture provides a textual entry into the symbolic realm of the Ao Naga mind. The 'text' needs to be reconfigured and re-read by establishing the intricate links in its surface representation. The spheres of Ao Naga life are demarcated from the given configuration of the text, and one could try to separate the 'private' and the 'public' spheres of Ao Naga life even though such markers are not readily available (Mills, 1926: 71–161). What Mills names as 'domestic' could possibly provide a basis for wider arenas of life, by streamlining the values, practices and habits of the domestic sphere. Conversely, the domestic sphere can become a sustainable ground for continuance of the practices in 'public' life. Even without strictly demarcated spheres of the 'private' and 'public', Mills' preferred coinages such as domestic and other spheres arranged the text in such a manner that it envelopes distinct spheres of life. We propose a reading of the Ao Naga domestic realm, as described by Mills, in order to experience the sphere of domesticity as the microcosm of intricate linkages of various symbols which also sustain practices in wider spheres, thus giving rise to their specific domesticity. What constitutes the sphere of domestic in the Ao Naga life? We designate two levels: (*i*) the material cultural resources; and (*ii*) the representational types available in language. We take these two levels of constitution of the domestic not because they erect the limits of a designated sphere but because they provide a route from the 'concrete' to the 'formal'; the specific transition to cognizable 'forms' that stand as the finished products of their 'domestic' realm. Further, the specific transition from one level to another bears the process of linguistic appropriation of their life-experiences that sets their horizon. Mills' textualization of their horizon provides an exploratory poetics of their lives, the meanings of which need to be disseminated.

The village as a place of inhabitation is 'surrounded by a belt of bamboo clumps and light jungle' (Mills, 1926: 71). The name of the village represents a spatial feature: *Changtongia* derives its 'root' from a kind of thin bamboo called *chuchuo*. In a way the name of the village and its surroundings get identified, and the name acquires its ostensible reference. But the demarcation of the village paths by fine spear-oaks brought during the present villagers' migration here retraces their long forlorn footprints in the well-ordered plantation of these trees. One can read an ecological balancing in a chosen place of habitation, the synchronization between the natural surroundings and the planned arrangements within a village that give rise to a creative imagination reflected in the acts of naming the place and its natural/cultural objects. Interestingly, a village name such as *Yongyimsen* recalls the memory of long-departed *Konyak* settlers with its new connotation as 'new village of the Yong people'. The Ao Naga way of naming reveals a synchronism between the present and the past.

Naming suffices the fundamental purpose of the binding together the settlers of the village and it spills over onto certain organized functions. The 'defence' of the village is secured by making 'fences'. 'The fence, made of wooden stakes lashed together and bristling with *panjis*, stretches right around the village (Mills, 1926: 72). Such fences are necessary for the safety of the village and are marked in a festival called *Atsutsu Kimak* or *Urang Kimak*. There is a strategic planting of long creepers whose tendrils are trained down the bamboo, which are used to thwart enemies. Such a defence strategy links up defence with certain beliefs and norms—such as the belief of growing creepers and the participation of the community in making fences. What is revealed here is the continuation of the practice of growing creepers as a custom, because its discontinuation would weaken village defences; thus many plants, which would otherwise have become extinct, are being preserved. How does the preparation for defence become a domestic affair? Firstly, by the participation of the community in the erection of the fences and, secondly, the day becomes one of celebration as every young male participant visits the dormitories of the girls and is offered rice beer, converting it into a 'domestic' occasion.

The observance of community works, and the customs related to it, is obligatory. Even the growing of certain plants serves the double function of defending the community, as well as being a symbolic ratification of defence plans. Moreover, such symbolic and customary observances, performed as a part of a common goal, partially constitutes the realm of the domestic, while an act of celebration of the real work through reception and festivity adds the 'intent' to the symbolic. A symbolic performance without its celebrating mode does not acquire a decipherable meaning in the domestic sphere of Ao Nagas. Therefore, the domestic sphere is in no way limited to a piecemeal symbolic act of the individual; unless it is opened up to a collective celebration of a work, meant to serve the common purpose, it is never completed.

As a part of the defence preparations, the Aos make a spacious building near the village gate but inside the fence, 'often over fifty feet long and twenty feet broad', which serves the purpose of a guard house as well as clubhouse (Ibid.: 73). These buildings are called *morungs*, and serve the special purpose of assembling the male members for war as well as for get-to-gethers. The morung symbolizes a special reassembling of domestic spaces compounded with the taking of collective decisions in the face of urgencies.

Moreover, it re-integrates one and all—the sharing of everyday moments of joy and sorrow and strengthens interpersonal relations. At the same time, by prohibiting the entry of females in morungs, society imposes among the members' readiness to act against any odd occurrence. Perhaps the prohibition of entry to women is enforced strictly because the main purpose is to keep the men in readiness for battle. Women do not take part in battles. Morungs signify a specific character of domestic defence so that the domestic is divided in terms of 'defence' and 'festive' purposes; both are sometimes strategically integrated and sometimes separated, in order to separate task-specific spheres of domestic life without affecting the general male-female relationships. This is reflected when morungs are rebuilt. On the last evening of the completion of work, the girls of the other phratries, with whom the young men of the morung consort, assemble in front of it and walk round it six times singing (Mills, 1926: 76–77). Afterwards, they are entertained to a feast outside.

It appears that the morung, with its frontal location near the village gate, acquires a kind of sanctity. Moreover, with its strictly defined norms of prohibition of entrance to females, while maintaining the homosocial world within, the morungs also becomes a site of celebration when the festivity takes place outside it. What, then, is the significance of the demarcation of zones of homosocial duty and companionship among the males, and of an outside space of celebration with women of other clans with whom the males are acquainted? It indicates a kind of self-discipline, both in maintaining the defence of the village as well as restraining the heterosocial relations with women who they are acquainted with. This act of self-discipline constitutes male domesticity, which is never complete without the celebratory moment of female participation. Further, it portrays the norm of permissibility for the self-disciplined males to socialize with females, and the moment of celebration signifies a fulfilled moment within the act of self-disciplining. It also shows the completion of an act as a moment of success that acts as a moment of celebration. This kind of normative regulation of festivity comports a learned and cultured behaviour. Thus, domestic life incorporates the aspect of discipline and learning, mixed with the pleasure of free-mixing and colourful celebrations.

Apart from the functional aspects of domestic life, its aesthetic component is no less fascinating. Music is an essential component in every aspect of their lives, representing the direct interrelationship between society and creativity. One can perceive that music consists not only of tunes and voices, but also contains the ultimate resonance of a sought-after mitigation of a materially-rooted necessity. There is a tale that tells us about the *Changis*, an Ao clan, trying to 'prove that they are in no way different from other Aos' (Mills, 1926: 76). They possessed a drum, but 'jealous of the tap-tap sound that the *Chanke* women produced when making pots, which rivalled its fine note, the drummer ran down a steep slope and turned into a stone'. This tale reveals an intrinsic attribution of 'value' in the creation of musical instruments; of the gratification of refined taste reflected in the apparent sense of contention between refinement in the tune of the 'tap tap' and the 'drum', in which the drummer is underrated and gets converted into another form. The end of this tale demarcates the identification of 'sensibility' and 'no-sensibility': a 'stone' representing the lack of sensibility and the 'death' bringing out the pathos of not being refined enough in the production of tonalities. Perhaps the subtle distinction between the tune of making pots—the vibrations of which had a greater frequency, producing a variety of notes, and being a female innovation, while the drums beaten by a male producing monotonous sounds, lacking the quality of music made by pot-making—generated an aesthetic angst that sought its end by turning into something beyond sensibility. This aspect of the refinement of task and aesthetic sense operates at the level of pleasure and satisfaction among the Ao Nagas. Later, every *khel* (clan) owned a drum. Let us reflect on Mills's elaborate description of the drums:

> They consist of huge logs, slit along one side and partially hollowed out. One end is carved to represent what is undoubtedly a buffalo's head, with horns lying back along the drum...The tongue of the buffalo often protrudes and turns up against the upper lip, and, as if to personify the drum still further, a human face is often carved on the tongue (Ibid.: 76–77).

This description of the drums and the personified motifs on it signify purposive social and cultural performances. At the level of representation, these drums and the motifs closely relate to the domestic moorings of the Ao Naga life. It is important to consider the spatial arrangements of domestic space and its functional correspondence with certain social and cultural patterns. Mills locates the organizing principle of division in the villages in terms of morung and *muphu* with the principle that its inmates can never be drawn from more than one muphu. A muphu often contains more than one morung, each occupied by one or more clans. According to Mills:

...a man usually describes himself as belonging to such-and-such a 'morung', rather than to such-and-such a *muphu*, for, though a 'morung' never draws its inmates from more than one muphu, a muphu often contains more than one 'morung', each occupied by one or more clans (1926: 83).

A muphu is like a cluster of members, sharing the same language or belonging to the same clan in contrast to members who have later migrated to the village. Customs also vary from one muphu to the other. Muphus are called khels in Nagamese, which, going by its Assamese meaning, would mean a village organization with distinct families, clans and individuals, ordinarily sharing a common geographical territory like the same village or locality.

This principle of organization leads to the distribution of settlements in various ways. What is significant is the difference in social and cultural behaviour that can be traced back to the different muphus within the village. The difference is maintained by the special location of the various muphus within the village, with trespasses leading to internecine warfare and trouble. There is a functional integration of society by its demarcated interior, without which differentiates could not have been maintained. Between one muphu and another there is a boundary that is constituted by a fireline.

Another significant area of domestic preoccupation is the performance of 'rituals' in which various functional divisions of society are assigned a definite role. The performance of certain common rites and rituals brings about the coordination between different muphus and morungs. In a way, these rites produce the societal whole at the level of their performance, even though the rites often include the specific differential markers. *Phuchung* is a ceremony that is a ritualistic invocation of the corn spirit or field spirit, through an act of oblation at the end of the harvest season, in which the husband and the wife play distinct roles. Another important ritual is the reaping ceremony, during which the family undergoes the tension of whether or not it is going to get the expected amount of corn. There are occasions of sacrifice and ritualistic invocation of corn spirits in order to protect and ensure the reaping of the harvest (Mills, 1926: 112–113).

The sphere of the 'domestic' in Ao Naga life is an open space, where family chores are performed, involving participation in the community, on the one hand, and the determination of domestic duties based on community differentiations, on the other. The Ao Naga life never manifests itself without a community orientation, making a closed privacy impossible. Therefore the 'domestic' as described by Mills includes public acts; it becomes an extensional sphere that contains the functional distinctions of various family members.

THE CONSTRUCTION OF NARRATIVE SELF: ANGAMI NAGA MEANINGS

J.H. Hutton's remarkable work on the Angami Nagas discusses what he terms as Angami Naga superstitions. He describes these as: (*i*) whosoever approaches the foot of the rainbow will die; (*ii*) it is dangerous to plant cacti (*Euphorbia antiquorum*) as it will cause a storm; and (*iii*) a man's stomach aches when someone at a distance is ransacking his property. No concrete reasons were given for such belief-statements that apparently assume some form of closure (Hutton, 1921: 251). What is interesting is the narrative that links up of a statement of belief with another belief. The explanation given for the cause of death by touching the foot of a rainbow is that it is the work of the spirit residing in the rainbow. This interpretation gives primacy to the concept of the rainbow spirit that enacts death; another line of interpretation could be a narrative reconfiguration of the sight of a rainbow that suggests that the colour bands of a rainbow manifest a spirit. However, such an explanation does not have an expected consistency and hence appears like superstition to an observer. Belief represents a narrative and fictional nature in which narrative becomes the medium to link up disparate phenomena and entities. The notion of the 'spirit' in the rainbow is invoked to explain the death caused by touching the foot of the rainbow. Again, the 'foot of a rainbow' is an imagined construction to signify its declining semi-circular arch, a visual illusion or spectre that gives rise to such narrative construction. It obviously lacks the usual narrative elements such as rhetoric or trope, but bears an important characteristic of the narrative, by presenting an explanation that leaves an 'inexplicable' that has to be accommodated by belief. In the same extract, the cause of stomach pain as someone is molesting one's property presents a metaphorical picture of one's mutual loss, which can be best described in terms of a physiological attack corresponding to the act of ransacking of one's property. Two kinds of explanations can be attempted in this regard. In the first belief, the visual representation gives rise to a strategy of containment, and in the second, causal correspondence between 'pain' and 'molestation' established through an analogous equivalence represents a belief about natural causation. How do these explanations acquire the status of belief?

Given this introduction to the nature of Angami Naga belief, one can try to see the play of such belief in the narrative construction of its genealogy. One can try to locate its internal connections and designate how certain specific concepts evolve in the Angami Naga mind. Hutton relates a tale about their origin which he titled 'Tower of Babel', obviously an elusive title. Hutton talked about *Ukepenopfii*, the primal mother, who, instead of dying, transmigrated to heaven. Her progenies thought of keeping in touch with her by building up a tower through which they would reach heaven and speak to her. At this, the primal mother thought of the hazard of everyone wanting to get a gift from her! So she advised them to build the tower in a manner that those working at the site spoke different languages, so that they would not understand each other. When one instructed his co-worker to bring a piece of stone, he would fetch water or a stick. As a result, total miscommunication and chaos prevailed amongst the workers with mutually unintelligible languages. The tower was abandoned, but what remained are the different languages of the tribes. One can read here a metonymic connection between different tongues and tribes through the communicative confusion. In yet another version of the story, Hutton brought out the ethical quandary of reaching impossible heights within the self-inflating paradigm of power:

> There was once a country under a powerful chief with great armies and the people thought they would mount up to heaven by building a ladder of wood. So they builded [sic] a stair, and made the stair very high into heaven. Now the men who were up at the top asked for more wood and men who were below made answer [sic], 'There is no wood, shall we cut a piece from the stair?' So the men at the top not understanding what they said gave, 'Aye, cut it.' So they cut it and the ladder fell, and great was the fall thereof, and they that builded [sic] it were killed (Hutton, 1921: 265).

The ethnographic significance of this tale can be unravelled by turning to the narrative. One can perceive the play of symbolic and metaphoric events. The very act of constructing the tower in order to communicate reflects the descendants' sense of terrestrial space, a space in which they stretch out by climbing the tower. It represents an upward journey. This effort to re-establish the link with the originary mother produces a gradual upward displacement. This signifies an inversion of temporal sequence and the effort to go back to the beginning of creation, which is an imagined retreat in a terrestrial space. The making of the tower signifies continuity and a symbolic construction of the lost time path. The tower becomes a traversing symbol, and the stair signifies that the flight is never cut off from the ground. At the same time, the stair grounds the moment of climbing into the real space. Can the reader try to get an answer as to why the journey to heaven was never completed? Does the narrative give an answer? Clearly, the answer is not at all evident. It calls for a hermeneutic imagination to retract the layers of meaning in the incomplete journey to heaven. It presents a tale which is the ultimate in going back to the origin, but always remaining unfulfilled in the 'given' space and time. The kind of break introduced in the communication between Ukepenopfii and her descendents, and later the breakdown of the whole symbolic device, in an effort to complete and reach out to the ultimate goal of touching heaven is a voluntary acceptance of the impossibility of accomplishing the journey. The whole narrative is a reconstructive effort to retrace the lost genealogy of the community. It simultaneously produces the effect of an imagined continuity of history and disorients the continuity with a rupture that desecrates the tower, with the disappearance of all the fantasies around it. This again serves the purpose of re-establishing narrative continuity with the descendents from the original Mother. The loss of the link in an interregnum is compensated by an imaginary journey through time that internally recaptures the depth dimension of continuity. Moreover, the final fall of the tower reveals the situation in the present outside the imaginary; but, at the same time, there is the symbol of historical continuity.

This is an attempt on the part of the Angami Nagas to reconstruct a lack or a loss through narrative explanation, the economy of which fills the gap between the present experience of an event, and another collateral event, without a mapped terrain of reproductive activity. The narrative also produces several events that give it a certain direction, communicating an intentional meaning of the community. But it is never the logical-causal relationship of events alone that determines the 'total' meaning of a narrative. Rather, it is a surplus over the cognitive and material resources introduced into it through a disposition of belief that regulates the flow of meanings. The Angami Naga narratives cover up the disjunction between events, not only to produce a belief at the level of ideas but also recontextualize it in the concrete practices of narration. The narrative hermeneutic sustains a belief in its currency. What is philosophically interesting is to think of a way to systematize the traces of belief in a comprehensive mode. Does the Angami Naga body of knowledge provide a way to form a chain of all such disparate and disjointed beliefs? Apart from a teleological resolution of disparity between the various sorts of beliefs and the amalgamating role of narratives, the gamut of social practices is the field in which beliefs are placed. Thus, it is apparent that beliefs form a set of praxis that determines the social interrelationship within the Angami Nagas.

Head-Hunting

Given this kind of belief–practice interrelationship, the 'queer' phenomenon of 'head-hunting' needs to be explored at length. How are we to understand this phenomenon of head-hunting? Hutton's elaborate explanation of the phenomenon in possible terms, such as ensuring the death of the enemy by slashing the head, head-hunting as part of the game of hunting, the cult of human sacrifice, and so on, all covering from purposive to ritual necessities, does not give a precise explanation of the phenomenon. We would like to point out that head-hunting is visualized by ethnographers as an act of rage and barbarous cruelty, as experienced by the early colonizers who fell victim to it. This aspect of first falling victim to the practice and then observing it from outside makes it a subject of representation in English ethnography. Moreover, the British instituted a civil rule in order to stop the practice. This act of representation in colonial ethnography painted head-hunting in denigrating terms. However, it should be remembered that the Nagas always head-hunted in enemy terrain and human heads were celebratory symbols of their victory, which was associated with the number of heads one could collect from the enemy troops. Apart from this feeling of valour and prowess, there was nothing mysterious about it.

We can make an intertextual reference to a story that also gives an aestheticized representation of hunting, in which an event like cutting off one's head signifies an ecological sensibility, a return to an intimacy with nature. Hutton (1921) offers a tale, 'The Travelling Companions and the Grateful Doe'. It goes like this: Once upon a time, there was a hunter who used to go to hunt with his fellow countrymen and never missed a chance to collect a lot of booty. But whatever he used to hunt was taken by the fellow villagers, without giving him a share, though they themselves never killed many animals. One day he saw a big doe, a barking deer. While others asked him to kill the doe, he refused to shoot it. What happens then is almost magical. He was going along the road when a snake came out, turned into a beggar and asked him where he was going. The beggar expressed his wish to join him as a companion. Soon a frog came out in front of them, became a man and also asked where they were going. The frog-turned-human being and also desired to become their partner in travel. Then, as they were going along, the doe turned into a very nice girl, washing her hair in the river, and she wanted to know where they were going. They replied that they were going to travel and so the girl decided to join them.

After reaching a country, the hunter and the girl married, and the hunter went to a Sahib, and the Sahib said to him, 'If you don't make a water-field and make rice grow in it in one day, I will kill you with an hour's grace'. With this order from the Sahib, the man became very harassed and narrated it to his wife. Immediately, the wife told him that she would prepare the field for him, but he would have to cut her head off with a *dao*. But the man refused. According to Hutton:

> But at last she persuaded him to cut her head off, and when he had done it he felt very sorry and started weeping. But his wife had made the field and grew the rice and went back to their home and cooked their food and waited for her husband, but he did not come. So in her request the beggar man and the man who had been a frog went to call him, but he remained hesitant to come. Finally when he came to their house after a lot of persuasion, he, to his utter surprise found his wife there ready with food, as she used to be always (1921: 271–72).

She (the doe) offered all of them some food to eat. After they had eaten, she told them that they should now go back to their places of origin, their old homes. She told the man that once he had saved her life by not shooting her and now, she in return had saved his life and her job was over. Then she became a doe again and went off to the jungle. Similarly, the frog-man became a frog again and went back to the water, and the beggar became a snake and crept into the bushes. Finally, the man was left all alone and he came back to his own home.

Though the narrative has a number of clues, we shall examine only a few: the tale represents a transition from the hunting and food-gathering stage of life to settled agriculture. This is present in the hunter with a gun refusing to shoot animals and the huntsman not getting his share—a negative presentation of contempt for the life of hunting. The subsequent change into a traveller represents a moment of wandering in the process of transition. The accompaniment of various non-human species during the travel is the desire of those species to be freed from the domination of man. At the same time, this aspect of travel acquires a psychoanalytic depth, by re-enlivening the immediate past of hunting that moves the hunter-traveller beyond the act of killing them, a transcendence from the baggage of the deposits from the acts of cruelty, a self-renewal that embraces a new mode of production. It is the Pauline capacity of men in expression that reconfirms man's intersubjective kinship with animals and other species through which they are transformed into human/huwoman beings. Therefore, the transition from the hunting–gathering stage to the agrarian stage is also a transition of human beings from negativity to complementarity.

We need to recall the moment in the narrative when the hunter refuses to cut off the 'head' of his wife, a doe in disguise, and then does so and is traumatized by the experience. This traumatic experience has to be underlined in understanding the practice of head-hunting. At one level, it is an act of bravado against one's enemy to succeed in a battle, and, at another level, head-hunting is the jouissance in the act of battle. What this tale expresses is that 'love' is the 'double' of hunting; that is, translated in sociological terms, kinship bonding through an act of marriage (here the marriage between the hunter and the doe) is the double of hunting. This is evident in the narrative as it mobilizes an instance of love and killing, the subject of which is the disguised doe, an apparent antinomy of action leading to an inverted relationship between man and an animal in disguise. The positions of the two different species occur in an identical place without the abolition of the already continuing relationship of Eater and Food, Killer and Killed. Hence, this chiasmus is invoked in the act of killing one's beloved, accompanied by a deep sense of guilt and pathos. This internalized sense of guilt and pathos goes into the weeping and apathy that the man went through when he killed his wife, but this whole event is necessitated by the 'dictate of the Sahib'. In the dictate of cultivating the field and growing rice, the colonial white man commands an action and the native Angami performs it, and in performing it he took recourse to a difficult arrangement, reflected in the symbolic acts of killing the wife and hunting of the head. These are no longer acts of jouissance, but gainful acts in the context of the given narrative which make possible an imaginary fulfilment of the wish of the sahib. It is also an act of sacrifice, consistent with the Angami belief that ensures a rich harvest. Incidentally, the same is believed to follow from an act of head-hunting.

This is only one way of linear reading of the narrative in which one can see the effect of transformation, by retaining some core aspect of the belief related to head-hunting. What is even more revealing from the narrative is the happy return of animals and other non-human species in their own form to their own homes, signifying the deliverance of all the sub-human species through the act of cutting off the head of the wife. One can read here the trace of the belief of deliverance of the dead if their heads are hunted, which treats one's returning to his own abode as a substitute for reaching heaven. The Angami Naga belief that head-hunting and the subsequent sharing of flesh leads to a good harvest is a mode of symbolic return. The metaphoric play of the word 'return' not only signifies return in terms of a rich harvest, but also a return to the victorious, in the spirit of being useful to them. In other words, in terms of the Angami belief, the appropriation of the 'head' in the course of head-hunting was a beginning of a new cycle of creation.

Another salient feature of the 'return' of the various species to the jungle signifies the distinction between the 'jungle' and the 'plain': the excursions of the traveller into the agrarian mode of life, and the cultivation of the land of the plain according to the dictate of the white colonial Sahib, marks the triumph of the modern mode over the traditional mode of living and the break with the life of the 'jungle'. The contentment that appears on being successful in the agrarian mode of life is a celebration of the Sahib's command and superiority, and the image of a dismal hitherto existent mode of life begins to prevail. It highlights a new predicament in Angami life. The image of a traveller, more significantly a wanderer instead of a hunter, implies a moment of transition in which the community is without a warrant. The warrant is from the Sahib who gives the command and the traveller conforms to it. This new relationship of carrying out commands is introduced in Angami life with the onset of the British presence in Nagaland.

What we shall read further is the sense of an end provided in the narrative, of course with the sense of a beginning. Between these two senses, there is no moment of stasis in which one can fix a moment for a practice that may seem evil to an observer. Hutton's (1921) narrative does not have such a moment of fixed figuration, and the narratives of the Angamis set a dynamics of self-creation and its mechanics of abandonment and replenishment.

What Hutton's text does is to represent the transition from hunting–gathering to settled cultivation as an episode of history, but without all the contingent features of how the community undergoes a moment of transition. The contingencies cannot be fully explored in a space of narrative representation.

EXPRESSIONS OF MAKING THE WORLD

Moving from the narrativized representation of ethnography, one can only peep into the modes of expression, creation and narrativization of the tribal populace by taking an interpretive effort. Verrier Elwin's *The Arts and Crafts of Nagaland* (1986) discusses the artistic expression and skills in representing Naga art. One interesting aspect is the removal of the differences of kind between, say, a work made of bamboo and a piece of poetry. The usual nationalist interpretation of creativity, in terms of labour in the process of production, cannot explain the act of artistic representation that remains as a special moment of creating another reality. A cultural explanation of the creation of art, in terms of the relationship between the artist and the art, needs to widen in order to encompass the artist's social conditions, labour and so on, and can be trans-cultural. But in the ethnographic representation of art, the descriptions involved in the act of creation help us interpret it. There is an ethnographic continuum between the world of the creator, the act of creation, and what is created; all singularly different and yet related as an inseparable continuity/discontinuity in the space of creation, to emerge into what is called 'Art'. This ethnographic continuum gets transformed into a work of art. A self-interpretive 'pre-understanding' preceding the work of art situates art in a cultural perspective. This ethno-specific pre-understanding act is simultaneously a hermeneutic backdrop and an experiential world of the tribal community. Verrier Elwin mentions an Ao folk tale about works of bamboo:

> Once there lived a magician, who was known by the name Changkichanglangba....When he was alive, he used to tell the people that if they open his grave on the sixth day after his death, they

would discover there something new. On the sixth day, after his death, when the grave was opened out, all the designs and patterns of basketry work were found there. The people copied it and started practising it (1986: 71).

In Ao Naga society, basketry or something made out of bamboo carries with it a cultural memoir. It represents an ingrained custom of discovering the art, designs of which arise from the grave, a house of finished endeavours of one's life. In a cultural sense, art works as copies of designs from the grave of the creator magician, and produces an altogether different meaning than its surface appreciation. Such a narrative backdrop provides the specific cultural context for understanding the specific criterion of art in a specific society. At a universal level, the connection between magic, discovery in the grave and new designs represent a discursive framework within which art, as the motif of death, is the 'gift' of death, a gift in an absolute sense. At the narratological level, the voyeuristic subconscious in a conception of a work of art is a different experience that subdues 'death' in the work of art, which otherwise remains as the ultimate existential motif of art in most universal-rational cultures. This kind of subsumption or sublation of specific human experiences in works of art, through a narrative appropriation in a tribal culture, arrests the precedence of anthropocentrism over art, euphemistically treated as a separate area of creation over life and death. The making of the world as 'creation' in a tribal context, frees creation from the pathos of life and death and makes it an 'experience' that remains immanent as a motif in a tribal-making-of-the-world, which is otherwise inverted as a transcendental realm in the rationalist tradition.

Another way of a making of the tribal world, as exemplified in the Konyak representation of human figures in Konyak woodcarving, is an act of inscribing the figure on something—piece(s) of wood (Elwin, 1986: 62). The inscription of human figures in this naturalistic mode presents an image of the human which is free from discursive spaces. It is an open presence before one's eye. Art here is bare human existence free from its 'essences', 'thoughts' and other nuances, and is also not a still object. Its vitality lies in its imprint without any extraneous experiences or nuances. Let us consider the Ao skirt which is woven to embody one's social position and function. An Ao skirt that has three or four designs in each of its two breadths—which represent material richness, and its lack of such elaborate design represents poverty—stands as a mark of one's individual position in the society. Thus, what it makes visible is that the clothes are markers of social status not in an economic sense, but in a sense of socially celebrating ones role in society. The link between dress, design, colour and social position is a culture-specific artistic imagery, a symbolic demonstration of the social realm. In case of Chakrim and Khezama Angamis, the fourth line in their clan, according to Elwin's ethnographic representation, 'denotes process not in war but in love' and may be worn for any one of the four following achievements:

(*i*)   an intrigue with a married woman living with her husband;
(*ii*) a double-barrelled intrigue with two girls; or
(*iii*) with two daughters of one father; or
(*iv*) with a mother and her daughter (Elwin, 1986: 29)

These kinds of social and individual events find symbolic denotation in Angami clothes. Does it mean that they wear clothes to represent these kinds of events and motifs? One plausible answer could be that what the cloth presents in its lines and colours functions as a 'dominant motif' of society or the individual, thereby making the cloth or the process of making of the cloth an inseparable point of one's social world. Here again, artwork conserves and presents the life-world meanings, and without this necessary life-world meaning artworks cannot be understood. One can say that the artwork remakes the world for the tribals, not to live in it, but to give life to the artwork. The lines are typical indexes that are employed as the paradigmatic representation of tribal society.

The semantic of 'making the world' by the tribals in North-East India is contained in their oral culture. The reality is constituted by a collective memory archive that retains the thematic through collective 'speech-acts', 'narration' and 'recitation'. All these ways of retention through modes of communication are ways of speaking to the world. Elwin (1986) cited some of these oral poems in a translated form. His translation remains as an act of representing them in their ways of speaking. The poetic narration and its accompanied rhythm and musicality sustain the spreading of the word. Speaking out in poetic narration is an act of the constitution of subjectivity, within which the speaker and the one who is spoken of are located. It is dialogical in the sense of presenting the subjectivities inscribed within the oral narration as subjects constituted by an experience of exchange and sharing. Poetry signifies a play of pretension and retention of this experience. This play of pretension and retention is a play exceeding and inhabiting the structure of experience in language, itself an experience of poetic movement holding a double register of a 'poetic intentionality' and the structuring of this intentionality in the play between signifier and signified. The poetic intentionality is manifested in the situational dialogue, while its structuring is a fictional reconstruction of the dialogue in a mode that expresses its rhythm. It is a sublimation of the poetic intentionality that arranges its signifiers at the level of the intentional, while its oralization recalls the movements within the intentionality to structure it in a poetic mode. Tribal poetry surpasses the initial dialogic intentionality by way of structuring this intentional in 'orality'. Orality surpasses the limits of the written and translated textualization as done by Elwin. An example of how it takes place can explain such a feature. A *Sangtam* song describing the process of building a new village reads:

> Building village anew, we Sangtam, first, of all, clear tiger's' excreta then cut the big trees. Sacrifice dogs, next enrich village bringing mithuns and bulls. Cut fields and cultivate after cutting big big trees. (...) Buy mithuns with end of harvest. Invite villages at feast in winter, slaughtering mithuns, spreading our name and fame thus far and wide (Elwin, 1986: 110).

Elwin considered the cutting of the jungle as a quotidian act performed to build houses, taking it as it is. Elwin's comment, 'Tiger's excreta, of course, does not carry any inner significance here except custom' (Ibid.), does not recognize the retention aspect in referring to clearing the Tiger's excreta. What other human custom can be a source of retention of such an essential act during the building of a new village? It indicates an invocation of memory as a part of the play of retention and pretension, as house building is an act of pretension. The effect of the whole narration is a

recollection of a life-world context that enters into poetic intentionality, producing a flow like 'cut big trees', 'cutting big big trees'.
Poetic intentionality signifies an arousal represented in lines such
as 'Buy mithuns with end of harvest'. Intentionality also puts into
play archetypes of Sangtam life-world that acquires uniqueness in
its exploration of the habitat. It is sung in the manner of coordination
of the job of setting the new village. Hence the tonal variety arises
from the variety of work that is actually done in the process of
setting up of the new village. The fleeting impact of such a tactile
motion is presented in a situation of joy that goes with the
organization of village feasts with invitees who spread the name
of organizers far and wide, a gentle gratification of Sangtam sense
of hospitality.

This sense of reaching out to a tangible goal is an outflow of
the event surpassing the limits of the text, as the desire of the
community hangs like a dangling spectre. The last part of the song
is even more 'cosmic', revealing the desire of attaining a universal
home, appearing as a culturally informed determination of the
completion of the village:

> Look, O Sangtams Crying the universe.
> Ongugo[16] the bird singing (and) singing human being alike.
> Voice of the universe, you and yourself heard or not?
> Step forward, universe for you [everybody].
> On your death die not universal tune
> [Hesitate not] Think and feel for humanity (Elwin, 1986: 110).

The motifs of 'crying the universe', 'voice of the universe' and
'feeling for humanity' present an elliptical movement of life,
fulfilment and death, ingrained in the motif of the 'universe', in its
stillness, permanence and infinite vastness. The motifs of the
discrete qualities of life-world stand in passivity to the motifs of
the illimitable universe and listen to them. Listening to the cry and
voice of the universe is simultaneously the expression of an
innermost desire and the desire to attain it; a drive to sublimate
oneself in this universal cry or yearning, that is, a total merger in
dialogue. One cannot but appreciate this mode of world making as
an innermost act of dialogue in the tribal culture. As Elwin suggests:

The poem carries a deep meaning of harmonious character and philosophy of life. 'Universe crying' reflects a tragic sense here, for people are in isolation from each other that is against the law of nature...The bird's singing that enraptures human hearts, which in turn, cannot help responding to it, no matter in their own words, are this idealized and emotional atmosphere and spirit of feeling between the two (Elwin, 1986: 110).

What Elwin reads here is the tribal practice of singing themes that concern the universal and the cosmic, acting both as an inspiration and as a construction of the world in the highest form of yearning. Such themes are sung in a meeting with other singing creatures deriving enjoyment in responding to each other's tunes. It transmutes the relations between humans and other species and between humans and the world. The poetics of the Sangtam mind represents a universal humanity of coexistence and communion. This universalization of a home motif in poetic and musical form is 'architectonic'.

Apart from such architectonic constructions, the 'ways of world making' of the ethnic cultures lead to a fictional and artifactual reconstruction in ritual texts and codes. Tribal art is more artifactual than fetishized because it embodies those aspects of culture that desire to exceed its signification. The figures of tribal creativity culminate in the experiences of life and make it ready for living a life. Along with the living man and woman, the figures of tales, painting and sculpture in the tribal world live a life with the community and their meanings are ethno-ecological, entering into the discourse of collective memory and signification. This embeddedness of the world they make signifies the 'roots' of tribal culture.

Notes

1. Collective subject 'types' are produced as the 'Other', who is identified in a non-self mode. It is a way of putting the psychoanalytic question of desire of ethnic communities in their historico-cultural condition of being under domination.

2. Mediation in language takes place by way of distinguishing the 'actual', 'possible', 'contingent', 'concrete', 'non-concrete' and the relations of modal nature.

3. Artifactuality describes the fictional mode of construction of 'facts' that are multiple-dependent entities. It knits together various concepts and practices of a culture by way of their 'dependence' within a culture. For example, Apatani Mida as a generic name exists for ritual performances for the well-being of a married daughter and her groom from her parent's side. Mida also induces the gifts like seeds and its signification of children to be born out of the marriage in a ritual text and context. Ka Rngiew is another such artifactual generic construct that characterizes virtues both at the level of the individual and also of a collective.

4. The conditions of maintaining an identity can fail or be fulfilled independently of 'artifactuality', it can be maintained by way of transmuting dependent signifiers of a culture. Identity acts as a metasignifier for all the artifactualities of culture. Reduction to certain characteristics is a reduction to contingencies that does not require reduction, as it keeps open the possibility of assuming any of them.

5. This agency cannot be located within the public/private dichotomy, but only in the in-between spaces that cannot reduce the polarities of a relationship; the agency remains 'dialogic' and 'mediative' by decentring the 'subjects' of contestations.

6. The notion of 'agency' could be identified in terms of certain specific markers, but it could not be completely determined.

7. 'Subject of power' signifies a 'subject' in relation to what it is not by way of its will or repression of this will.

8. The social life of the subject is constituted by an exterior, which is repressed within an inscription of self or community

9. This disposition of/off specific artifactual elements of a world is a disposition of/off the idealized language of identity. Articulation invokes such idealizations.

10. Such fractures are produced out of cleavages between power and subject in so far as subject resists the differentiating logic of power.

11. 'Complementarity' is a Derridean concept which signifies the play of differential elements that do not allow any one of the concepts to represent without the Other and thereby displacing oppositions between them. This dependence between terms produces only an effect, not an opposition between cause and effect.

12. Principle of transference means an act of substitution of one concept for another in order to attain a common objective. In psychoanalysis, transference means substitution of one mental act in a mental state that does not produce the act.

13. From S. Lyngdoh's remarks on the concept of *un long briew man brion,* which means human in the fullest sense of the term

14. Habermas notion of 'life-world' as a closed concept signifying within one's language or within the possible tripartite division of the world between subjective, objective and inter-subjective spheres of life.

15. Remarks by J. Klongwir interpreting region as the 'person itself'. See Sujata Miri (1998: 52).

16. Elwin's note states 'local name of a bird like the weaver bird'.

2

Return of the Native

Ethnic identity remains ridden with a split at its heart. The resultant dilemma is whether to maintain roots in consonance with the tradition or whether to maintain an identity, despite the ongoing changes augured by modernity. Politics of culture does not make this dilemma a central question in understanding identity, rather perceives it unilaterally, as a moment of making culture an instrument of survival by an ethnic community. While such a view takes ethnicity as just a matter of claiming roots, it does not address the question of retention of the already owned cultural forms but for the question of survival. Modernity paves the way for such 'opportunistic' survival by providing a free space for the perpetuation of native meanings with added value. It does this by constructing a criterion of judgement, stemming from the internal standards of a particular culture. Such internal standards cohere with the current demands for articulation of native meanings. The question is: how does a uniform criterion of judgement arise within a community that enforces a collectively-agreed interpretation of cultural meanings? Is it because there is an already shared life-world?

On the plane of assertion of a common ethnic identity, the way members identify and define themselves seems to be more a political than cultural mobilization of a set of markers, which provide the easy plank for feeling an ownness towards these meanings and signs. But this whole politics of culture bypasses the sources of meanings embedded in a particular culture, to facilitate a ready and handy appropriation of cultural meanings by its own members. Culture seekers recognize this as a loss of roots, while it is celebrated as change wrought in a new time. What results is a gradual uprooting of cultural meanings from their native sources. In contrast, 'cultural politics' refuses to give in to a changeable self-identity in the interest of an opportunistic survival, but *looks back* at its 'interior' to discover its own 'language' and to make others hear its 'voice'. The onslaught of modernity in providing native voices a mere 'self-representation' in terms of cultural referents is *resisted* by re-making a native self-pitted against its images, constructed by an alien process of appropriation.

Such a mechanism of re-appropriation gives the native a representation useful for the purpose of re-describing his self-identity. This process of re-construction of the self-identity marks a simultaneous assertion of native sources of meaning as well as its re-description within the deconstructing processes of identity in modernity. On the one hand, it turns into a process of emptying out one's own cultural resources or the native referents in order to exhaust it against the overpowering processes of modernity; on the other, it reconfigures the native identity with a heightened commitment to roots at the level of articulation of identity. The 'Ethnic' resurges not against the non-representation of native referents but against its appropriation in the making of modern culture. It resists a mix between the native and the alien and obstructs the modus operandi of utilizing the native as an ingredient of the 'modern'. But this resistance is not anti-modern in character just because it resists the processes of loss of the native within modernity. Rather, it designates the *struggle* of the native to survive on her or his *own terms*.

In the context of North-East India, it is an imperative to trace the construction of identities to map out the processes of 'politics of culture' and 'cultural politics'. 'Identities' were constructed by the colonizers as 'subjects' of ethnographic disciplines and later brought under their rule as a set of (dis)obedient subjects. These identities, treated as 'tribes', further became the 'subject' of nationalist discourses and, as 'citizens', they were determined by the capacities and constraints of 'state' discourses. As decolonized subjects, they now share the vision of 'India' as Europe's Other and 'Europe' as India's Other, while they position themselves as the Other of *both,* with respect to their otherness from both 'Europe' and 'India'. As post-colonial subjects they write their history through various articulations, alternative to the construction of national identity, to struggle against the politics of appropriation. This struggle invites a lot of resistance and reprieve *from* the dominant system. In turn, with their already shifting horizons of self-location, they expose the inane nature of India's state discourses, where the premise is mostly the idea of a unitary nationhood. As against this, they position themselves in various modalities, and, as collectively articulated communities, they struggle for their 'place under the sun'. What comes into play is the content of their native self through a constant re-configuration within the strategies of politics. As the politics of the modern 'nation-state' has been turned into a politics of appropriation, their language of resistance harps distinct claims of their identity, such that the reconfiguration of the self jibes well with the strategies of politics as a form of *cultural politics*. The strategies of such articulation have so far been successful in undercutting the processes of domination.

CARTOGRAPHY OF INVASION

Colonial ethnographers had explored the inaccessible terrains of human habitats of various parts of the 'hills' of present North-East India. Their writings on lives of various smaller communities were 'official' and acquired authentic status as part of their project of ruling these people and the areas they lived in. The encounter of the British with these smaller communities was initiated through their insubordination and resistance against the former's presence, which always gave the latter an alibi to lead a military expedition and bring them under their control. The British perceived them to be wild, savage and disobedient communities that needed to be penalized and disciplined. The will to dominate them emanated from the perceived superiority of the British and their assumption of authority to rule over the natives. Further, the British intended to protect the frontiers and borders of the territories they ruled; therefore the hills of North-East India were of military and strategic importance to them. The British conceived the hill areas as physical spaces to be included within their empire, and once included they desired to gain sufficient knowledge about the communities living in these unknown territories. The knowledge about such people became an inseparable part of the will to rule them. This resulted in preparation of British texts and narrativization of the communities of North-East India. In case of North-East India, the idea of invasion came later than the first phase of British annexation of the Indian mainland. The British decided to explore the territory of North-East India only when they felt that their rule could be justified on the grounds of establishing law and order in an otherwise different terrain as was here. Especially, since hill people of North-East India had historically remained unsubjugated by any major dynasty or power, their history and culture was very different than rest of India. The physical, cultural and administrative features of tribes living in inaccessible hills posed a difficult challenge for any would-be ruler. So, the burden fell on the colonizers to evolve a suitable knowledge-based idea of administration. The British therefore adopted a different strategy by choosing those officers who had a greater flair for anthropology than for military expedition and administration.

The colonizers had grafted this strategy of rule on the text of the description of the landscape of North-East India. *The Provincial Gazetteers of India: Eastern Bengal and Assam* is a text grafted with signs of conceptual subsumption of the aforementioned areas (Allen et.al., 1889). The landscape of these areas provided a canvas to *draw* the 'subject-ed' landscape itself with dots, marks and nuances and the text bore these traces. The author assumed an all-pervasive vision to draw the landscape as if aspects of the landscape are one with the authorial plotting of the space. Physical space is created in the text by placing 'places' within the text, the 'place' being earmarked by the author. Such earmarked places mark the presence of space with authorial/textual marks. This mode of 'represented' landscape formed a landscape of 'colonization'. The very emplotment of the landscape turned into a visible exterior for colonial desire, as the exterior turns into a concrete body of knowledge for the desire to be embodied and emplotted. One can exemplify such emplottings in the narrative. For example,

> From west to east at right angles to the upper portion of this tract, in Assam proper, stretches the Brahmaputra valley, which forms an *alluvial* plain about 450 miles long with an average breadth of 50 miles. About the centre of the valley there is a tract of *mountainous* country known as Mikir Hills...The Brahmaputra, through the greater part of its course, is bounded on either side by stretches of *marsh* land covered with *high grass jungle* (Allen et al., 1889: 6).

The words emphasized exhibit the colonial marks on landscape in the body of its text. The claim that such plottings are an emplotment of colonial desire can be further read from the aestheticized feature of the description. The aesthetic is spread out over the narrative of a picturesque landscape known as Brahmaputra Valley, bounded by hills on the north and the south. On a clear day the snowy peaks of the Himalayas glisten in the sunlight. There are rivers, woods and pools on every side of these rice-fields fenced with bamboo groves. The slopes of the lower hills are covered with forest and the rivers that flow on the plains issue through gorges of exceptional beauty (Ibid.: 3).

This aesthetic with its usual narrative qualifiers inscribed on the textual body of the landscape exude the pleasure of the text, an authorial ploy to narrativize the 'natural' that offers a field for marking the cultural. At one of the moments of marking the quality of life inscribed upon nature, the text comments, 'During the rains the greater part of western Sylhet lies under water, but in Cachar and eastern Sylhet the conditions of life are less unfavourable' (Ibid.: 8). This shows how the natural determinants of cultural life or quality of life find a greater importance in the narrative of the landscape. For example, Sylhet, categorized by the text as a 'deltaic' place, acquires a sense of abundance and richness in terms of meaning, which later is turned into a site of production of tea. Also 'delta' maps a connecting route through river to various centres of commercial importance. This kind of implicative employment of landscape markers remains as one of the most important textual strategy of colonial Gazetteers. For the subjugated people, the knowledge schema of the Gazetteers was nothing new, except that it was not formal and it did not arise from the gaze of the ruler.

This landscape of nature not only yielded one kind of field for representation, but it provided the backdrop for a contingent representation of 'culture'. The same Gazetteer incorporates comments on Hinduism, Vaishnavism and Saktism (Allen et al, 1889: 52–53). The Gazetteer picked up an unquestionable assumption that Hindus were divided into believers in Vaishnavism and Saktism and conversely Vaishnavas and Saktas were Hindus. Vaishnavism is described as 'a revolt against the pretensions of the Brahmans and the licentious rites of corrupted forms of Saktism' (Ibid.: 53). So far as pretension of Brahmins is concerned, it goes well with the prevalent disposition to think in a similar manner on the rise of Vaishnavism, and to that extent it is a reproduction of the prevalent stereotypic idea of Vaishnavism. But as far as terming of Sakta cult as 'licentious' is concerned, it is another stereotype created by a Brahminical critique of Saktism reproduced in the colonizer's text, and the justification of such a coinage through the use of the expression 'corrupted forms of Saktism' conflates both an insider's perspective as well as an outsider's perspective. How can one call the prevalent form of Saktism 'corrupted' and by what criterion? So far as the reading of Vaishnavism as a 'revolt' is concerned, its anti-Brahminical tirade drew much of its support from the Saktas, but the later proselytizating of Saktas into Vaishnavas was again a Brahminical ploy. The Gazetteer mentioned that the presiding priests of Saktas were Brahmins, who were the 'great proselytizing agency in Assam' (Ibid.: 53). The text hails their role as that of civilizing the aboriginal tribes, just as their colonial masters do (Ibid.: 54). The text distinguishes priests by their loyalty to the government and appreciates their enlightenment and liberality of thought. Given the culture of purity and Brahminical obscurantism, the praise does not sound genuine, yet the colonizers draw a tacit ideological and moral support from the priestly order (Ibid.: 54).

Such homilies are replete in the British text, identifying a friendly class of subjects as opposed to the rebels or the dissenters, thereby marking an epistemic access to the ground reality of the subject country. Attribution of quality and obedience to the masters went together to wield a justification of British presence as a culturally necessary outcome. That the colonizers' own identity is formed by the colonized is amply demonstrated here, as attributes of 'liberality' are freely deployed in an otherwise unfriendly terrain for the British as colonial masters. The project of colonization shares an intercultural understanding of each other, which in the first place is in the form of an enlightened respect for the other till the rule is settled. Brahmins as a priori subjects of rule are represented in typically elite markers of British society, juxtaposed over the yet to be fully colonized society. Brahmins as the recognizable 'Other' of the subject society are a source of rationalization of the structure of power that is supposed to emerge. The text performs several functions here simultaneously. It produces the colonizers' categories of thinking such as 'proselytization', 'civilizing influence', 'enlightenment' and 'liberality of thought'. The tone of appreciation for the role of priest in the text is a tacit linking up of the emergence of new social elites with the liberal, proselytizing, civilizing and colonizing motif of the colonial author. The moment of conversion and the moment of revolt are juxtaposed to produce a temporal backdrop for the current history of colonization, and this mode of totalizing appropriation of the past of the colonized is directed at blurring the effect of colonial politics/ideology. Within the text, colonization acts through the canons of cultural appropriation (here the appropriation of Hindus and Saktas under Vaishnavism) that remains as the 'unconscious' of the colonial text, to produce a historically evolved mode of domination. This discloses the politics of culture that is textualized within colonial texts. The colonial text acts as a 'writing machine'[1] that assumes an authoritative voice to recreate the past through narrativization, in order to position the colonized subjects within a continuity without empowering them to distinguish the past and the present.

At the crux is the historiographical question: how to separate the textual unconscious of domination from the colonial text in order to recuperate the native in her own mode? This also becomes a key question in locating cultural politics of the native. In the example just cited, conversion to Vaishnavism, according to the colonial text, was the source of replacement of Brahminism and Saktism, which does not show the position of the native. The replacement of one faith by another supposedly revolutionary faith is a transition in which the natives are represented as passive receivers. What dominates here is the phenomenon of conversion from one creed to another by submerging the story of those who were converted. This exemplifies a kind of colonial strategy of *muting* the native subject. It is further reinforced in the dominant colonial motif of civilizing missions, liberalizing ideas and so on, attributed to the priests of proselytization. This slant of the text is loudly presented in the notion of civilizing the aboriginal. This slant becomes even more vivid when the Gazetteer speaks of the 'number of unconverted 'tribesmen' in the Surma Valley and the Brahmaputra Valley (Allen et.al., 1889: 55). What the text opines about the tribesmen in the following words is remarkable in stereotyping their conditions of life:

> The tribesman [*sic*] have no special preference for their own form of religion, and take fairly readily to Hinduism in the plains, and to Christianity in the hills. Conversion would, in fact, proceed rapidly, if not for the natural reluctance of these primitive people to abandon pork, liquor, and the freedom of intercourse between sexes permitted by their own religion (Ibid.: 55).

This is how the colonizers gazed upon the tribes as a mass of uninitiated, uncivilized and un-indoctrinated people readily available for any attempt to convert them into a different mould. The reluctance with which the text talks about the tribal ways of life is borne out of the cultural difference encountered by the colonizers. The representation of tribes as addicted to liquor and sex in the colonial text clearly portrays the abject rejection of tribal mores of life by devaluating it from a supposedly superior cultural location. Here also, powerful colonial stereotypes such as lasciviousness or alcoholism bring out the construction of moral justifications in enslaving or subjugating the tribes. The imputation on tribal religions for granting the sanction to all degrading practices produces a favourable justification for conversion.

(DIS)PLACING THE NATIVE

The construction of social space in terms of cultural inferiority/ superiority is the mark of colonial politics of culture. Colonial politics of culture makes use of the prevalent valuational structure of the colonized societies in order to build up the place of the colonizer as the ruler. This is a strategy of legitimization of the colonial ruler through internal norms of the colonized society. In this process, the colonial text alludes to the dominant social norms that already act as a naturalized source of power and control within the colonized societies. The overwhelming reason for such an allusion is the ready acceptance of such existing norms at the level of common sense within the colonized societies. The colonial text also differentiates between the 'natural', 'social', 'cultural' and 'political'; a mark of introduction of disciplinary boundaries in the body of systematic knowledge; but more than that, it served the purpose of colonial representation of the natives confined to differentiated spheres of life.

This general description of colonial construction of the physical and political space exhibits the British mode of developing systems of knowledge erected on such spaces. This could be seen as the technology of epistemic dominance. One example shall suffice. One can read the following representative British record entitled *Shendoo Raids on the Chittagong Hill Tracts* as a 'text' semiotically:

> The country is almost unexplored,...impenetrable cane brakes lying between Manipur and Cachar on the North, and the Arrakan Hill Tracts on the South, and between the Chindwin River on the East and the Chittagong Hill Tracts and Hill Tipperah on the West...people from a mingling of clans, speaking so far as I know, dialects of the same language, who are known to us by various names—Kookis, Lusheis, Pois, Shendus, Chins etc. (cited in Reid, 1983: 3).

One can read three different layers of description in this text: firstly, identification of physical space through direction and places; secondly, description of the nature of that space, which is an internal characterization; and thirdly, identification of hills, people, language and names by employing physiognomic and cultural markers such as 'high hill' and 'common language'. The enclosement of the third into the second is the source of a derivative discourse, as the names of various tribes are known through the use of common language, making language the marker for such identities and then enclosing it to the location of high hill villages. This reveals a moment of structuration, a typical colonial mode of identification and subsumption. But the description of high and low hills does not entirely capture the elaborate physiological description of space; rather it remains *unspecific* while denoting the location of various communities. The description of location on high hills presents a sense of unfamiliarity and formidability in the text. The politics of culture of the British can be looked upon as a pathos of unfamiliarity through which they expressed a passive desire to rule over these communities. The semiotic construction of physical space is an act of charting out a terrain for that desire to be manifested in 'raids' that the British conducted in Mizo Hills, Naga Hills and other Frontier Tracts. The British way of disciplining was through defeating various tribes of the North-East in a way that ultimately aimed at their subjugation. Therefore, they were transformed by the British from being native to subjects of the empire.

Such a categorical shift in the position of the native tribes of North-East India provided them with a cognitive apparatus to identify them as subjugated under the mighty prowess of the British. Therefore, the colonial politics of culture consisted in turning the native into subjects and make them see themselves as subjects under the superior rule of the British. The image of the British as superior in terms of their 'prowess' generated several impacts: firstly, it dislodged the chieftains and kings among various tribes; secondly, it forced them to give up certain 'uncivilized' practices; and thirdly, it gave them the identity of a free and independent people. The last especially resulted from the British policy of 'leaving them alone' in their own style of life and using some of them for the purpose of defence and labour. This limited use of a defeated community by the British was so strategic that it kept room enough for the natives to think of themselves as sovereign unto themselves as well as being useful to their masters. Mr McCabe's expedition to North Lushei Hills brings out this aspect of British colonization. Reid quotes the Report of 1891–92 that described McCabe's expedition as 'The Complete Pacification of the North Lushei villages west of the Sonai River' which mentioned:

These operations against the Western Chiefs were followed by the erection of a stockade at Sonai Bazar and a 'Promenade' in the Eastern Lushei country, i.e., on the east of the Sonai River. The purpose of this was not punitive, but rather exploratory so as to make...acquaintance of the Chiefs and to locate the sites of the different villages and also to inform the tribes that they were now under the control of the British government and that they would have to pay revenue....McCabe expressed himself, at any rate then, as entirely satisfied with the results, though...careful to observe that it was 'too early to prognosticate what absolute effect this promenande on the Eastern Lusheis would have or whether house-tax would be paid without demur after next harvest.' Be that as it may, he could show that he had increased our topographical knowl-edge of the hills, he has obtained local information about the coun-try and the people: he had entered into relations with the Chiefs, who had agreed to pay house-tax and supply rice and labour, and he had shown that a force could march from village to village and rely upon obtaining Lushei coolies and supplies, the latter an im-portant point (Reid, 1983: 21).

This rather long passage is full of affirmations that iterate the whole context of the expedition and its impact in turning the 'natives' into 'subjects'. One very important aspect is represented in the descrip-tion of the nature of the expedition, which is termed as 'explor-atory'. The duplex movement of the expedition through 'stockade' and 'promenade' expresses the strategies of overpowering the natives by mere show that produces subjection in them; and events such as collection of taxes show everyone that the colonizer intends total 'subjection', yet giving them a chance to reciprocate through paying taxes as a mark of their allegiance. This new found allegiance and reciprocation from the colonized gave them the stature of free subjects within the colonial structure; and this is how they were 'informed' by the colonizers that 'they were now under the control of the British government'. All other 'impacts', such as victory of the British, were enumerated in the last few sentences of the passage. But the colonizers were not all too happy with what McCabe hinted at about the probable repercussion of punishing some Lushei chiefs such as 'Khalkam, Langpunga and Thangula', who were convicted for conducting raids on the plains of Cachar. Such a backlash was averted as the first two chiefs committed suicide in Hazaribagh Jail; such an act could hardly evoke any anger among the Lusheis. This perspective of the colonizers exposes their inner fear of a possible backlash from the natives that would have arisen due to the former's desire to punish the natives. At the same time, it absolved them from the responsibility of sentencing the chiefs to death, which would have made them 'culprits' in the eyes of the colonized. One can locate here a 'politics of culture' in which the colonizer needed a good self-image in the eyes of the colonized, and an unopposed acceptance of their diktat by the colonized was the source of a sense of fulfilment of their desire. But the question is: how could such a strategy of self-fashioning be realized through the colonized? Or how could the colonized recognize the colonizer in such a superior mode? The British assessment of how such a self-image would be successful was not only based upon their obvious successes, but also depended on investing 'power' successfully on the 'colonized'. Mr Davis, Superintendent, North Lushei Hills remarked on the occasion of his handing over charge to the next incumbent Mr Porteous in 1894:

> I always held the Chiefs of villages responsible for the behaviour of their people....any course of action which tends to discourage any litigation amongst a people like the Lusheis is worth persisting in or they would soon become like Kukis, in the Naga Hills, who, having been, by neglect on our part, practically emancipated from the control of their hereditary chiefs, are the most litigious tribe in that district (Reid, 1983: 41).

This investment of power in the native chiefs became a source of reducing the anxiety of colonization and such investments were intended to produce subjectivation under the rule.

The politics of culture here was in the form of justifying the exclusion of colonizers from the native societies, that went both ways: of giving power to the native rulers and controlling them from above, and of freeing the natives from their own chiefs in order to empower the natives, as among the Kukis in Naga Hills. But the colonizers needed to exercise caution and calculate risks both ways. Their own exclusion from the native societies despite being their rulers needed to be covered up through a process of subjectivation that ensured a stable order within their rule. The calculated refrain in case of Lushei Hills on part of the British, in not allowing the subjects to litigate against their chiefs, was also a suppression of any possibility of rebellion as individual discontentment often took the form of community resistance. Therefore, the British policy was to contain litigations within the rule of the chief and control them from above. Thus, the politics of culture, during the time of annexation mainly consisted in not intervening in the internal affairs of a tribe, but controlling them through some intermediary power from above. The British sought to brighten their image by being just and kind to the natives in order to establish the political superiority of their rule upon the already existing rule of tribal chiefs.

One can read here how the British as colonizers negotiated their cultural power by maintaining a cultural distance created through a mechanism of control from above, so that the culture of the colonized remained in an altogether different sphere not to be intervened through overt political power. At the same time, retaining chieftainship in the interest of managing the natives from within by their own traditional chiefs exhibits a practice of liberalism towards native culture, while displaying a calculative attitude too. The colonizers allowed the restraints and prohibitions within native culture to continue to exist so that native culture would not intrude into the space of colonial political culture. Therefore, a cultural logic operated as a supportive mechanism of political control, which one can decipher from the British policy of fortifying the rule of the chiefs.

Manoeuvres of the Empire

The British kept the native cultural sphere separate from the colonial political space. This was even more evident from the fact that they considered the hill areas such as Mizo, Manipur and Khasi Hills as 'frontiers' and categorized these as excluded, partially excluded and unadministered areas. The colonizers only wanted to protect their assets inside the 'frontiers', such as tea gardens that paid for running the colonial regime (Mackenzie, 1979: 302–314). Such a notion of 'frontier' as a limit-point for protection of beneficial areas and activities reduced the various tribes of North-East India into people of not much interest and importance. Therefore, attributions such as 'wild' and 'savage' signified gross devaluation of their cultural position, and regular punitive action by the British succeeded in producing a sense of devaluation among the native cultures. This was manifest in undermining the spirit of native resistance by the British. For example, the British deplored the rebellion of the Kuki chiefs against forced labour and the recruitment of such labour corps for employment in France in 1917. 'Forced labour clearly violated basic human dignity. But then the 'rationale' by the British for penalizing the Kukis was not the said rebellion but the raids that they conducted on the Nagas. The British intention was to stop such raids by punitive measures, which would ultimately subject them to surrender before the rule (Machenzie, 1979: 80–81). Such apparently justified pleas made by the British served their ulterior purpose of colonization, but they knew very well how to disguise the actual purpose behind the veil of such justifications given to repressive measures. The ulterior purpose of colonization becomes evident when the British displaced the same Kukis to various places as a front against other tribes. For example, Kukis were dispatched to North Cachar Hills to act a buffer against the Dimasas resisting British invasion. The case of Khonoma, a legendary Angami village unique for its 40-year-long resistance against British intrusion, exemplified how the vanquished were dehumanized by the victors. What happened after the fall of Khonoma has been described by Verrier Elwin in the following words: 'Wonderful terraced cultivation confiscated and its clan dispersed among other village. The result was that the dispossessed villagers found themselves not only deprived of their homes, but confiscated of their settled cultivation....The result was widespread sickness and mortality' (1961: 22).

This kind of destruction of their livelihood practices by the British had a far reaching impact on displacing the native. Such displacement was far more barbarous than what was done by the most brutal savages of the world. The civilized savagery of the British was far more powerful than the natives' indigenous ways of embattling and resist the former. The civilized ways of British consisted in making use of native territory and their cultural norms for the advancement of the colony. The strategy of winning over the native chief either by military power or by manoeuvre was the means to secure supremacy over them. Natives were cowered to death and destruction and could scarcely resist the British, often giving in to their might. The entire corps of the British waiting on the Hill tracts of the North-East discussed various strategies and reflected on securing their supremacy. Thus, the British knowledge of the natives was aimed at attaining only this goal.

The knowledge claims of the British were also circulated to subjugate native claims of knowledge, especially military and administrative forms of knowledge, which were directly utilized to undermine the natives' claim over their own territory and engage them with a responsibility to protect the interests of the British Raj. In negotiation with the Lushei chief Vonpilal, Captain Stewart, the then Deputy Commissioner of Cachar, made him understand that it would be unwise to expand his territory near the tea gardens up to Sonai, later elaborating on the British plan to annex the Lushei territory. According to colonial logic, even if the Lusheis thought of themselves as an independent people they could not have had an independent territory of their own; the reason being the absence of a natural boundary between the Lushei hills and the southern boundary of Cachar on the one hand, and between Lushei hills and the sea on the other. As the water point was supposed to be the natural boundary and the Lusheis drank water from a river flowing into the Barak, one could take them to be living within Cachar. The Deputy Commissioner of Cachar, therefore, was in the right stead to bring Lushei hills under the control of British rule by pushing the southern boundary of Cachar as far as it was thought proper. One can locate here the expansionist desire of the empire by playing on geographical factors to such an extent that the cultural distinctness of Lusheis could be subsumed under the demarcations of political control. In other words, the justification for expansion of colony into Lushei hills was given in terms of a concept of geographical boundaries, in which human beings do not play any role. It is the geographical factor alone that determines the legitimacy of demarcating cultural and political boundary. This is an example of colonial determination of geography as a system of knowledge that produces truths congenial to desires of power (Mackenzie, 1979: 299–300).

Here, the colonizer effaced the territorial location of the Lusheis and created an epistemic distortion of the social boundary of their home. It advocated an opening of Lushei Hills through the southern boundary of Cachar and prescribed the inclusion of Lushei territory within Cachar, with the cogent reason that Lusheis drank water from the river Barak. It upheld a concept of a natural boundary in order to facilitate British annexation up to the boundary till the sea. This whole passage produced a deliberate colonial travesty of the social and cultural boundaries of the Lusheis. This kind of production of a deliberate miscognition on the part of the colonizer was intended to produce similar cognitive distortion among the natives so that they turned oblivious of their own cultural and social grounding. The process of colonization produces such involuntary forgetting of the crucial markers of one's cultural landscape, as it drives them to other territories and even generates a desire to dominate others in their own territory. The continuation of Lushei raids on the plains of Cachar even after British annexation did not find a place in British accounts, while public memories are replete with such marauding raids in eastern part of southern Assam's Cachar district. The blueprint of British annexation of Lushei Hills was therefore conceived by naturalizing their claim over Lushei territory. This was how the British undermined the social and cultural boundaries of the Lusheis. They advocated a policy of seclusion for the tribe, taking a leaf from what the government of United States did in dealing with Native Indian tribes. Their thoughts on tribes were suggestive of the creation of a special agency, legislation and tribunal for managing affairs pertaining to tribes like Lushei and other Kukis (Mackenzie, 1979: 428).

This exhibits how the British intended a total subjugation of the tribes in the manner in which native Indian tribes were cleansed by the white settlers in America. The British further intended to bring every subject community and tribe such as 'dangerous Mussulman', 'intriguing Manipuris' and 'wild hill-tribes' under a common territorial jurisdiction. The logic behind such a demand was reflective of colonial arrogance: wherever they (British) had wished to extend their rule, they wanted every subject to completely submit to the rule (Ibid.: 430). It is interesting to note that colonial laws did not provide any rights and liberties to the subjects, but their expected complete submission to the diktats of the rulers.

Such a proclamation of what 'ought' the Empire do fledged its wings on an imagined territorial jurisdiction up to watersheds of the Bay of Bengal and Irawadi in order to wield an iron law of power. This instrumental territorialization of various tribes and communities within British rule was accomplished by way of actualizing various plans of the British. But the British perception of the loyalty of various such people exhibited a kind of inner scepticism and tension. Categories like 'friendly' and 'hostile' employed by the British to identify tribes on this side or that created confusion for the administrators. Tribes that were considered friendly were imagined to have virtues as an 'uncorrupt child of nature'. Tribes that were found hostile were supposed to incarnate all possible wickedness. In effect, the British thought that they could depend implicitly on the friendly tribes in all frontier matters. The fidelity, peaceful habits, gentleness and truthfulness of these so-called friendly tribes were contrasted with the turbulence, cruelty, and treachery of their opponents. Within this imaginary picture of virtues and vices of tribes, the Lusheis were considered hostile because of their frequent raids on British subjects. Other hill tribes who had accepted British domination were, as a matter of colonial policy, pitted against such hostile tribes. The friendly tribes were settled in a buffer zone between the territory of the hostile and the areas governed by the British. The British planned settlement of friendly tribes on the borders of those areas which were more vulnerable to attack by hostile tribes. What turned out to be more intriguing is the interrelationship between the so-called hostile and friendly tribes, as they shared the same clans despite being located across impassable physical barriers separating them. This is how the Lusheis and tribes hostile to them did not exactly behave as enemies in supporting the plan of the empire to control the hostile Lusheis. The colonial imagination about friendliness and hostility with tribes, therefore, proved to be more unreal than true (Mackenzie, 1979: 426).

Here, the colonizers are suspicious of their own 'make-belief' subject tribes, and such a suspicion mixed with the wish to wield absolute power over them through legal and political means shows the construction of an episteme in which certainty is derived from the fact of total subjugation and total fidelity to the Empire. But the ground reality represented the subversive possibility of a completely opposite situation such that the self-created myth of superiority got busted. This showed an unstable core of the colonizers' perception of themselves, apart from their detached suspicious attitude to-wards the native. At the moment of encountering a rebellion, this British attitude was fully represented. The 'politics of culture' of the British, in ordaining them a superior position of strength, was fraught with the fear of losing due to some disadvantageous factors. At the same time, it assumed undermining the strength of the native, often by derogatory references to their culture. Talking about the Kabui Naga uprising of 1930–31, the British official records stated that the uprising was caused by the introduction of a new religion among Kabui Nagas by a messiah king called Jadonang, who proclaimed that worshipping the new found god *Bambo* and His power would help them overthrow the British and take revenge on the Kukis, supposedly friendly to the British administration. In response to such preparations for a rebellion, the political agent of the British posted in Manipur decided to make an armed demonstration and proceeded with a column of Assam Rifles.

> In year 1930–31 occurred the unrest connected with the rise of Jadonang, a Kabui Naga, who started a new religion and induced the superstitious Kabui Naga to *believe* that he would overthrow the existing administration and enable them to take revenge on the hated Kukis. The political agent decided to make an armed demonstration in February 1931 and proceeded with a column of Assam Rifles to Kambiron where Jadonang had established a temple for his new found religion. Jadonang's temple and idols were destroyed and Jadonang had meanwhile been arrested in Cachar from a hideout. He was then handed over to the Manipur authorities in March. They had tried him for the murder of four unarmed Manipuris, probably as sacrifice to his new gods, in 1929 and was hanged on 29 August 1931 (Reid, 1983: 86).

In the British strategy of pitting one tribe against another, one side would be treated as offenders and the other as victims, and the British administration would come as the saviour of the situation. This was how they created the strategy of punishment and discipline that supported the idea of subjugating others. At the same time, the colonial power could hide behind such a facade of giving protection to the weak and repress any rebellion. This exhibits the politics of playing the perceived 'Others' against each other and then negotiating from a distance through necessary means. In the case of Jadonang, the same policy of penalizing the offender against other unarmed communities such as Kukis and Manipuris provided the punitive evidence to hang him. But such a formal judicial construction of a rebel as an infringer of law and order did not really conceal the fact of cultural devaluation. The British indictment that Jadonang was inducing a new religious belief among the Kabui Nagas added a cultural content to his rebellious role, and the British could perceive that. Therefore, they destroyed the temple and the idol that symbolized the source and the strength of native resistance and trummed up the charge that four Manipuris were sacrificed at the altar of these idols. This was tantamount to intimidating the Kabui Nagas culturally, by unleashing an attack on their cultural symbols and undermining it as superstition. The strategy of the British was to de-legitimize the new-found cult of Jadonang that articulated resistance by turning the practice of human sacrifice against the cult in order to debunk it wholesale. This also marked the colonial modernity that undermined the gods along with the hero of the resistance by an iron rule, that of Reason and Law.

The British demolition of the idols of Jadonang evoked greater reactions. A lady called Gaidiliu, who wanted the Kabui Nagas to get back their lost freedom, carried Jadonang's unfinished task forward. She escaped attempts by the colonial administration to arrest her. Each disappearance created a flurry of unrest among the Kabui Nagas and they strongly believed in her message that the Nagas would be able to establish a 'Naga Raj' all over the hills and could rule over the Kukis. The most significant aspect of propagation of her message was that a large number of *Maibas* or medicine men cropped up in every village; it was they who had spread the word that benefits could be gained from following the cult. There had been a mixture of sorcery and other magical powers in the Jadonang cult with its martial and rebellious overtones. Although Gaidiliu's mobilization of Kabui Nagas could not go beyond arming them with spears and daos, the tremendous power of her sorcery and magical feats projected her as the embodiment of God and as one elected to carry out the unfinished task of Jadonang.

Gaidiliu was captured in 1932 and was given a life sentence. What is significant here is the evaluation of the rebellion by the British as 'semi-religious' and 'semi-martial', and the special mention of usurpation of the power of village chiefs (Reid, 1983: 86–87). Indeed, the invocation of a new cult was necessitated by the British presence, with its tacit alliance with the Kukis. Both these factors necessitated a re-articulation of Naga identity represented in the imagination of the 'Naga Raj'. But the attitude of the British was typically reflected again in their gross debunking of the Kabui Nagas, representing them as a culturally undermined community in colonial texts.

There was simultaneously another facet of British politics of culture in which the British intended to project themselves as the 'messiah' of the savage tribes and derived satisfaction in sympathizing with them. Reports of such activities could be read as texts of colonial grandeur, contemplation and nobility. Such texts contain the self-representation of the colonizer through which they also gave a representation of the colonized. Apart from the dwindling and deceiving imagery of a hostile native that challenged the ideas of stable British rule, the colonizers had also fallen for the creation of a benevolent image of themselves among the natives. The figures of such benevolence emerged in the form of some British officials who crossed the line between the colonizer and the colonized by way of proffering the solitary image of a philanthropologist or saviour among the natives. The master-narrative of colonial triumph situated such instances of benevolence and empathy in a special form of mention. In Alexander Mackenzie's (1979) elaborate chronicle of colonial rule, he documented some such ecstatic moments of colonial triumph experienced in benevolence by compiling a reportage titled *Work in Bengal Jungles* or *Lewin's Proverbial Philosophy*. *Work in Bengal Jungles* (cited in Mackenzie, 1979) stated that government officials, freed from formalities of laws and regulations, could develop relevant knowledge about every aspect of the life of hill tribes of the eastern frontier of the British colony. Mackenzie mentions that such officers had an unflagging interest in tribal life and wrote volumes about them.

This ethnographical and anthropological description of the hill tracts of the eastern frontier are then the assertion of one of the most vital colonial motifs in representing the colonized, which brings out how the colonial power operated. It operated without location, identity or boundaries with such an anonymity that is also ubiquitous, answerable only to 'God' (Ibid.: 583). These tracts written by colonial officers were published in *Pioneer,* a periodical that covered the experience of British officers posted in hill areas of the eastern frontier. One example of how the knowledge generated in the *Pioneer* helped the expansion of the empire lay in subjugation of the Garos and, more positively, in teaching the Nagas to grow potato on the rich terraces of Barail hill range. It was possible for the colonial administrators to let the world know about the sacrifice of many devoted to the cause of establishing rudiments of civilization and progress among tribes that lived in a state of animality. According to reports published in the *Pioneer*, many such lives suffered from fever and other deadly diseases. Many of the colonial administrators spent their lives for the sake of people that the Government controlled in the areas covered with jungles (Lentricchiaa, 1982: 50–51).

This makes clear how colonial power wielded its authority through moral actions—actions that resulted into the good of the native, which in turn stimulated a pregnant self-designation of 'power' to rule by turning the natives into subjects who required the rule for their well-being. Both the authority and the native are planted in a relationship of the ruler and the ruled in such discursive production of benevolence and service. What many foreign-funded as well as nationalist NGOs do today is somewhat akin to this colonial benevolence: building up social capital by turning the woes of a populace into a cause. Even an elected government does not desist from establishing a contractual relationship with its citizenry in terms of being a benevolent giver. The best way to pursue a distressed populace into being an ally is to act as a provider. Such a strategy succeeds because it carries the gift and grace of benevolence, to ensure unfaltering support from an otherwise disobedient mass of people.

The texts of *Pioneer* is a mimetic reproduction of the 'self' of the colonizers in terms of a greater moral latitude than just being the ruler, the wielder of power. It produces an image of the self in which the colonizer sees himself more as a concerned human being than a mere ruler. Circulation of such texts also obfuscates the power already assumed in interpolation of the native within that mimetic text. Here, 'politics' assumes its 'reality' from the symbolic codification of power within a culture of benevolence and service created by the colonizer for self-designation and assumption of 'power'. Once again this finds a close analogy to rulers pursuing a policy of reforms with a human face. The whole idea is to project the identity of the rulers as humane and not as oppressors. This human face of the colonizer is an assumed moral authority that could widen the space for recognition of the colonized and give them a cognitive frame of reference to identify themselves within it.

The colonized as 'rebels' subverted that colonial frame of reference, and a greater degree of control by the colonizers within that frame produced the muted and incarcerated identity of the colonized. Therefore, one way of allowing the colonized greater reflexivity was to produce moral codes and pedagogic devices in order to make them feel elevated and secure. For such a purposive making of the 'self' of the colonized, the colonizers accommodated them within their rule. The politics of colonial accommodation based itself upon benevolence and pedagogy to the colonized so that their reciprocation was ensured; and it generated a culture of benevolence and kindness to be reciprocated by an equally sympathetic response from the colonized. The British intended a politics of culture that sublimated possible reactions of the colonized in an enchanted, obedient and rule-following response that could be articulated by the colonizers.

Production of Knowledge as a Means of Subjugation

The colonizer could succeed in producing such effects by epistemic and cognitive control of the colonized within a structure of knowledge. This was done through the construction of knowledge systems and their disciplinary circulation within the overall domination of the British. One such colonial text of knowledge is available in the reportage *Lewin's Proverbial Philosophy*, in which it was mentioned how Col. T.H. Lewin, a colonial army officer and administrator posted among the Chin people inhabiting what is presently the territories of Myanmar, Chittagong and Mizoram could become successful in producing a system of knowledge by extracting the native wisdom into it (Mackenzie, 1979: 583). Native proverbs that served the purpose of determination of various actions of theirs gave rise to wisdom specific to their identity. Such proverbs were collected and translated by Lewin in order to create a system or a store of knowledge that made the native mind more intelligible to the colonizers, as well as serving the purpose of regulating them according to their own system of belief. The text talked of several proverbs. Lewin compared and contrasted these Khioungte proverbs with English. For example:

'Food refused when offered, search in seven houses and you will not find' was appositely compared with 'He that will not when may when he will he shall have nay'. We were also introduced to the following: 'If I must die I must die, but do not touch my top knot, as the peacock said,' very neatly capped by Leech's, 'Take all, take money, take life; but spare, Oh, spare my collars!' In the present collection we find many proofs that human nature is after all very much the *same* whether it is trained in the woods of Chittagong or amid the leafy lanes of England. 'He got angry with the rat, and set fire to the house' is the hill man's way of 'cutting off his nose to spite his face'. The Englishman 'shuts his door when the steed is stolen', the Khioungtha lets his pot fall, and then tucks up his waist cloth. At home 'the bad workman quarrels with his tools,' in Chittagong 'the unsuccessful fisherman curses the river, rough people lay the blame on their dress'...'Caulk a new boat, beat a new wife' is atoned for by 'prop up old house, cherish an old wife' (Mackenzie, 1979: 583).

Throughout the text, examples of equivalence between the native and the English are construed through linguistic–semantic similarities, but it brings out the appropriation of the native in the linguistic mode of the British. It also meant the primacy of linguistic communication over the native speech forms, in which the space between the 'literate' and the 'oral' is merged into the British propensities of meaning. The text represents native proverbs tinged in typical English meanings. This construction of communicative cultural meanings out of the native cultural resources acts as a material for colonial cognition of the native. This is a transformed native context constructed in the British way, in which the native had to know her own meanings from the meanings endowed to it in a colonial text. Apart from meaning, the logic of proverbs is also transformed from its native contexts to the context of Englishmen, and thereby to the universal context. For example, an Englishman's 'shutting the door when the steed is stolen' represents a metaphoric way of covering up or taking caution only after an immediate loss. It further presents a mishap caused by others. But this context cannot be extended up to the point of an actual sequence of carrying a pot and the moment of its fall resulting from the loosening of the waistcloth, because when the hands move to hold the waistcloth the pot drops. One cannot say that the fall of the pot occasions the tightening of the waistcloth; rather one could see that the waistcloth loosens because the entire attention and effort is concentrated on carrying the pot, which in turn results in the fall of the pot. On the one hand, the carrying of the pot is the cause of loosening the waistcloth and, on the other, the loosening of the waistcloth happens because of carrying the pot and results in the pot falling; and then comes the moment of making everything all right. In the native context, the relationship between the carrying of pot and loosening of waistcloth is not that of a door and a steed which are linked up by a different sequence of activity, but the stealing of the steed only causes an apprehension of how to shut the door, which is a post-facto motive. In the native context, the consequent action follows from a natural incapacity; while in the English context, the consequent action follows by way of sudden arousal of intelligence and carefulness. The translation of the native into the English appropriates this sense of naturalness and replaces it with its cultural opposite, as loss caused by artificial extraneous factors like stealing is bound to make the victim look for some solace after the event. This is how *Lewin's Proverbial Philosophy* (mis)represented the native and levelled the significant cultural difference in translation in such a way that the English could not perceive the natural helplessness of the native. It draws a bland equivalence between the case of stealing and the case of loosening of waistcloth in terms of meaning. Looked at from another angle, the English could only imagine the native in a problematic context, in which the native charts her own ways out.

Such problematic contexts are clearly different for the native than what the English administrator perceives, as the lessons the natives derive involve reference to a direct situation. For example, the failure of a fisherman to cross the river and the experience of seeing rough people blaming their dress are certain predicaments of a difficult nature; while 'a bad workman quarrels with his tools' is just an expression of bad temperament resulting from one's failure to come to terms with one's own fault. The fisherman realizes that he failed before he crosses the river, while the rough people in the native scene make an excuse of their dress; and in both cases there is no deliberate intent involved. In the quarrel of a bad workman with his tools, there is primarily a manifestation of a quarrelling instinct; while in the native context a quarrelling spirit does not exist. 'Cursing' and 'blaming' in the native proverb cannot be understood as a kind of 'quarrel' in the British context; it is not only a gross equivalence of meaning but also far removed from the native context. But the English claim to understand the native in this way only shows an arrogant ethnocentrism that fails to recognize its own limits, and aims at appropriating the larger gamut of senses available in the native context by funnelling it down to a narrow British context. Despite the incompatibility of the contexts and radically different nature of expressions of problems, the translation glosses over these significant differences. While the English context is more formal and proverbs turn into precepts, in the native context the description of the event is bound to the situation and proverbs are neither 'precepts' nor 'maxims', nor even 'thumb rules' that are invoked in facing the situation. Rather the native proverbs represent an existential problem that disturbs their wisdom and such disturbing occurrences do not provide them with a thumb rule to act upon.

The translation of these native proverbs in English by Captain Lewin is part of the will to know them and they are known in terms of the colonizer. Most native meanings are driven outside their text when equivalence is established with English culture. Such an understanding through one's own terms produces a sharp division between the knower and the known. The English attains the superior position of the 'knower' and the native remains as the 'known'. This is what could be called an act of epistemic appropriation of native culture by the colonizers. It also distinctly exhibits the two distinct frames of knowledge—colonial knowledge and native knowledge—and the association between the former and the latter ruptures the latter, disembedding it from its moorings. This is how the native becomes the Other—the 'object' of colonial knowledge. The colonial knowledge reproduces the native in an authoritative way by claiming validity of such reproduction or representation. Lewin's translation as a mode of reproduction of the native text enriches the treasure of colonial knowledge in a way that remains invisible to the native. The native is doubly displaced, first by a displacement of native terms of reference and then by being reproduced in terms that replace him. The native becomes invisible in this process and what becomes visible is a figuration of a being called 'native'. This is how native is turned into a signifier within the processes of reproduction of colonial knowledge.

Another example from Lewin's text shall make it clear how the 'native' becomes the signifier of colonial knowledge. 'Native', as known in the terms of the colonizer, is a transmuted identity created in the image of the colonizer. The colonized seeks her 'native self' as a memory of the image given to her by the colonizer; and in this way attribution of nativity to the representation of the native draws similes from the colonizer's texts. This secures an image of the native and projects it to the colonized. Such images are reciprocally entrapped within a narrative representation. Therefore, what remains as Other to the colonizer comes also as an Other to the colonized. The women, in particular, become the site on which the colonizer engraves an 'otherhood' within the colonized, and this is done by way of showing the relationship between man and woman among the colonized. Thus, the colonizer interpolates its patriarchy in the native in the process of appropriation of the native social relations, turning the native as an Other to itself. But it cannot accomplish this otherization of the native without imaging an Other of the native within it. Natives as the Other of the colonizer are erased in the Other of the native within themselves. One such duplicated Other is brought out in the open by Lewin's text. Lewin's translation of the native proverb 'prop up old house, cherish an old wife', is inverted into an equivalence with 'caulk a new boat, beat a new wife' that reveals the technologies of colonial otherization of the native. The Other within the colonizer, who is 'caulked and beaten' is inverted in the Other of the colonized, 'propped up and cherished', reinvented and equated into being 'caulked and beaten'. The Other of the colonizer is inverted into the Other of the colonized, in exchange to the Other of the 'colonized' being turned into the Other of the colonizer. The Other cherished by the colonized becomes 'beaten' by the colonizer to reveal what 'violence' an innocuous looking translation performs. Surely, the colonized cannot shut his door when the steed is stolen by the colonizer. He can only let his pot fall and let them only tuck up his waistcloth. The colonial eulogy and self-praise for such a wonderful way of understanding the native comes from Lewin as he goes on to suggest that the native mind was in no way very different from the 'Western understanding of Man'. According to Lewin, one just needs to scratch the Western notion of Man in order to discover the universal human characteristics, that is, the very same common human nature. If one could identify such a common human nature, the widest difference of race, religion, culture and language seems to be superficial. By obliterating cultural differences, Lewin appropriated the distinct cultural forms of hill tribes, even if they show up substantial difference in terms of proverbs reflective of their culture specific wisdom. Lewin tried to interpret these proverbs as a different version of the same wisdom that Western culture reflected in many of the proverbs available in English. He considered proverbs of the tribes as reflective of their simplicity, while such proverbs in the West represented artificial culture and conventionality. He understood the difference between the Western culture and tribal culture in terms of a rather naïve binary opposition of simplicity versus artificiality (Mackenzie, 1979: 583–84).

One does not require an Edward Said to tell one how the West produces its Other in the Oriental 'natives', for one also does not require a Michel Foucault to grasp that 'The historicity of such discourses lies in the use of reason to discover a deep truth about ourselves and our culture, which has to hide its history in order to function as a goal for us' (1982: 260). Only Lewin's texts are sufficiently provocative to grasp that colonial texts discover a deeper truth of human nature to hide its history of colonization. Lewin, an officer posted by the colonial administration, tries hard to keep the mask of a dispassionate learner of the cultural nuances of the colonized society. This is because most of us cannot face reality, as centuries of literature and the relatively new science of psychiatry tell us—we usually manage to deceive ourselves. When the masks slip, a human often has a breakdown because the truth(s) are usually too poignant and painful for us to grasp. So, if one is a colonizer and one realizes what one is doing, one would have to quit or go mad. George Orwell did leave the Burmese Police Service. Similarly, most upper-caste Indians accept the myth that the caste system is consensual and has a benign aspect, and that Hinduism is very tolerant. Lewin's extensive learning of colonized culture reveals a similar kind of masquerade of knowledge that serves to disguise the brute force of power. It is reported in the *Pioneer* that there is scarcely an incident of hill life which proverbs do not utilize or illustrate (Mackenzie, 1979: 583). When a village feast is organized it is said that just as dry vegetables smell in the pot in the same way cold people thaw at a feast. The miseries of people who suffer raids by hostile tribes have always felt that a relationship of subjugation and slavery is like a thorn under the nail. If a human being lands up in a strange and possibly hostile clan it is advised that s/he should take the strut out of her walk before entering that strange village. If s/he cruises through a strange river, it is intelligent and cautionary on his/her part to take down the flag from the mast. Describing the difference of the familiar and the unfamiliar, they believed that in their own village a crow could be a cock, but in an unfamiliar village it could only be a hen. The message is that nothing is sure and certain about an unfamiliar place and nothing can be taken for granted. Such pieces of wisdom that drop from the lips of the colonized provide succour to Lewin's scholarship and ideas.

This report on proverbs of caution and apprehension of danger by the natives mentioned in the *Pioneer* exhibits the colonial endeavour to know the mind of the colonized. Lewin's text signifies the sympathy of the ruler for the ruled as they try to see their response to difficult situations in life. This is simultaneously a critical searching into the mind of the Other. But the most authentic mode of knowing the Other is by knowing how she knows her own language. Lewin focuses on some such proverbs: 'Do not talk on important matters to a man just off on a journey'; 'Seek no quarrel with one just awakened'; 'A thousand ants can carry an earthworm so the words of many turn a lie into truth' (Ibid.: 583–584).

Lewin's text assumes a body in order to construe a body of knowledge for the natives for whom knowledge remained discrete speech-acts. Certain performative attitudes are represented in such discrete speech-acts, such as determining situational dos and don'ts. This performative attitude follows a self-description of one's own language, as the native believes metaphorically that speech assists wisdom, in which the language of speech contains wisdom. But at the same time, the elusiveness of words in falsifying reality or constructing truth or falsehood is represented metaphori-cally when the native says, 'A thousands ants can carry an earthworm, so the words of many turn a lie into truth'. This represents a metaphoric way of understanding how language can be used to construct reality in a certain way that bears veracity from the community of speakers. A lie is construed in the manner in which language is spoken by many, which simultaneously presupposes the singular authenticity of truth. Lies are associated with plurality of voices, while truth is determined to be singular. Obviously, such a framing of native wisdom is a self-reflexive gaze of the native on herself.

Colonial ethnography records these self-representing moments and makes use of such interpretations in grounding the colonial ruse of power. Knowing the native in the mode in which the native knows himself removes the distance and unfamiliarity with them and establishes a kind of linkage through which colonial discourse is formed and channelized. Such colonial discourse mirrors the native in order to make him conscious, and such an act of stirring the consciousness of the native makes him feel the presence of the colonizer. Further transmission of native knowledge by the colonizer produces a kind of confidence in the native which is enjoyed by the colonizers in establishing their epistemic dominance. The moment colonial production of native knowledge can establish its truthfulness, such truthfulness can not only give legitimacy to their rule but can also sustain the normative authority of the colonial power. The entire process involves a politics of culture in which correct understanding of the native culture empowers them and endows them with the capacity to produce a cognitive apparatus for the native. As if the colonizer holds the mirror in which the native can see himself, the moment the native sees his true representation from the Other, he accepts the presence of the Other. What produces the impression of truth is the colonial textualization of native ways, the ways that are very much known a priori by the native himself, but the colonial representation of such self-knowledge manifests the truth of it. This is how colonial reproduction of native knowledge produces the 'truth effect' in the native, something that is radically different than the a priori knowing of their truth by themselves. All this is done in a way that the natives can see a true representation of their convictions, beliefs and values in the colonial text. But the colonizer hides this strategy of travesty by way of bringing home the truth of the native in such a way that it tallies with the home truths.

The aim of such an epistemological framing of the native overdetermines the politics of culture present in colonial ethnography. As both the 'truth' and the 'travesty of truth' remain to be the choice for such politics of culture, the choice can assume forms such as commentary, documentation and so on, to come to a specific mode of representation. Such representations, in turn, contain within themselves specific hermeneutic strategies of the politics of power in order to determine the meaning constituted for the colonized, and also have bearing on the native sense of history, which are interiorized into colonial texts in order to make the native live within that sense of history without giving her or him an alien sense of being colonized.

POLITICS OF CULTURE IN A SALVAGE MODE: HUTTON'S REPORT ON NAGA HILLS

J.H. Hutton's *Report on Naga Hills* (1986) presents a travelogue from an ethnographer who restored many of the lost symbols that attained mystic, iconic and figurative meanings in the Naga society. The text resists any attempt to tamper with such symbols to undermine the past of the Nagas. It frames an image whose contents refer to other contents outside the frame; its structure denotes something that cannot be encompassed, and, at the same time, its gross objectification in photography and pictures brings it in their pristine state to the image market of modernity. Therefore, Hutton appears to the present as an ethnographer who *salvages* the Naga images before their irrecoverable disappearance. Hutton's report is strengthened by pictographic and photographic textualization that bears an urge to grasp the fugitive at the moment of extinction. It seizes moments from time so that each image is a record of salvage, freezing actions and fixing beings against their transience. But then Hutton foregrounded the explicit relationship between the photography/pictography and the object in a narrative cognition, in which the making of signs by the Nagas is negotiated through the figure of bodies and structures. Hutton's gift of Naga images serves as a metaphor of disappearance at a moment when photography assumes a hegemonic power over its subjects. The politics of culture that roots itself in a dominant symbolic order can easily subsume these photo/pictographs to patterns of interpretations and communications that alienate it from its life-world context, and gives an authenticity that lies prior to the present and, therefore, turns the whole fund of images into a broken continuum between presence and absence. The politics of culture makes these images look like the figure of the mystic world or icons of a ravaged pre-history, the place of which is that of an authenticity based on time, disjointed and fractured between the past and the present.

Hutton's reportage about field-houses built in the form of buffalo horns in Konyak villages and his explanation of buffalo horns as 'fertility symbols' decoded the symbolic relationship between fertility and agriculture (Hutton, 1986: 7). But such houses as signifiers also speak of the relationship between the material and the cultural, the latter inscribed on the former. But the houses looking like thatched shrines for effigies of the dead are explained away by Hutton when he says, 'the dead are intimately associated with the village crops'. Such decoding makes death merely corporeal, realized in terms of enhanced productivity, shorn of its effigy-symbolic, in which the body of the dead reappears as fetish. Through such fetishization the perversity of death is normalized at the level of culture that subverts the association of fertility with death enhancing the crop. Here, culture through its fetishes emerges as overpowering death and the effigy-symbolic of death transcends the impressionistic boundary of good harvest. All these layers of meaning are fetishized not in the fetish itself, but in the photograph of a cultural fetish. The meanings attached to the fetish of the body in the effigy are reified in ethnographic texts in its picto/photograph. Therefore, there is a *double fetishization* of cultural images in its representation, on which the politics of culture thrives. The politics of culture suffers from the blind spot of concealing what the natives see and it fetishizes the native-symbolic with a privileged textual decoding. The symbolic and ceremonial cutting of hair among the Konyak and Changs is evaluated by Hutton quoting Marco Polo, who, according to Hutton, would have called the custom as a very evil custom and a parlous one, and the latter describes the rationale of such 'hair-cutting' as advantageous for 'verminous country'.

Once again, the politics of culture manifests repeatedly through undermining the 'other' culture, especially the coinage 'verminous' which represents a sense of cultural indictment.

The possibility that needs to be decoded here is the native way of warding off the stigma of falling sick, suffering from loss of vitality, depletion of male health or female pollution, which got coded in the rite of hair-dressing in a specific way. Especially for the women, 'hair' signifies puberty, sexual purity or even the holding and release of spirits deemed to be good or evil. Therefore, the act of hair cutting is a means to satisfy all these considerations attached to it. Thus, the cutting of hair encodes masculine domination and feminine disposition. The politics of culture continually re-inscribes dominant categories and discourses through reference to a fixed relationship of difference, manifested in the textualization of partial meanings and a further stigmatization of the native stigmas through these meanings. The way Hutton called the practice of the cutting of hair as advantageous to 'verminous country', substantiates this kind of 'travestying' of native meanings. Such travesties are incorporated into the larger body of belief. For instance, when inquiring into why a cow's skull is placed between buffalo horns in the case when Nagas fail to hunt the head of an enemy, Hutton identified affinity of Nagas to cows analogous to Hindu practices. He opined, 'In case of the cow, it seems possible again that one is in touch with some pre-Hindu belief that has been incorporated elsewhere into that...receptive system' (Hutton, 1986: 14). This exhibits how a reference to some more significant (according to the ethnographer's consideration) and dominant system of belief, within which he tries to position Naga belief. The visual experience of the presence of heads in Hutton's report and their pictorial presentation as 'tattoo' closes up the text in repetitive swirls. But how such tattoos represent the figures of naturalistic imagination of the Nagas, how the aesthetic of the tattoo produces the motif of living in a fortunate way, are all muted into the politics of imagination of something 'grotesque', the imagery of a visual modern society. Hutton's silence on these aesthetic nuances merely reproduce the picture of such tattoos constituted by its correspondence with heads or tusks of some animals on the body of a warrior (Ibid.: 24). Hutton sees similarity between tattoos in terms of its designs such as when he mentions about a 'tattoo' in *Yonghong*:

I noticed here a face tatoo [*sic*] which I have occasionally seen before in Phom villages, probably on runaways from further east, and which is, I believe, worn in Tobu. In the form I saw here it is a line running from the forehead down the nose, at the tip of which it broadens out, with three dots on each side. Tobu, I think, wear it the other way up and extend it to the chin as well (Hutton, 1986: 24).

Hutton extends his field of vision by way of drawing resemblance with others, a typical ethnographic mode of encoding an item universally as a mark, here again, downplaying the location of such marks. When Naga tribesmen engrave 'tattoos' on their bodies or on things that are a part of their lives, it assumes a specificity that cannot be so easily seen in other figures. Otherwise, such tattoos are treated on the same scale as 'all triangles have three angles', a kind of monastic truism. The apparent similarity at the level of the figurative does not produce an indistinguishable resemblance; rather, the resemblance figured in it is un-contained in the figurative. Similar tattoos on two different faces belonging to two different locations can produce a cultural difference that cannot be retrieved through a language of similarity.

Once a meaning is fixed in such a way it produces 'quandaries' that make meanings irretrievable. Talking about the head ornament of the males at *Angfang*, Hutton noticed that the buffalo horns had been replaced by a brass version; and for those whose heads had been taken away by enemies, this was represented in the form of an effigy 'whose top of the head was high and rounded, instead of low and flat and the horns were absent'. Such fixation of meanings reduces the aesthetic of Naga emblems and effigies into mere visual objects. That the figures are more than a copy of objects is demonstrated in the figurated carving of objects such as the 'Y' post called *Yimtsang* by the Sangtams. Such figurated objects present both the figure and the object and attain a 'name' in language. Therefore, one cannot term it as a stone erected in the honour of this or that, but what has been carved out as 'Y'; this is neither the figure Y, nor the object 'Y', nor something that it symbolizes. The figure acquires a new language, a sign unrepresentable in the linguistic–objective mode. Even the tattooed parts of a body are markers of an inscription different than that part; the figure that is borne out of that part through tattooing

intensifies this gap between the body and the figure. A representation of such figures in language can only be figurative. The
tendency to link such figures with certain obvious functions makes
it essentialist, which represses the figurative. Hutton's example of
'a smallish erect stone put up by a *Yimtsung* inhabitant 'because
it was a nice one', commits such fallacies when he says, '...people
sharpened their daos on the top of it'. Even such a mundane activity
involves the appreciation of the particular shape of something that
is erected, and the beauty of that shape indicates a kind of
subjectivity that perhaps cannot be equated with honing the dao on
it. Such subjectivity goes into constructing something like a
memorial erected in the honour of a dead chief, which represents
a more comprehensive symbolic meaning. Hutton's picture of the
'memorial to a chief of Chinghori that represented the rainbow' is
symbolic of the rain that comes only when a really great man dies
(Hutton, 1986: 57). Its accompanied array of clothes and ornaments, a long row of Y-shaped posts and the skulls of slaughtered
cattle, all in the memory of the dead chief produces a total meaning.
But comparing such a narrative claim with actuality Hutton observed:

> The chevron does not really look a bit like a rainbow, being angular
> and the two sides crossing at the top, having a sort of foot sticking
> up at each end, but it struck me that it might have something to do
> with the passage of the soul to the next world, as I think the rainbow
> is called 'the spirit's bridge' by some Naga tribe and the Semas also
> call it Kungami-Pukhu which one translated as 'sky spirits leg', but
> 'apukhu' means bridge as well and the latter is a much more reason-
> able translation (Ibid.: 58).

This appreciation of the tribal symbolic marks a method of comparing meanings in modalities. But such modalities are complemented in terms of ruling the tribe. Hutton gives the example of
disobedience of the village headman of *Rishetsi*, a Sangtam village,
who did not produce his son who had committed the murder of
a British subject a year or two ago before Hutton arrived there. The
village headman promised that he would bring his son to Kohima,
but Hutton says, 'but probably won't'. This apparently innocuous
event tells a tale that British administrators could exercise their

power in a retributive way, showing that they could assume the image of 'humane power' in order to control the natives. This intimacy with the 'native' represents the soft and persuasive aspect of British rule that could humble the native in a subliminal way. It did not emphasize the gulf between the ruler and the ruled but it involved gentle persuasion, dialogic in character (Hutton, 1986: 65). There is no fear, even if there is a bit of gratuitous fear of penalizing, which represented the 'cultural empire' that the British intended to build in India. What the British intended in the context of North-East is to imprint their perspective and, thereby, exorcise the native point of view. Such a cultural empire weaves together the gaze on the subject through their aesthetic as well as moral spheres of life.

IMAGING THE 'CORPOREAL'

Haimendorf's *Return to the Naked Nagas* (1974) is a work based on his extensive tour and notes on the landscape and humanscape of distant villages of Nagaland that he visited in 1934 and 1969–70. Therefore, a reading through the text presents the visible interior of these sites that Haimendorf had visited. The reading connects 'visit' and 'vision' in a spectacular manner that gives the reader a vantage point into the corporeal aspects of Naga life. This mode of writing assumes a complete pictorial representation of the marked field of vision to codify it in language. There is nothing within that field of vision that perhaps remains invisible, and this mode of assumption compels a reader to decode the images of the corporeal and explore whether there is nothing invisible even within the corporeals. A cursory reading of the text calls for a discounting of this explorative possibility, but, even while discounting that, one has to identify the textual distinction between corporeal and incorporeal, visible and invisible, and one has to read through such negotiations between the two sides.

The very first chapter entitled 'The Naga Hills' represents Haimendorf's encounter with the Nagas in a hospitable and charitable way. The encounter occurs in the backdrop of Naga habitat. The habitats are slippery paths through rocky passages that are covered with overgrown bushes with prickly creepers. But such a narrow alley emerges into an open space. But more than what met his eyes lies there where he 'recognizes',

> '...representations of cattle, pig's heads, women breasts [sic], dance ornaments and human heads, these symbols of successful head-hunting which for the Angami belonged to the past...'(Haimendorf, 1974: 9).

One can read here Haimendorf's recognition of things that have been already represented, his return to these items. His return occasions a representation of the represented, mixed with surface-level recognitions. In a moving and remarkable experience of how he was welcomed as a guest, Haimendorf expresses non-understanding of the language of his host and the queer verbal communication between him and his guest. But the clear and explicit gesture of welcome by the host by way of offering Haimendorf rice-beer and later presenting him a cock when he returned to the bungalow, is an experience recorded by him as being honoured by the Nagas as a guest. But so far as linguistic communication is concerned the absence of a language is what Haimendorf seems to leave aside as something ambiguous. Language that remains beyond visibility, apart from smiling at each other and murmuring of some words, 'which, however remained equally unintelligible' (Ibid.) to both the guest and the host remains as some ostensible linguistic behaviour, even without a glimpse of what transpired in that behaviour. Language emerges as 'invisible' in its corporeal manifestation. It occupies the position of a tangible entity, which is both visible and corporeal at Haimendorf's surface-level cognitions. But at this level of corporeality only the forms of the culture-specific codes of *hospitatility* of the Nagas remain visible.

The predominant ethnographic desire is to represent, but what is represented cannot always fulfil the desire. What the text 'speaks of' is a language that represents. Can the text speak a language which it supposedly represents? Haimendorf's representation of *Tevo*, the descendent of the founder of the village, as a repository of 'virtue' draws an equivalence between 'Tevo, the virtue of the village' and his own representation of 'Tevo' in the context of the Angami village (Ibid). This is how 'virtues of Tevo', the virtue of the village, gets circumscribed within ethnography. This circumscription within the text assumes the form of the real, and this is how corporeality of the real and its visibility are merged within the text. While virtues arise in actual social praxis, the circumscribed 'virtue' in the text is a meaning-construct that appears 'visible'. Similarly, Haimendorf's description of the 'feast of merit' creates a quandary of 'meaning construction', in which the sacrifice of a large number of animals for arranging a feast for the entire village community presents a visible performance of the feast. The construction of a monument signifying the conduct of the feast, as an act of symbolic fulfilment of something great, narrates the concept of 'merit' within the Angami context (Haimendorf 1974: 14). But this whole act is symbolic in character in such a way that it gives rise to definite meaning in the Angami context, and more than that, it enacts the satisfaction of desire of the Angamis. Do the mystique of association of such feasts with the 'symbolic' of fulfilment, and its transcendental flight into the symbolic continuation between life and death, reveal how the 'world' is disclosed or made by Angamis? Can Haimendorf's text represent those invisible sources of signification that fulfil the native mind? What needs to be noted here is the 'intentional fallacy' that Haimendorf commits by giving the authorial point of view and by ignoring possibilities of alternative meaning (Ibid.: 18). Further, one also needs to remember that a text is a message that is clearly perceived as being distinct from a 'non-text' or 'other text'. It has the peculiar property of belonging to a culture and the text cannot be taken outside the culture to which it belongs. Haimendorf's representation of Angami feast cannot take the text inside Angami culture beyond a point. The point, as P.K. Mishra remarked about Haimendorf and other colonial ethnographers, is:

The officers travelled in style, escorted by guards, retinues of coolies to carry their baggage, groceries and other items of luxury, clearly sending *messages* as to who they were. In 1936, Furer Haimendorf arrived at Manipur Road Railway Station with sixteen pieces of luggage to do anthropological fieldwork. In other words, the relationship between the observer and the observed was that of the ruler and the ruled. The data had to be produced by the observed. The critical question is how far was this relationship of power reflected in what the British anthropologists chose to write about and what they wrote (Mishra, 2003: 28).

Haimendorf senses the presence of Homeric time in Nagaland and contextualizes the whole feast of merit in the universal mode of megalithic culture. He concludes the note by saying that Angamis had forsaken the habit of head-hunting, which was an apologia for 'colonial modernity' to celebrate the present sense of moral superiority in rejecting that 'aspect'. In textualizing such a moment of rejection, 'head-hunting' becomes the symbolic marker of a stage of civilization, a 'given' in characterizing the Nagas.

The conjunction between re-enactment of a traditional performance and its visible nuances are represented in terms of determination and distinction, while such representation can hardly cover the 'depth dimensions' of actual performance of these rituals. Therefore, the text maps them onto a visible field, and images its nitty-gritties in an act of cognition. Only an inkling of the depth-dimension is possible through the narrative. For instance, the narrative about how the Ahom kings used to annihilate the Nagas was supplanted with an episode of an absconding Ahom king marrying the daughter of the chief of Tanhai, of Konyak Naga country. Haimendorf mentions that the people of Tanhai do not forget to point to the stone that served the exiled Ahom king as a seat. But then he interpreted the event by giving an inkling of its depth-dimension when he concluded that Naga culture had been more humane than the proud rulers of Ahom kingdom. This also gives Nagas a recokning that the cultural difference between Nagas and Ahoms is insurmountable (Haimendorf, 1974).

Through this culturally affinitive event, Haimendorf drew a stark distinction between Ahoms and Nagas when he attributed greater humaneness to Nagas, thus imaging them in a distinct categorical way, which perhaps contradicts the images of Naga as 'head-hunters'. Haimendorf mentioned how the heads of Nagas were hunted by the Ahom Kings. This reversal of a stereotype is an ethnographic strategy by which the images that are given to a community could be partially corrected.

Reading of the 'motif' is another usual ethnographic technique to weave the 'text' from the threads of the 'corporeal'. The text images the corporeal by reading through such 'motifs'. The sacred birds, lions, elephants, snakes and humans carved on the gable of a morung in a Konyak village, were taken by Haimendorf as some 'motifs'. The invocation of a concept of 'motif' purposedly represents the mind behind such carvings, and its textualization reproduces the 'motif' as something present in these carvings. This is a kind of motif that remains present in the objects. But the motif that floats in the text such as 'narrow paths' and 'thick jungles' within which Naga villages are built produces the textual signifiers of such representations. The mimetic representation of such images, motifs and rituals in ethnographic texts assumes a form of actuality by relegating the 'signifiers' of the text. In representing the festive attire of a group of tribesmen, Haimendorf says:

> Their slim bodies, more elegant and supple...and even their fantas- tic head-dress did not weaken this impression. Boar's tusks, goat's hair dyed red, monkey and bear fur, and great hornbill feathers were all in some way or other attached to the small cane hats perched on the tip of their heads (1974: 35).

Such description of ornaments and attires made out of parts of animals preserves an exotic tribal imagery that serves the taste of the observer. But then there are two distinct layers of representation here. Firstly, all those items represent some Naga meaning and their arrangement on their bodies establishes a meaningful relationship between the body and the environment. Secondly, their textualization assimilates that meaning into what is visible and conceived as 'beautiful'. It upholds the look of it, 'what' and 'how' of that 'look' without representing their meaning. Haimendorf highlights the 'look' when he discovered a man standing out in that motley crowd who looked much more luminous. In Haimendorf's words,

> One man, with head-dress of a monkey skull framed in boar's tusks, seemed to stand out from all this motley crowd...But it was his self- possession and his composure, even more than his head-dress and fine ornaments that distinguished him from those surrounding him (Ibid.: 36).

The narrative of look perhaps betrays the allusive meaning that Haimendorf expects the reader to empathize with him. When he describes the head-dress in animalistic images it creates further surprise, as the ethnographer is not able to reconcile his surprise at seeing a man with 'princely bearing'. The ethnographer tran- scribed the vision in certain allusive terms that are available only in the 'text', obviously an act of authorized description that slips from the coherence of the meaning-construction by the Konyaks. It further points at the aporia between two levels of representation: the representation of what the people themselves represent (artefacts) and what the people represent. Any authorized description at both these levels is bound to slip out the coherent meanings imbricated in it. The attribution of supposedly civilized princely qualities in that distinguished persona of the Konyak chief is an act of imaging that transfers the whole meaning to a 'visual field' created within the text. This visual field within the text is where the colonizing look posits itself, and this becomes the field of substituting the voyeur with the aestheticized image of the chief. The meaning transferred within such a visual field is a meaning of how the subject authors the meaning of the subject, and a narrative shift from the objectified exterior to aestheticized interior is what sustains the distance of the subject from what is communicated to it.

What ethnography articulates is a narrative strait that fills up the space between the desire of the subject and the location of its Other. The Other as a subject only becomes an impressionistic replica of the subject and that is how the Other looks the way the subject looks at him. The civilized image of a Naga prince surrounded by 'primitives' is the kind of image that gives fictive satisfaction of the desire of the subject, and the narrative representation produces the 'figure' of that image. The figure resembles the figure of the primitive, and yet, in its princely and beautiful figuration, takes over the meaning generating contexts of such 'figures'. The ethnographer speaks of a 'figure' that loses out its generative context, and through such 'figures' the ethnographer speaks of the distinctiveness of a kind of people, the Nagas in this case. This is an instance of ethnographic appropriation of a Naga figure within the space of decontextualized European representation. Here again, the 'corporeal' touches the height of being 'visible' to an observer in his own terms, thereby disappearing from its sheer corporeality into the imaginative figure of being 'visible' in its own context. The language of ethnography creates such 'invisible' corporeality. Haimendorf mentioned 'morung-feelings' (1974: 57) among the Konyaks, and the practice of war and head-hunting as a life-sustaining force that resists epidemic and disease. 'Death' was described in terms of such feeling. Even when the ethnographer spoke in the cultural idiom of the native, the gap between the language of the ethnographer coined in a different cultural idiom and the native cultural idiom remained unbridgeable. Haimendorf mentioned two distinct modes of mourning, one in the case of death of a person from a morung—with whom intermarriage is possible—as not so grave, and the other in which the frequency of death blurs all feelings and interrelationships (Haimendorf, 1974: 51). It produces a stark comparison with the culture to which the ethnographer belonged. Haimendorf observed that the Naga attitude towards death was conditioned by their falling terminally ill too frequently. Hence, Nagas became insensitive to incidences of death (Ibid.: 60).

Not only is this gap created between two different modes of cultural reception, but it also pervades the ethnographer's representation of a community. The gap remains a visionary narrative of the corporeal realm. The line between the 'corporeal' and the 'incorporeal', the 'visible' and 'invisible' manifests more clearly between such events of life and death. The gap of the language between the ethnographer and the native further creates a gap between the corporeal and the incorporeal, because the ethnographer's limited field of vision fails to perceive the native vision of death as corporeal. For the ethnographer, death is the end of corporeality, of life; but for the Konyaks, the native death is a continuity of life and hence absence in death is filled up with rites of disposing the body within the village despite the rotting smell of decomposition. The rites such as severing the head from the body was associated with a belief that a part of the soul resides in the skull while the other part goes back to soil. The mixing of the body's bones with the soil brought out a visible destruction of the soul from the living body to the land of the dead, where it continues a similar style of life like when the person was alive. Haimendorf could not have described this entire continuum from life to death with an ostensible reference to the rites associated with disposal of the body, and the obvious stench that the body as a 'corpse' created. Haimendorf blurred the visibility of the death as corporeal among the Nagas by starting from a premise that 'death' is a kind of vacuum or absence for which one suffers grief. This obvious difference of cultural idiom produces gaps in understanding the language of the native life.

Haimendorf further accentuated such cultural difference in a piece entitled 'Heathens and Baptists' (included in the same book), Haimendorf's exasperation at the Baptists in the sudden cultural contrasts that they introduced by forbidding many of the Naga cultural practices also could not overcome the epistemic distortions that it produced. The insertion of Christianity as totally opposed to Naga cultural ethos was represented by Haimendorf as what we earlier described as a 'split' in their ethos. He tried to present it through the eyes of Nagas and described that village life after the presence of missions had seemingly lost much of its colour and entertainment had become monotonous. For the younger generation, condemnation of Naga culture by the missionaries had created an alienation from their roots, as youngsters started devaluing their own tribal cultural practices. The effect of such devaluation lay in projecting Christianity and tribal culture as two opposite poles; nothing was built up on what is valuable in tribal life. This debunking of the tribal cultural roots had emerged as one area of disharmony between the old and the new, consequently acting as a setback to Naga society as a whole. Conversion to Christianity could in no way bring back the colour and joy; rather, it contributed to a loss that remained irreparable in village life of the tribes (Haimendorf, 1974: 49).

Haimendorf could identify again the fast disappearing traces of Naga culture under the superiority of Christianity and could see this disappearance through the eyes of the native. Therefore, in the case of intrusion of Christianity as something 'alien', the visibility of disappearance of certain cultural traits went on unabated. Correspondingly, the 'native' perhaps had seen himself as the subject of that alien perspective with the increased visibility of himself. This was a condition that Haimendorf articulated by looking into the interior of Naga culture; and this was a moment when 'aliens' could see the 'inside' from an insider's perspective. Some of this was also because Haimendorf was writing at a time very different from when Hutton was writing. In a sense, Naga culture now is much more visible in the public sphere than it was during Hutton's time. Because of this difference of time, Haimendorf could locate some of the action of the Church as totally violative of the minimal elements of Naga culture. He took pains to represent instances of distortion. He pointed out that the American Baptist mission had no sympathy for either the aims of the government or for the precious elements of Naga culture. Many of the old feasts and ceremonies that the Nagas had, according to Haimendorf, are in no way conflicting to the beliefs and practices of Christianity. Especially, agricultural festivals of the Nagas could have been adopted within Christian religious practices and could have been given a new meaning. Retention of the old within the new religion could have proven to be of greater cultural vitality. But Christian communities desisted from such a convergence between the old tradition and the new faith (Haimendorf, 1974: 51).

Haimendorf mapped out this enforced depreciation of Naga culture through the imposition of rigid norms of Christianity by the missionaries, bringing out the implications of such an imposition. He stated in a nostalgic tenor that while the Ao prayed to the supreme deity for a good harvest, the Christian faith did not allow for such a prayer (Ibid.: 51).

Haimendorf images the clash of cultures in the form of a sudden disruption in the ethos of Naga life and the substitution of their indigenous faith by Christianity. It had its practical consequence of even affecting productivity, as indigenous productivity was grounded in a system of belief that determined the output. The substitution of a new faith struck at the bottom line of Naga culture, asking them to produce without its cultural moorings. Haimendorf is averse to celebrate the pallid process of changeover to a different faith, and as a resistance to it he celebrated the moments of realization of Naga hopes and aspirations expressed through their traditional rites. In commenting about the dances associated with head-hunting, Haimendorf described:

> Voices carry far into the night, and the rhythm that they bear resounds in the darkness, gripping the singers and blending them one and all, till they finally merge in the unity of the dance...The pallid skulls watching the dance from the front of the morung are also symbols of this harmonious alteration of death and life,...they are in death magically linked with the happiness and prosperity of the village (Ibid.: 177).

This description is 'holistic' and blurs the visible differentiation between various forms of performances related to rites and functions, bending it to trace the 'primordial' in which the corporeal and the incorporeal are merged. Still, the gap between the language of Haimendorf and the language of the native persisted when he interpreted the whole dance of head-hunting as a 'primeval instinct', a kind of metaphysical surge overwhelming the act of the ritual. But then he returned to the naked to decipher the translated version of a song about *him*:

> The Sahib came as the wind, as the storm is, he over our land; he brings heads to us all, all men give him thanks.
> Here stay the heads; from Pangsha are the slaughtered enemies (Haimendorf, 1974: 178).

At the same time, the unquenchable and unmitigated temptation of the ethnographer to write about the colonized with an inexhaustible interest demonstrates the colonial imagination of benevolence.

ENCOUNTER WITH CHRISTIANITY: EMERGING FORMS OF DISCOURSES

The interiorization of the native is culturally produced. The ethnographic text merely redraws a marked history of the natives, in which they are *represented*. The interiorization generates a subject who inhabits the hermeneutical space already produced by the act of interiorization. This hermeneutic space is a space of contestation between appropriation and expropriation. It is also a space for counter-appropriation in which the subject expressly reclaims a self-defined position. Colonial texts interiorized the native by way of their appropriation by the colonial cultural influence, manifested through the encounter with the West through the early influence of Christianity in the region. Christianity with its hermeneutical approach was a useful tool for the missionaries to reinterpret the histories of the world to the natives. Such hermeneutical approaches became an all-encompassing affair for the early mission to develop an acceptable interpretation of indigenous religions and institutionalize it under the Church. This had generated a discourse of conversion in the Christian language of love, compassion and revelation that evolved a more acceptable and plausible understanding of the life-world. It was a first-time interaction and interface between Christian and native cultures that emanated a new discourse of conversion. It produced a mix between the Christian and the native faiths in a transformatory or transitional mode.

Christian theology comprehended and overcame the native ways of world-making by replacing it with a better understanding of the truth and the good. Native ways of world-making did not present a concept of God that leads to salvation. Further, Christian theology principally aimed at explaining the native faiths over natural phenomenon and replaced these faiths by way of demonstrating the order of the universe, nature and human life. Such an interpretation of the native world-view helped the tribes to examine their own faith critically and identify loose ends. Christianity, in turn, was interpreted in terms of the best and the noblest of human virtues. Christian philosophy in North-East India sought to explain the primary form of power in the world, along with the most basic human necessity 'not in domination, but in caring presence'. The Christian idea of deliverance of the sufferer by God—by way of Christ's suffering for entire humanity—provided the rationale to highlight Christ as the saviour. Such an appeal to Christ as the saviour was backed by Christianity's theological capability to explain the rationale of indigenous faith. This clearly established the superiority of Christianity as an explanatory framework that provided better answers to questions emanating from life-world situations. A memoir by a Christian missionary can represent the conversion of the native here. J. Meirion Lloyd (1991) wrote about the process of relating Christian theology with the native religious concepts. In a section entitled 'Biakin', Lloyd explained:

> It was some years before the Mizos in North Mizoram built their first BIAKIN as they called chapel or church-building...Biakin soon became the name for this new kind of building. 'In' means house and 'BIAK' is almost untranslatable. It means to speak to someone with a purpose in view, to interview or to address. But it carries religious overtones for it was the old Mizo word for worshiping through sacrifice. It is not the word for prayer or the word for praise or the word for preaching, but it can include aspects of all three. It is a good instance of the Mizo genius for inventing or adapting words (1991: 110).

What this explains is an adaptation through exchange of equivalent belief terms that constitute a cultural translation of some of the tenets of Christianity. Another description of such translation is through a collective experiencing and sharing of an event that initiates a theological explanation. Rev. Lalsawma's text entitled *Four Decades of Revivals: The Mizo Way* describes such an event:

> The Church at Zanlawn experienced an unusual spectacle in 1920. In a house meeting at night, as singing and dancing was in process, suddenly a great flash of light fell upon congregation with flakes of light, the shape and size of a rupee coin, showering and distributing among the people...But the flakes were ethereal in nature and they disappeared, except in the case of one girl named Lawmi who was said to have the power of holding the flake of light longer than others...in later revival meetings whenever she was in the right state to receive the gift. She was accordingly nicknamed 'Enghumi' (She who holds the light) (1994: 111).

The theological explanation of the phenomenon within the text fulfils the aim of revival which goes into the making of the text. The demonstration effect of the experience involves the collective, and Lawmi, who is later known as 'Enghumi'—a creation after the experience—is an embodiment of the mystique of God. Generalizing in such an experiential context of the religious belief in tribal life, Rev. Sylvanus Sngi Lyngdoh pointed out that the concept of '*God as Master and as love* and *tribal people as chosen by God*' are available within the tribal tradition (Puthenpurakal, 1996: 210–211). Citing the example of Hynniewtrep, Rev. Lyngdoh said that it was expressed in clear terms, '*Ban Synshar ban khadar ha ka hok katkum ka Hukum da ka Bar'*, which means 'to rule, to govern, to administer in God as much as he appears in creation, endowed as the Hynniewtrep are with God's power of the word and of Righteousness' (Ibid.). By this the tribals mean to say that they are to rule, to govern and to administer in and with God the Creator Himself.

What this description points out is the cultural grounding of Christianity that was accommodated within the tribal ethos. This mode of cultural transmission of something perceived to be destructive of tribal culture contradicts the foreclosed view that Christianity necessarily destroys tribal culture. Rather, what it inaugurates is best described by Julian Jacobs in the case of Nagas:

It would be wrong to see the Nagas as passive victims of a process of deculturation...Rather we may discern the ways in which Naga ethnicity is being actively and consciously moulded in the present era. What emerges is a vigorous sense of history and identity at the level of individual, tribe and nation (Jacobs, 1990: 176)

Therefore, the 'cultural politics' of Christianity was different from the colonial politics of culture that reduced indigenous culture to a mere object; while Christianity moulded the tribal meanings by taking into account available meanings within tribal cultures. Christianity emerged through tribal culture in order to transform it to a modern liberal culture that accommodates the spirit of individual brotherhood within it. It indicates the Christian spirit that produces a cultural difference within, to give the tribals an experience of modernity by way of a cultural give and take. The transaction was regulated by a relationship with the West that made them subjects of currents within modernity and opened up a window to look beyond the closed space of other dominant cultures.

SELF-REPRESENTATION THROUGH INDIGENOUS ETHNOGRAPHY

Ethnographic representation of the native culture and community produces a shift from hermeneutic enclosure of the community within a specific textual mode to an interaction with colonialism, leaving open the possibility of writing themselves by divesting the 'foreign' elements. The attempt to translate the indigenous culture within the whole of colonial or dominant culture is reversed in indigenous self-representation, as it not only lays claim on the specific historical and cultural resources but also presents an irreducible interior. Indigenous ethnography stands apart from the mode of appropriation in colonial ethnography. It stands 'outside' the 'sentences' of ethnographic representation and thereby allows the past cultural resources to come to the foreground. It produces a narrative of presentation and not re-presentation. Often, freedom of 'genre' in such indigenous ethnography marks a displacement from colonial ethnography. One good example could be a text called *Mizo Inchei Dan,* which shows how the various tribes in Mizoram present themselves (Anonymous, n.d.). The basic code of Inchei Dan, or dressing up, reinforces the intrinsic Mizo imagery of a perennial inseparability between the human and the hill. The presentation of the human body signifies an intimacy between the body and the nature that surrounds it and is described in the text in such a manner that topography and human-scape are invaginated into each other. Mizos wore *hruikhau* (bark or fibre of the vaiza and khanpui trees) before the use of *kaur* (shirt) and *puan* (cloth to cover oneself). A transition from hruikhau to kaur and puan signifies an incorporation of the hruikhau as a pre-symbolic presentation into a more symbolic kaur and puan, a graduation from undifferentiated affinity with nature to a cultural signification of that past. Current Mizo dress preserves this original symbolic source of dressing up in its new mode. The Mizo men wear puan in such a manner that recalls the function of hruikhau in its complete wrapping of the body. The wrapping of the body of the male is functionally linked with prowess in hunting in the forest, which is an additional conservation of the past 'form of life', that is, the hunter's life. The wearing of the puan also marks the prowess of the Mizo man, with a special kind of puan made to honour the gallantry of a hunter successful in offering a feast of merit to the community. This is puan known as *thangchhuah* puan—the most prestigious garment signifying human attachment with forest and animals—a life-world encoded in the dress and the act of hunting gendered in it. There is a headgear for men called *chhawndawl,* a tuft of goat hair dyed red worn on special festive occasions as a head-plume recalling head-hunting during raids in the past. The dress of hunting acquires a special meaning on the occasion of Mizo men going for hunting *sakei* (tiger), maintaining a secret code name *sapui,* so as not to give an inkling to the tiger that it was going to be hunted. These delicate layers of meaning contained in the dress code of Mizo men lie in their attire in terms of internal meanings attached to their life-world.

The female dress code is not very different than that of the male; the only difference is that the female wears *siap-suap,* a short skirt. This short skirt is traditionally made of fringes of twisted strands of cotton. Ornaments in Mizo culture serve as class markers;

earrings called *bengbeh* are worn by upper class women. Another kind of hair-ornament for women is called *dawkhilh,* which looks like a hairpin and is made out of the root of plants. One can note here the emergence of stratification in Mizo dress code, signifying functional positions among men and social positions among women.

Pawis are another sub-tribe of the Mizos, who used to identity themselves as *Lai.* The Pawi women had a little more complicated dress code compared to the Lusheis. At the initial stage of evolution of the dress code, the Pawi girls used to wear a short skirt made of cotton strand called siap-suap, which also is worn by Mizo women. Siap-suap has a special use in *pownfew*, which was worn as an inner-skirt. It is knitted as an apparel in pownfew. The *arsihui* is worn by Pawi women and is a special type of petticoat, which is knitted as a longer apparel. So far as the dress of Pawi men is concerned, they wear *hnawkhal*, a raincoat made out of long strips of leaves ingeniously twisted together with the ends hanging down. *Huathawh kawrfual* is an overcoat worn by Pawi men on some special occasions, which is indicative of their social status or position. This mode of ethnographic presentation of the self constitutes a definite kind of cultural politics of centring the self on tradition and presenting the distinction with modern dress, Western or otherwise,which are no longer designed from plants, flora and fauna. Even the so-called ethnic wears marketed with a special price do not represent their ethnographic sources, as these are merely designers' products. The ethnographic description reads like storage of aestheticized meanings associated with dressing, which acts as an important means to present one before Others.

Such indigenous ethnographic resources become the markers of cultural politics for the tribes of North-East India. For example, the taboos associated with ethnic communities produce a distinction between the sacred and the profane. Taboos also identify objects and animals with definite significance, which is other than their significance in themselves. Verrier Elwin wrote about *Adi* taboos:

A number of taboos are connected with animals. Suppose a hen hatches out a brood of chick...the woman who feeds the mother hen is in a state of taboo and must not cook. If she does, she may get too hot and the chicks will die. Nor may she fetch water, for water falls from above, out of a bamboo pipe and the force of it might kill the chicks (Elwin, 1991: 24).

Taboos, such as those just described, are the content of belief in a tribal/ethnic community, the cognitive and epistemological back-drop relating itself to situations of life. The taboo of the Adi here reflects a concern for the life of the chicks just after they are hatched. The reasons why chicks die are unknown, and they attribute causality on the wrongdoings of the woman who is supposed to care for the chicks. There is a combination of biological and spiritual aspect of life that act as a cultural force in the sphere of belief.

Such resources of indigenous culture go into making ethnocultural characteristics that represents itself in a creative way. Tribal handicraft, art and woodcarving in the North-East are presented as human subjects affected by many natural and supernatural forces. Elwin's presentation of tribal artifacts, such as a 'Konyak figure of black wood with a band of cane coloured red and yellow and a tail of black hair', marks such subjectivity embodied in what are otherwise mere artifacts. In the Konyak tradition, such a figure 'should be first placed in the village dormitory when a village is established' (Elwin, 1986: 67). Similarly, the figure of a *Sherdupken*— a masked dancer—presents an ethnic imagery of how the commu-nity dances to dispel the evil influence of spirits (Elwin, 1959: 226).

Such figures of ethnographic representation give rise to a perceptual world that stands outside the textualized reproduction of cultural objects. Such cultural objects acquire their represen-tational form from within ethnic culture to become objects of ethnographic concern, which wishes to reclaim the resources by an act of projection before the world, and does so by the very act of figuration. The act of figuration does not present a familiar figure, but a graffito of the familiar. Verrier Elwin's representation of two Konyak woodcarvings—one of a female and the other of a male figure—present a juxtaposition of these two primary kind of gendered figures upon the wood. The cutting of wood to shape the figures brings back a total cognition of one's own self within Konyak society. The faces of the figures are carved following Konyak facial features. This is simultaneously a self-portrayal as well as production of a field of vision to have an imagistic self-representation. The plasticity of such figures presents a stable social identity through gendering. The gender markers are never suppressed in such representation of stable identity, as if without such marks on the body the otherwise plastic features get defamiliarized in the representation (Elwin, 1959: 63).

Various kinds of tribal attire also encompass certain signifying practices of the tribe. Verrier Elwin (Ibid.) cited the case of the *Timchunger* Naga having more than 12 kinds of clothes, each attached to signify various kinds of social functions like hunting and war. The distinction of colour and knitting distinguishes men of various strata and merit. With the greater disorientation of tribes from their life-world, there is no direct relationship between 'signification' and 'practice' anymore. In such a contest of detribalization and acculturation, the signifying marks embroidered on cloth itself assume the role of signifying practice. Even though the reference of such signifying practices is vanishing from tribal life, the continuation of such signifying practices becomes the visible marker of distinctness of the community. The plethora of red-coloured shawls with embroidered patches of band acquires a 'value' not only in terms of an identity marker, but also in its aestheticized representation as an independent art object.

Reclaiming Indigenousness

The crucial question of cultural politics is how the *signifying practices* or *ethnic markers* of a community *affect* its identity and its relationship with the Others. The question also relates to the nature of contest between ethnic, tribal and communitarian identities, with identities construed by the state to bring into focus how ethnic communities are positioned. Further, this positioning is an act of claiming the identity vested in them, which calls for a political positioning of their culture so that it is not appropriated in the currents of domination. Although the life-world of the ethnic communities is affected by the modern state, social identity and social relations—these produce what is called the 'subject effect' upon the community. Such an effect is realized in the structure of the community that undergoes drastic changes, such as the emergence of elite and non-elite classes as poles. This has its disparaging divide between the two classes in cultural terms, which signifies a new mode of legitimation and evaluation within the community. Even at a moment of rejection of some of its traditions, the new criterion of value usually augured by the elites remain alien with respect to their culture, groping to find its grounds within the culture. One can call this situation a kind of detribalization or decontextualization of tribal 'form of life'. Although it does not mean a wholesale merger with others radically different from them, it opens up another way of signifying the already existing practices. The utility and use of a large number of traditional tribal objects— from attire to musical instruments—come into a newer strategic use to signify the tribal life-world in the context of encountering an alien cultural practice. Therefore, decontextualization does not uproot the identifying premises of tribal life, which are their cultural practices. Decontextualization brings out a moment of renewal, bringing together radically new combinations of the old and the new within the cultural practices of a tribal community.

Here is a crucial dimension of positioning themselves as one among the multi-cultural identities with 'Indian' tradition, a task set out by the nationalist cultural politics. With an invigorated rise of ethnic consciousness, the rejection of a common assimilative cultural tradition by the tribals resists canonization of their culture by the dominant 'centre' of Indian culture. Contrarily, starting from within one's own tradition and remaining fully attached to it, the tribals of North-East India are negotiating their cultural tradition with others within the multi-cultural fabric of the Indian situation.

Cultural politics of the North-East Indian tribes resists the onslaught of nationalist-statist politics of cultural devaluation, canonization and homogenization by way of self-representation and maintenance of traditional community institutions. A cult like *Doini-Polo, Seng Khasi,* or the celebration of *Gangngai* by *Rongmei* Nagas, stands as a resistance to such processes of Hinduization or Christianization. The participation of Christian Hmars and Lusheis in traditional festivities like *Butu khuong Lawm, Chalpou kut, Mim Kut* or *Chapchar Kut* brings back a renewed sense of tribal identity. In this sense, self-enclosed tribal communities need to be revaluated from the perspective of giving them an independent recognition and freeing them permanently from the possibility of overt and covert cultural domination. Even though religious converts do not participate in rituals associated with such *kuts* (festivals), they are organized thrice in a year covering sowing, harvesting and reaping at three different times of the year. The agricultural festival, Chapchar kut is celebrated for reaping, which normally takes place during the period between mid-October and mid-November. It generates a lot of jubilation and merry-making among the tribes of Mizo origin. The celebration takes a secular character going beyond religious chores. This internal secularization is also a part of cultural positioning of the tribe in a self-conscious acceptance of something 'better'. No Mizo can isolate herself from the almost 200 years of Christian influence in bringing about a sense of modernity, at the same time retaining a sense of age old identity by the continuance of some of their signifying practices. Similarly, the division between Seng Khasi and Christian Khasis is not a water-tight division, as many Khasi practices explore the spaces 'in-between' and into both the traditional and the new form of life. This aspect of positioning between the two modes of practice to negotiate the two enlarges the space of tribal identity in a mix between the indigenous and the exogenous.

Another aspect of cultural politics is a mode of questioning ethnic practices and the practices of the state from the point of view of a political affirmation of identity. An influential section of the Khasi society has questioned the marriage of the girls outside the community. The Khasi Lineage Bill of 1996 suggests excommunication of those Khasi women who marry outside the community. Therefore, 'cultural politics' assumes a closure of ethnic identity in order to resist domination. In the case of deciding the official language of Nagaland in the late 1980s, Nagas opposed the case of *Nagamese* and instead preferred English. The logic of this preference was obviously the greater influence and utility of English in contemporary India, even though for all practical purposes Nagamese acts as the lingua franca in Nagaland. If something like English, being the culturally dominant, can resist domination from other Indian communities, then they would choose such a culturally dominant symbol. In the sphere of public culture the tilt towards English as a language instead of Hindi, Western dressing and media items have the same reason of preference. But the preference here is for greater sense of freedom attached to the Western mode of life, with a greater sense of pleasure and hedonism that act without affecting their own cultural practices. This pattern can also be seen amongst the mainland elites. A rudimentary adaptation of the language and culture of the dominant has been the means of assertion of an identity led by the educated elites who are caught within the dominant cultural practices. Especially, the elites of marginalized North-East Indian communities never miss a chance of assertion through an alien, yet dominant Western mode. It takes them outside the ways of Pan-Indian mainstream cultural forms. Paradoxically enough, they choose such globally-dominant symbols that can only foster a sense of being different from what is 'Indian'. This aspect of 'cultural politics' goes into playing the politics of difference at the level of Indian mainstream, while it makes them subservient to the global culture industry. Strangely enough, belongingness to global cultural symbols helps a sense of recuperation of what gets lost within Pan-Indian national identity.

Apart from this area of inter-cultural transactions, there is an area of narrativization of tribal culture from within the practice of preserving undistorted grounds of tribal identity. Native intelligence, science, technology and medicinal practices merged with a commonly-shared history produce an ethnic space for the tribal community. This is an integral mode of life that preserves the essential markers of tribal identity. The native type of house, garments, weapons, utensils and ornaments constitute the location of self and community in culture in an integral and inseparable mode. A narration containing the events, time and space of all such items of life reinforces an eternal authentic signification for their own selves. This is how they know themselves. The revolt of Phizo, the daily events of struggle, ceasefire and prevailing uncertainty are all narrativized in the folk psychology, assuming a similar degree of relevance for them with other cultural practices. All these come as a collage, interconnected in a deeper cultural concomitance, but never presenting them as a fixed 'whole'. This flexibility of the real world for the tribals in which the stable markers of identity form a core sustains the cultural identity. The act of narrativization employs the most living cultural organism of language that repetitively sings the same song and poems to generate a 'taste' of specific nature with which the identification is umbilical. Languages run as the umbilical cord in sustaining the positive and living resources of tribal culture. The architecture of tribal language retains a specific depth-dimension of a particular mode of speaking, calling, appealing and expressing emotions through its timbre, and hence ensures the *presence* of an umbilical cord.

This delicate and vibrant interior of 'cultural politics' seeks a language of its own, different from the language of state politics. Cultural politics tries to attain a language that does not define a cultural community, nor decide about the justification of cultural claims. In North-East India, the language of cultural expression mixes with the languages of state, nation and ethnicity to contaminate the language of cultural politics. The desire to preserve and practice their own tradition gets negotiated in the criss-crossing of such several languages. Cultural politics provides an area for such criss-crossing. Negotiation and mediation with a dominant group or collective identity forms the first step of cultural politics. For the North-East, the crux is how to ensure recognition by the state of stable ethnic identities.

One crucial articulation is the description of an 'indigenous' status to be attached to the tribes. This coining is derived from the position adopted by the UN Working Group on Indigenous Populations, formed in 1982 (Imchen, 1996). The description 'indigenous' attributes the status of *original* people to a group of people who started their settlement in an area previous to settlement of people of different ethnic origins. This consideration of 'originality' comes against the possibility that such a group of original settlers were colonized and dominated by another group. Attribution of 'originality' rewrites the prominence or priority of the original inhabiting community against the emergent descriptions of domination that imposes its normative criterion upon them. The North-East Indian communities, expressing their own desire not only to retain their own cultural and native habitat but also wishing to live autonomous and independent lives, become the 'addressee' of this description 'indigenous'. But they become the 'addressee' in a specific recounting of history in the Indian context and also by their affirmations of identity claims. The UN Working Group seems to have adopted a 'clearer' position that advocates self-determination of the indigenous groups.[2]

For cultural politics, the starting point is an unhindered assertion of indigenous claims that requires a clearing space for removing all dominant interventions. The tribes of the North-East attempt at clearing the space by way of fighting out the cultural ripples or effects of domination as impressed upon the indigenous culture; often by way of identifying the state as the prime mover of such disruption that constantly images itself in the form of a unitary nation.

CONCLUSION

The distinction between 'politics of culture' and 'cultural politics' lies in the fact that the former signifies a subsumption of culture under the game of politics, while the latter signifies mobilization of cultural signifiers beyond a politically fixed identity of a culture. The former constructs a plot for political expediency of a dominating regime, while the latter contests that this politics of normalization reconstructs itself in an alternating mode. In case of North-East India, the colonial ethnographic construction of 'tribe' as a mute category of the powerless and uncivilized oppressed is inverted in the ethnic self-definitions and its categories like 'indigenous' that reclaim a past beyond the limits of a nation-state[3] (also see Chatterjee, 1994: 1–45). The emergence of the nation-state in post-colonial India, aiming at reducing such cultural self-definitions to a part of the nationalist definition of Indian identity, produces a conflict between the native and the nation. The supposedly greater and legitimate form of power and its attended episteme—centring an elite that presents itself as the 'nation'—indeed resolves this conflict in inter-elite terms, without addressing the exclusion of cultural wholes of ethnic communities. The smaller ethnic communities encode their resistance in the most legitimate terms and offer it to the state, which regulates this process of reduction into a nation only to contest its game of power and seek a sovereign and independent status. The process of marginalization of ethnic communities by the state consists in non-recognition of the independence of their specific mode of life and raising the statist agenda of taking the path of an inter-elite conflict. The state represents both this inter-elite conflict as well as reduction of ethnic identities into one national identity. This is how politics of culture brings forth a politics of marginalizing the ethnic cultures.

In contrast, cultural politics needs to identify a break from merely encoding the nation-state and its discourses in ethnic assertions, manifested in the multiple relationship of an ethnic community with its Others. The dominance of 'state' over 'nation' in matters of forming ethnic cultures begins with the advent of what is called nation-state, and hence 'cultural politics' needs to call it 'state-nation', that is, the imposition of a nation from above through the nation-state. Cultural politics implies the break with this process. Cultural politics needs to explore the multiple, diverse, fragmentary and unique moments of ethnic assertion with the disclosure of its moorings and use of such multiplicities in deciding its politics of identity.

An ethnophilosophical distinction between the two in the context of the North-East needs to emphasize greater meaning in the mode on which ethnicity manifests itself, as opposed to the criteria of (de)valuation evolved by the nationalist–statist and universalist discourses. The nativist perspective recovers the self-defined values from the rubric of suppression of the ethnic life-world, and the universalist perspective recovers a genuine universalist criteria of equality, by way of uncovering the cultural devaluation inscribed in the universalist criterion. Therefore, ethnophilosophy sets an agenda of recovering the cultural position of ethnic identities lost inside the universalist mapping of humanity. It carries an imperative for its Others to locate the point of drawing them under the rubric of domination perpetuated by the Other. It asks the Others to see themselves and read their history from their acts of denigration of the native. With this heavy burden of correcting the morals of the Other, the natives present themselves as 'persecuted', but the universalist discourse mistakes it to be their cry for liberation from the marginalized position. The crucial question is whether a dominant order can correct the criterion of denigration, inherent in its very superiority, by way of evolving certain normative criteria for justice. In the case of the Indian state-nation, such normative criteria drawn for uplifting the tribals draws its justification from the marginalized position of the tribals, thereby obliterating the imperative of knowing themselves as 'tormentors' and 'denigrators'. The dominant national conscience shrugs off its guilt by way of accommodation, while the systemic practices of the state disorient the marginalized tribal communities from their culture.

In distinguishing between the 'politics of culture' and 'cultural politics', ethnophilosophy sets the imperative of registering every bit of ethnic resistance to domination, hence reading strategies of domination in the texts that claim to represent the ethnic identities. Contrastingly, the imbrication of domination in ethnic texts sets the task of recovering the recognition of domination by the ethnic communities. Hence, ethnophilosophy's primary concern of delineating and espousing the contents of the making of the ethnic community falls in the gap between 'representation' and 'domination', requiring identification of 'cultural politics' against the 'politics of culture'. Such a gap can be conceptualized in terms of ranging free imagination of the community from the structures of inequality and domination that depend on strategies of representation of the self. Strategic negotiation with the powerful Others often brings dividends for passive, neutral and activist 'cultural politics'.

Notes

1. Giles Deleuze's concept of 'writing machine' refers to an identification of writing with social processes as a metaphor of 'machine' that generates social processes.

2. Quoted in Imchen (1996). from UNESCO, Commission on Human Rights, preliminary report on the Study of the Problem of Discrimination against Indigenous Populations, Chapter II, para 17 (E/CN. 4/Sub.2/L. 566).

3. Reclamation is an act of critique of the claims on past history by way of different imaginations of nationhood.

3

The Native and the Nation

Jawaharlal Nehru-Verrier Elwin's Philosophical Anthropology

Located within the nation space, the natives as social groups, as we have discussed in Chapter 2, mark a space of 'Otherness' and difference. How such a space emerges remains the central question in charting out the relationship between the Indian nation and the North-East Indian communities—the former being the universalized 'nation-form' and the latter being subjects in their specific location. The nation-form as constituted by the modern bourgeoisie is differentiated in two main functions, namely, economic and symbolic/ideological. As none of these functions converge on the other but merely act together, nation remains simultaneously a social as well as an ideological form comprising the collective and the individual with their particular cultural, historical and economic characteristics. It is through the nation-form that these characteristics exist and transform each other in order to modify the status of all other communities in such a way that allows people to produce themselves continually as a national community (Balibar, 1990: 329–30). Although the nation-form includes people of the North-East, there are struggles for recognition of their distinct social identity in terms of rights in the spheres of culture, politics and economy. This struggle is carried mainly by the educated elites among these communities who learn the language of articulation of rights in the civil and political sphere. Such aspiration for recognition of rights makes the state treat North-East communities as autonomous and self-sustaining—their own modes of life, cultural symbols and traditional institutions largely accepted by the post-colonial Indian State (Swain, 1996...). A non-conflictual, non-dominative and non-interventionist attitude towards the distinctness and ingenuity of the North-East Indian communities marked the tone of the nationalist discourse. Jawaharlal Nehru and Verrier Elwin represent two simultaneous and interrelated approaches of this discourse. Nehru intended to involve the North-East communities into the making of the nation, and Elwin aimed at upholding the distinct style of life of these communities. The Nehurvian state aimed at becoming a good mediator between these two aspects of nationalist ideology, and it had set out certain policies and practices in its goal of emerging into a nation. Nationalist discourse intended to mould itself in order to provide a space for re-articulation of the native communities from the already-produced subordination, and thereby heal the scars produced within colonial politics of culture. In a sense, nationalist discourse intended to give rise to a cultural politics of representation as against colonialist misrepresentation. Jawaharlal Nehru's articulation of this cultural politics construed the nation as a space for living together in full dignity. It had a non-alienating effect on an already existing sense of alienation and difference.

In order to strengthen the accommodative spirit of nationalist discourse, Verrier Elwin delved into the most important issue—that of the protection of the native cultural ethos. Elwin worked towards this direction by constructing ethnographic canons of interpretation that would reflect self-critically on the nationalist discourse. These canons had historic, philosophical and political economy aspects on which Elwin developed a human science of nativism, to help understand the North-East Indian communities. Thus, Nehru's nationalism of recognition and respect for such communities was supplemented and strengthened by Elwin's humanistic canons of ethnography. The two together inaugurated a significant break with the colonialist–statist discourse embodying culturally-loaded notions of primitivism and superiority. The nationalist state, however, largely remained irresponsive to the humanistic approach of Nehru-

Elwin, as it tended to ensure a self-same reproduction of markers of identity within a homogenizing process, operating through its territorial and administrative functions. But its functional apparatus needed to maintain the cultural boundaries between communities by way of providing a space to their institutions by creating necessary administrative arrangements. Often, the nationalist and the statist discourses blurred the distinct cultural and institutional boundaries between these communities in the official deliberations of the administrators. Still, the distinction between the two was manifested in the tone of each of these discourses and then in their respective effects. We consider the interface of the Nehru-Elwin discourse by exploring the grounds of their convergence and divergence. The convergence takes place between Nehru's cultural politics of accommodation and Elwin's ethnography of nativism, while the divergence is between Nehru's statist discourse of institutionalized accommodation and Elwin's quest for a harmony between the native and the nation that undercuts much of the imposing agenda of Nehruvian state.

DRAWING PARALLELS: NEHRU AND ELWIN

For a revealing comparison, one has to read Nehru and Elwin in parallel to demarcate the areas of convergence and divergence. The most important declaration of Nehru on the policy towards tribals contains five principles known as *Panchsheel* (Nehru's 'Foreword' in Elwin, 1959):

1. People should develop along the lines of their own genius and we should avoid imposing anything on them. We should try to encourage in every way their own traditional art and culture.
2. Tribal rights in land and forest should be respected.
3. We should try to train and build up a team of their own people to do the work of administration and development. Some technical personnel from outside will no doubt be needed, especially in the beginning. But we should avoid introducing too many outsiders in tribal territory.

4. We should not over-administer these areas or overwhelm them with a multiplicity of schemes. We should rather work through and not in rivalry to, their own social and cultural institutions.
5. We should judge results, not by statistics or the amount of money spent, but by the quality of human character that is evolved.

The statements as explicit and clear as these could be read in juxtaposition[1] (also see Kamuf, 1991: xiii–xliii) with an assessment of the overall characteristic of tribal people. In the last few lines of Elwin's *A Philosophy for NEFA* (1959), he listed out the qualities uniquely available among tribals. According to him, their simplicity, courtesy, hospitality, discipline and self-reliance are commendable virtues, so much so that they are bewildered by the advances of modern civilization. Most often one misses the point that one has to be cautious while serving them, while one can never miss the warm hospitality straight from their heart. This calls for sharing of the good with utmost caution so that it does not disturb the delicate ambience of their lives (Elwin, 1959: 287).

The similarity of perspective between Nehru's Panchsheel and Elwin's characterization of the qualities of tribal people is more than an accidental convergence. It points to a consensual sharing between Elwin and Nehru. Elwin declared at the close of one of his most original works, 'A Fundamental Problem' (Ibid.: 59–60) that if the administrators in the North-East Frontier Agency (NEFA) mix with the tribal people with genuine love and true simplicity, it is possible that the tribals would be able to adjust with the 'new world', a coinage reminiscent of Native Americans perishing in the hands of White colonizers (Elwin, 1959).

Elwin's commendatory approach towards Nehru's policy is definitely a mark of his deep engagement with the latter's line of thinking. What Elwin thought about the indigenous people finds its endorsement in Nehru's framing of Panchsheel, which provided Elwin with a practical handle to work with, and also contribute to his philosophic point of view. Therefore, a juxtaposition of Nehru and Elwin is extremely salutary in order to trace the mutual growth of their line of thinking and action. Referring to the passages just cited one can easily decipher Nehru's extremely sensitive and careful grasp of the 'problem' of the tribals. He repeatedly focused on the native and the indigenous characteristics of the tribals as a people or a community which should not be disrupted. Nehru was concerned about (to prevent) any tampering with the ethos of tribals/natives by extraneous factors. Therefore, he relied on an ethnical imperative of not disturbing the ethos of indigenous communities. The policy, based on his deep concern for the good of the native communities, was framed in a language of restraint to ensure that the distortion and disruption of the tribal ethos never took place. This emphasizes commitment for the unhampered and unimpeded growth of the tribals.

What Nehru prescribed in such policy formulations merely suggests certain ideals for the state and other agencies to pursue, not assuming the authority to define what is good for the tribals. To fully grasp the merit of such an open, flexible and non-interfering policy one has to ask the question: what was the impact of such a policy on tribal life? Nehru's framework devised a policy to facilitate and smoothen the path of self-development for the tribals and aimed at assisting the process in all possible ways. The nationalist perspective on tribals, therefore, envisioned self-development of the tribals, without any intervention from any exterior source, while ensuring assistance/help. Verrier Elwin represented a similar perspective with a contextual and specific focus on the tribals of the North-East, who were incapable of resisting intervention, and thereby almost adhered to Nehru's concern that was against distorting the tribal ethos by an interventionist state. This convergence of concerns between Elwin and Nehru takes two different routes: for Elwin it is more a down to earth position concerning the tribal ethos, while for Nehru it is more of programming the state with a cultural restraint. Elwin's aim of maintaining cultural distinctions gets transformed into the cultural positions of the Nehruvian state, which gives birth to a humanistic body of knowledge.

The impact of Nehru's policy on tribal life could be assessed by going beyond the limits of policy statements. The statements need to be detached from their assumed contexts and placed in contexts other than those marked by their author, who was conscious of the fragile nature of tribal culture. The authority of the state assumes a moral context of the holistic self-development of North-

East communities placed in their life-worlds. Such a moral context elicits most of the meanings of the Panchsheel statements. Apart from this, the statements assume the context of normative mediation by the state. To place the statements in contexts other than those marked by Panchsheel, Elwin's concern was twofold: assimilation of tribal culture within the civic life, and not making them second-rate copies of the mainstream. Elwin locates a great deal of conflict of values between rare and precious values of tribal life, such as courage, self-reliance and artistic gifts on the one hand, and modern medicine, agriculture and education on the other, and proposes a *synthesis* between the two (Elwin, 1959: 59).

Elwin, as we can see, gives priority to the specific cultural ethos of the tribals. In concrete terms Elwin described the impact of such a policy in affecting tribal life in the context of NEFA. For Elwin the spatial characteristics of areas within NEFA are extremely important. The foothills and the international border in the north were the areas where tribes were in touch with the people of the plains and hence the administration could carry out developmental works with comparative ease. But the central part of NEFA posed a difficult challenge, primarily because of lack of roads and communication, as the administration had to go slow in carrying out developmental programmes (Ibid.: 55).

The 'effect' of such a developmental perspective based on spatial characteristics was determined by Elwin through the criteria that he formulated: 'it is necessary to balance material gains against psychological dangers', and 'it is essential to give the tribes the time to adjust themselves, to allow them breathing space' (Ibid.: 116). Elwin further elaborated: 'It is the quality of the material progress rather than its quantity that matters', and that the 'effect' of development should not be judged by statistics but by the 'quality' of human beings that we produce, apropos Nehru. In order to evaluate the 'impact' of state policies, the critical aspects of preservation of the tribal ethos must be taken into account. This is because 'their quality of life is better in some respects' and the current agenda of the state should help this quality to grow further. This self-corrective refrain of the state, present in Nehru's discourse, always looks first into its own deviations. Further, the state evolves a contextual principle of embedding tribal culture in framing its developmental policies, with a slant that development should not cause a breakdown of values of tribal societies (Elwin, 1959: 116). Elwin recollects all these pointers of Nehru in order to implement or practice what has evolved in the latter's nationalist–statist discourses.

Nehru's critique of domination over tribals carried forward his moralistic concerns. Nehru was concerned about the ideas such as 'assimilation' and 'integration' that contribute to the elimination of tribal ethos. He opined that the civilized world is anxious about shaping the tribes in their own image and imposing its lifestyle on them (Nehru, 1986: 150).

This kind of cultural domination was something that Nehru abhorred in the case of tribal development. With utter criticality and abhorrence, Nehru made an objective study of the tribal situation and expressed his sympathy for the apprehension among the tribes— that they might be merged in the sea of Indian humanity, that they might have to give up their customs and ways of living and that they would be dispossessed of their land (Nehru, 1986: 150). Nehru intends to allay the feelings of the tribes by perceiving the sources of their dispossession and displacement. He takes into account the difference of culture and history of the North-East frontier tribes, and the way these had been shaped in their previous generations and in recent years. He agreed that the fault lay in the mainstream as well as in the circumstances, in not understanding them in their proper cultural and historical context (Nehru, 1973: 6–7).

The tenor of self-criticism in Nehru's observations writes the deep sense of guilt lying at the heart of civilization for the misdeeds done to the tribes in the North-East frontier. It also bears a sense of sharing the pain of those tribes who suffered at the hands of civilization. In effect, Nehru is demystifying the idea of civilization and trying to look at tribal lifeworld from an insider's point of view. These subtle senses of guilt and pain often reveal the dark underside of civilization in Nehru's visionary utterances, which reinforced commitment to the cultural ethos of the tribal people. According to Nehru, the feeling of separateness persisting among the tribes of the North-East frontier and North-East India in general is not sui generis, but misdirected interventions from the dominant nationalist discourse. He considered the fear of tribals as genuine, especially the fear of loss of cultural distinctness by being drawn into the vortex of nation-making. It becomes further clearer when he cautioned that in the process of doing good to the tribes, if excesses are committed, it neither does good to the doer nor to the recipient (Nehru, 1973: 4).

This aspect of Nehruvian nationalism brings into the open a humanistic grounding of national community, within which a statesman like Nehru and a tribal could be human beings. Nehru is not only opposed to muting the tribal into submission but is also opposed to majoritarian Hindu chauvinism that aims at creating a homogenized national community (Nehru, 1989: 2–11). For Nehru, the key is to preserve the variety of communities and cultures in the making of the nation. The coupling of fellow-feeling and preservation of diversity was aimed at contesting the homogenizing tendencies within nationalism. Nehru's apprehensions about the role of the state in enforcing and imposing a homogenizing process of development took into account the historical precedents of annihilation of tribal culture by civilizations to suggest a discourse of sympathy and care for the cultural distinctness of the tribals. Such apprehensions of Nehru recalled the longing for a vanishing tribal life along with its ecological and cultural environments, which were translated into designing a policy of non-intervention and help towards the tribals.

Tribals: Caught between Nehruvian State and Nehru

One can note here two significant aspects of Nehru's policy: one, he did not want a strong state approach, but a slow process of growth that ensured participation and helped the growth of a sense of belonging among the tribals towards the nation-state; two, he wanted the nation-state to remain respectful toward their ethos. What Nehru worried about was whether a tribal could retain her identity in the process of nation-making. In other words, Nehru could foresee the dangers of state intervention, without which it would not be possible to draw the tribals towards the nation. This was the irresolvable dilemma in Nehru's nationalist positions.

Nehru's discourse from above could restrain the state to some extent, but it could not ensure the desired line of development. The Nehruvian nationalism of recognition and respect produced a kind of separation of tribal communities from non-tribals and the extent to which the state intervened in the process of development increased the differences. The discourse from above merely represented the finer aspects of tribal culture in Nehru's words, but it could not satisfy the aspirations of the tribals. Further, Nehru's discourses about cultural distinctiveness of the tribals treated them as human beings, but could not represent the language in which they spoke and thought. Nehru represented this *distance* mode of nationalist discourse, probably with the greatest finesse and delicacy. His words were full of pathos and metaphors. He said, 'Above all, they are a people who sing and dance and try to enjoy life; not people who sit in stock exchanges, shout at each other and think themselves civilized' (Nehru, 1973: 6–7) *His empathy for a people who sing and dance makes him to distinguish between tribes and the so-called civilized. This distinction presents a romantic imagination that constructs an alternative to the civilized, the natural and cultural space where tribals live. The space inhabited by tribes, for Nehru, is not just spatially and temporally different, but it is a spur to an imagination beyond the so-called 'civilization'.* As he said, 'The call of the jungle and mountain has always been strong with me, a dweller of cities and of cities and of plains, though I am, and I gazed at these forests and jungles, fascinated' (Gopal, 1983: 518). Thus, Nehru contrasts himself as one who is *not* a dweller in that site. This external gaze of Nehru represents the non-presence of tribals within the body of nationalist imaginations, for which it needs to map the tribal habitat out there in the hills. This distancing, of course, produces a lot of empathy and appreciation with its spacing into a different terrain:

> My own predilection is for the mountains rather than for the plains, for the hill folk than the plains people. So also I prefer the frontier, not only in a physical sense but because the idea of living near a frontier appeals to me intellectually (Nehru, 1973: 2).

Repeatedly, Nehru's markers like 'frontier' abstract a space for the tribals, bringing out a sense of inhabiting a different space—an exotic space different from the other living spaces. Moreover, 'frontier' as *metaphor* brings back the notion of an unknown site inhabited by strange people, giving another fillip to the nationalist imagination of a *margin* and an *exterior* at the margin. In imagining a 'nation' among the tribals, Nehru mobilized such metaphors of style and place and blended it in his coupling and uncoupling of cultural distinctness with the idea of a national whole.

Such designators of nationalist imagination mark two culturally determined positions: firstly, that of placing it in a site of gazing; and secondly, situating it at the 'frontier' of the national landscape. This is what Nehru does when he talks about continuation of tribal cultural traditions, as if such a continuation ensures their place within the nation. Even talk about self-development and non-intervention merely produces tribals as subjects of nationalist discourse, as it puts a halt to statist intervention mixed with sensitivity towards their cultural roots. This posture of nationalist discourse simultaneously produces and maintains a distance with tribal milieu from within, as it does not ensure that tribals remain as tribals by being drawn within the process of building up a common national identity. The unified description of an Indian tradition does not include tribal elements as essential to it but incorporates it as a specific strand unintegrated with the national culture. So, it designates a place of difference within itself, an inclusion that retains its separateness, thereby giving it a peripheral place outside the core. This ambivalent inclusion of tribal culture within the mainframe of nationalist discourse is manoeuvred in Nehru's universalistic sympathies for tribals as a distinct entity, as a group of people surviving cultural annihilation. Nehru's specific positions bring out this ambivalence and split within the nationalist self—a dilemma between the statist and the nationalist positions that gets its impetus within the 'love' and 'fear' of Nehru, a contradictory state of psyche that Nehru articulated in his discourses.

When Nehru articulates this state of ambivalence, he is treating the already displaced cultural position of the tribals as their greatest impediment, an assignment of identity as mute subjects of history. Nehruvian nationalism transfers this immobility of tribal identity into a further displaced metaphor of the frontier, far removed from the centre of the nation. His empathy towards such a position signifies the failure or the lack of the nationalist discourse to overturn this marginalization and, therefore, his consciousness merges itself with the consciousness of marginalization. This is also a search for legitimacy of the nationalist discourse that cannot attain legitimacy without granting a place to the marginalized identities.

The crucial question is: how does the nation evolve to yield a place to the tribals within it? One has to answer this question within the limits of nationalist discourse. As Nehru positioned and framed his humanistic concerns for the tribals within the discursive limits of nationalism, one needs to examine the actual practice of such discourse in dealing with the tribals. Nehru's humanistic concerns had to face a critical test on occasions of taking up concrete policy decisions and actions on the relationship between the state and the tribals of North-East India. Certain instances shall suffice. On the question of the demand of the Naga National Council (NNC) for independence and sovereignty, Nehru stated:

> It is obvious that Nagas or any other tribes on our borders cannot have independence. But we are very anxious to give them a large measure of autonomy and to help them in every way while respecting their traditions and way of life. I am personally an admirer of the Nagas and I like many of their fine qualities (1986: 154).

This is a well-thought over policy formulation by Nehru on the aspect of retaining the tribals within the boundary of the state—a closure of the nationalist discourse. The state finds its priority over the demands raised from the political leadership of the tribes, and the question of a large measure of autonomy becomes an alternative to the question of independence. The demands of a separate nationality status with their own sovereign state was rejected by Nehru as he argued that whether India was properly to be described as one nation or two, or more, really did not matter, for the modern idea of nationality had been almost divorced from statehood (Nehru, 1946: 647).

This divorce between 'nationality' and 'statehood' indicates a strategy of containment on the question of nationality aspirations. The demand of Naga leadership for establishing a separate, sovereign state was contained or deterred by this nationalist strategy in which statehood remains above the nationality question. In designing a larger measure of autonomy as an alternative to independence, this primacy of the state is ensured by charting out measures to 'give' autonomy to the tribals of the North-East. In carrying out this kind of a statist agenda of giving autonomy, the Nehruvian state moves away from the commitment of helping the tribals grow according to their genius.

The silence of the nationalist discourse over the legitimacy of the state among the tribals produces a kind of invisibility of the state, and Nehru's Panchsheel describes the modality of tribal development with greater emphasis on their self-development. The criteria of autonomy and self-development become the inevitable option for the nationalist discourse to make the tribals subjects of the nation. Nehru's already existent discursive gaze upon tribal culture, that is, keeping it at the periphery, gets identified with the discourse of the Nehruvian state in giving them autonomy. The suppression of the demand for independence—raised from within the tribal communities—is an inversion of the concept of autonomy in order to impose it from above. An interesting comparison is with Burma, where the ethnic *Zos* are not considered by the Burmese as a part of Burmese nationhood; but, at the same time, Burma refuses to grant them any political autonomy. As the idea of citizenship in Burma revolves around ethnic origins, Zos are considered as neither here nor there. The situation is complicated in Mizoram as Zos are looked upon as migrant 'Burmese'.

Revisionary Strategies of the Nehruvian State

The strategy of the Nehruvian state in securing autonomy for the tribals includes measures of granting constitutional and legal protection, incorporation of tribal customary institutions as grassroot-level institutions, and so on. Another important aspect was to introduce modern fiscal and electoral systems through the customary traditional institutions. For the Naga territories, the Nehruvian state intended to constitute an autonomous district council, which did not materialize as the Nagas did not consent to such an idea. After much squabbling, the state of Nagaland was formed during 1963. The Act of Nagaland 1963 passed in the Parliament excluded the power to amend Naga customary laws and conventions and bestowed the judicial and penal powers on the Naga customary institutions. This clearly shows the strategy of the Nehruvian state in simultaneously creating an administrative governmental mechanism from above, while maintaining a traditional institutional set-up at the bottom. The strategy of containment of nationalist discourse was carried out by the Nehruvian state in giving the Nagas autonomy at the grassroot level while imposing its machinery from above, thus creating a hierarchical state. Similar strategies were adopted in case of Meghalaya and Mizoram, where people demanded this right to self-government. On the one hand, autonomous district councils were created and, on the other, the bulwark of a state was created.

The irony of the statist agenda of tribal development is that the state extended its networks of power upon the tribal communities by way of legally defining their place and imposing an institutional bulwark upon them. Nehru's nationalist commitment of ensuring self-development of the tribal communities in a non-interventionist mode got upturned in the process of containing the tribal demands for independence by way of creating a state at every place. An alternative to this could have been a different federal re-constitution of North-East which could have ensured maximum autonomy to tribes of the region. The procedural–functional aspects of the newly created state within the Indian Union took over the modest Nehruvian nationalist goal of tribal development without distorting their mode of life, and introduced a modern system of governance by further displacing tribal cultural mores into an institutional, legal and fiscal framework of the state. This *displacement* of the tribal cultural mores had actualized the fear of Nehru about the loss of tribal ethos with the onslaught of civilization. This inversion of the goals set up by Nehru also meant the actualization of the tribal fear about loss of their cultural ethos under the domination of India. It inaugurated a moment of *revising* the Nehruvian position of non-interference, by way of turning the focus on the power of the state in bringing about the desired goals of development. So the question became that of acquiring greater access to state power in order to govern development. These crucial shifts in terms of change of positions of the Nehruvian state from a policy of non-interference to a policy of greater governance came about in such a contingent fashion that it drastically affected tribal mores. But the nationalist goal of retaining the tribal ethos was not forsaken too quickly in tune with such shifts; rather, the effect of those shifts was neutralized to some extent by according a place to tribal customary institutions. This was intended to make them look much like the institutions of state vested with defined powers. The distinction between the state institution and customary institutions was bridged and blurred to such an extent that the latter started acting as buffers for institutions of the state created from above. But the question is: how did Nehruvian nationalist discourse justify such an act of overpowering by the institutions of the state?

One of the stock Nehruvian answers could be the pragmatic justification that the tribal people wanted their own state. To tackle the demands of the tribal people, the Nehruvian state could only resort to steps required for immediate crisis management. The duplex structure of state control and customary institutions produced a disjunction between the goals of the state and the cultural ethos of the tribals. Therefore, the whole debate over setting up of institutions of state centred on the pivot of sharing power between state institutions and customary institutions. The crucial question was whether the state was encroaching on the powers of customary institutions. The debate focused ultimately on maintaining a separation between institutions of the state and the tribal customary institutions. This separation acted as a justification to the Nehruvian measures for autonomy within the framework of state governance. Further measures for autonomy were not only a strategy of containment to the demand for independence, but also took care of the claim that tribal customary institutions function in a much better way than the modern system of governance.

What this duplex structure gave rise to was an upward mobility and contest within tribal communities to occupy positions within governmental structure, while traditional customary institutions maintained the already existing customary boundaries between the tribal community and other communities. Combining the question of non-interference with the tribal ethos along with the effects of creation of governmental state structure, the Nehruvian state left open the necessity to negotiate between the official statist sphere and the tribal customary sphere. But the Nehruvian state's wish to protect the tribal cultural ethos remains, as long as the customary institutions are kept outside the purview of the state. A state equipped with greater legal, administrative and other powers is much more powerful than customary institutions; and, therefore, the structure of the state ensures a hierarchy of power, as mentioned earlier, and the disjunction of customary institutions and the institutions of the state. This strategy of disjunction reveals that the Nehruvian nationalist discourse operated as a discourse of power in its ultimate evolution in the formation of governmental states, and this becomes evident in its iteration by Elwin in contexts that are not ingrained in Nehru's statements.

Nehruvian State and the Tribal Life-World

Nehru's philosophical anthropology of tribals as 'a simple folk' and as 'a folk who loves to sing and dance' stretches across situated contexts of polity, economy, culture and history. The image of the tribal as a community of forest dwellers and as the sons and daughters of nature dominates Nehru's nationalist discourse (Gopal, 1983: 606–07). Nehruvian nationalism intended to produce a reception of India as a liberating force among the tribals. The agencies that have the tendency to appropriate and destroy tribal cultural mores were restrained in Nehru's vision on tribes. Nehru represented a tribal life-world as a cultural domain, and believing it to be an element in the making of the nation he naturalized such tribal roots as a legitimate ingredient of the composite national identity. Initially, he drew it as a form of ethnic geographical ingredient, to be later elevated to a civic-territorial component of the national identity. As a civic-territorial component, Nehru considered tribal areas as a space of precious heritage that would grow in its own genius to gradually emerge into a greater cohesion with the nation. Nehru granted tribals a volitional space in order to facilitate a closer articulation of the space of power. Once the frontiers inhabited by tribes were fully incorporated within the national boundary, what was needed was the reconstitution of a horizontal cultural space to organize volitional space for communities. Often, Nehru's narrative was an articulation of the silence of nationalist discourse:

> We must remember that...experience of hundreds of millions of Indian people did not extend to the tribal areas...we were not allowed to go by the old British authorities, so that our freedom struggle did not reach these people. Rumors of it reached them.

Sometimes they reacted rightly and sometimes wrongly...The result is that we have been psychologically prepared...for various changes in India, while those frontier areas were not so prepared (Singh, 1987: 20).

Nehru's re-articulation dissociates the tribals from the freedom struggle, but affiliates them to the nation as a 'polity' and as a 'society'. The sense of affiliation generated in the tribal communities, relative to their own institutions and related to the nation as such, was a sense of being in full possession of itself—'producer and product of fully a conscious exercise of an undivided power'. The inclusion of tribals within the nation and its late individuation were both part of the Nehruvian imaginary constitution of the nation that was granted a self-evidential status. Therefore, natives such as tribals were spoken of as an autonomous entity within the self-reproducing nation. Nehru's nationalist discourse separated tribal societies from the political constitution of the nation, but made it a part of the minimal social constitution of the nation, which was the ultimate source of political institutions of independent India.

The Nehruvian state introduced affirmative discrimination by following a policy of reservation or quotas for tribals in education, employment and electoral purposes. Further, Nehru introduced an 'inner line permit' system for tribal states of the North-East in order to preserve the distinct cultural and social life of tribes from intrusion by others. Most importantly, the permit system allowed people from other non-tribal communities to settle temporarily for certain purposes and it did not allow them the right to purchase land in those areas. The obvious reason being the possibility that the tribes might be disposed of their cultural and natural resource base. But this Nehruvian policy of protection of tribal cultural ethos could not ensure what it intended, as a greater investment of power through the state machinery had upset Nehru's ideas. The tribal life-world suffered heavily owing to the introduction of the state-sponsored agencies to govern development. Nehru's philosophical anthropology of the natives therefore consisted in maintaining a disjunction between the nation and the state, even though the action of the latter had wholly changed the terrain of Nehruvian nationalism from a cultural artefact to a political articulation. When the natives contested such an inversion of Nehruvian nationalism, the inherent duality between the state and the nation widened by making the state an oppressor.

What was left as ambivalent or unresolved in Nehruvian nationalist discourse was a set of mutual oppositions between 'nation' and 'state' through the various tribal and state institutions along with the possibility of domination over the tribals, which found their resonances in Elwin's holistic discourse. The tribals spoke through Elwin's ethnographic narratives. The absent Others of Nehru's discourse became visible subjects in Elwin's shift from 'speaking for' to 'speaking of', which also meant a shift from nationalist– statist columns of power to horizontal furrows of the life-world of the native. Elwin's 'speaking of' did not exclude the context of the state that turned the tribals into citizens; rather, the iteration of Nehru's utterances was meant to invoke the context in which the tribal life-world could be spoken of. As subjects of Elwin's ethnography, tribals were the natives of the nationalist discourse— the citizen subject whose biography is inscribed within the genres of Elwin's ethnography. This mode of speaking of the tribals by Elwin produces not the self-same tribal citizens of the nation-state, but an unstructured community that contests the structure of the nation-space. Just as the silence of the nationalist discourse speaks about the communities that were beyond its discursive field, Elwin speaks of them through their absence in the discursive field, which he does by iterating Nehru's pronouncements within a re-created discursive field that embodies an ethnographic description of the tribal communities.

In the context of 'detribalization' through government machinery and other modes of cultural domination, Elwin quipped, 'We have not only to build up the peoples' pride in being themselves, but, more important still, to build up their pride in being Indian' (Elwin, 1959: 146). He also locates a sense of difference generated in the process of making them 'Indian'. He points out that the inherent sense of superiority—created by rapid advances in technology and military capability—is the main source of insensitivity in overwhelming people of the hills by the mighty Indian state (Ibid.: 145).

This process of cultural domination results in 'detribalization', manifested in the 'inferiority complex' of the tribals, presenting a scenario of reversal to the goal of 'developing tribal people along the lines of their tradition and genius'. One needs to distinguish the anxiety of being disoriented by the dominant discourse of cultural invasion by the West from such anxiety about tribes being swallowed by the moves of detribalization. Nationalism offers a cultural resistance to the West, while tribal development in India faces the discourse of nationalism that tries to appropriate them within the nation-state. Therefore, Elwin had needed a counter-discourse of resistance to nationalist ploys. Elwin exemplifies such counter-discourse in terms of detribalizing effects. When some developmental work is carried out, for example, with the construction of roads, Elwin observed that developmental measures such as roads could be a curse as well as a blessing to tribal people in more than one ways. In some places roads may become the means of exploitation and corruption, while in other places it brought in diseases, moral decline and cultural decadence. It made easy for the money-lenders, merchants, liquor vendors and lawyers' touts to venture deep into the hills and forests. Elwin contended that more than bringing money, roads take money out from the hands of tribes, tempting them with consumerism (Elwin, 1959: 74–75).

In perturbation over the gradual erosion of the tribal mode of life by the advancing forces of civilization and state, Elwin intended to retain the characteristics of tribal communities. In the context of abolishing the practice of *Jhum* cultivation in the NEFA, Elwin opined that the way of dealing with the problem is not to forbid Jhuming altogether, as it would be an undue interference in the life of the people and would cause psychological and material impoverishment (Ibid.: 88). What he proposed as a way out was to obliterate some of the initiatives launched by the state and to explore the 'middle way', such that 'modern science could assist tribal economy without destroying it'. This highlights his sensitivity towards the tribal form of life. Moreover, his reaction to some of the cases of adverse and negative effects on tribal culture, as just exemplified, is a contrapuntal way of securing a cultural safeguard for the tribal communities. Elwin's assumption of speaking through the iterated pronouncements of Nehru is a mode of speaking about the tribals through the nationalist statist discourses, the addressee of these pronouncements being the state itself. Elwin quotes Nehru:

'It is obvious', says Mr. Nehru, 'that these areas have to progress in their own way...No individual can grow in alien surroundings, habits or customs...We have to find a middle course. And that can only succeed if people are in harmony with it and co-operate with it and there is no element of compulsion about it. That approach also has ultimately to be applied through their own people (Elwin, 1959: 206–07).

The 'addressee' here is positioned within the discourse, spelling out the mode of action upon them. Elwin cites such discourse to situate it in the tribal context. This effect of situating Nehru in the tribal context means situating the statist discourse in the tribal context, and Elwin does this to make tribals addressees of this official discourse, even though tribals are not the direct addressees. Once tribals become the subject of such discourses, the 'nationalist' position of taking a 'middle course' to negotiate between the state and the tribal creates a space for intervention and interaction between the state and the tribal. Elwin articulated this space, showing the possibilities of disjunction between the agenda drawn by the state and the need of the tribal, demonstrating the incommensurability between statist agenda and the prerogatives of tribal 'self' and 'community' structures. Elwin pointed out that town bred instructors suffer from a deep sense of superiority when they come to train the tribal learners. The instructors do not easily give in to the demand by the learners to improve their technique and, instead, artificially impose their preferred ways on the tribals. Elwin contended that such impositions are a major reason for the failure to evolve ways that arise out of cultural and natural skills of tribes themselves. As a result, the so called superior skills imposed by town bred instructors results in a 'ours versus theirs' kind of cultural gap (Ibid.: 259–60).

Elwin located the 'incommensurability' in basically two approaches (Ibid.: 48, 146): one is that of developing tribals in line with the other non-tribal areas[2], and the other is the immanent sense of superiority (Ibid.: 260)[3] ingrained in the approaches of the state. Two examples are given by Elwin: one talks about the case of spreading education, which according to Elwin not only fractures the tribal cultural ethos, but also makes it reactive in many ways (Ibid.: 200).[4] Paradoxically, Elwin considered the modern education system as a means of homogenization with the modern culture of individual freedom, while simultaneously he imaged tribals to be 'liberated' from their backwardness through education. He suggested that the tribal elders should be prepared to bring about drastic changes in the tribal ethos through a modern education system. In this case, Elwin's articulation of the context for negotiation develops a background for modernity within tribal communities. It oscillates between a context for 'preparing the elders' and the context of 'modernization of the tribals'—apparently marking 'a conflict between generations'—while in a deeper sense reflecting the prerogative of the nationalist-statist agenda of moulding them to change in a homogenizing fashion. The projected 'good' in such changes mark Elwin's privileging of such an agenda, while it speaks of the fallouts of such a change. Elwin celebrates such a triumph of modernity by recommending the 'middle way' of gradually making the tribals adapt to such a change within the tribal context. But this makes clear the incommensurability of one of the circumstances of the statist-nationalist items in the agenda of development with the tribal context, which keeps Elwin on the look out for ways and means to prepare the tribal communities to minimize the impact of such changes. He foresees the reactions and impacts of such changes, flowing from the development agenda of the state. Elwin applies a strategy/procedure for containing drastic changes among tribals, thereby aims at making the state acceptable and tolerable to the tribals. He calls forth adjustment and adaptability from the tribals in order to tackle such a process of directed change. Another example of 'incommensurability' is the approach of the state, which is more visible and direct, in the dealings of the officials with the tribals. Elwin remarked that our own cultural inhibitions and food taboos are responsible for conveying a sense to the tribes that they are disliked by us. He cautioned the officers not to give an impression that the tribes were looked down upon for their habits of eating snake, beef or monkey. He cites the example of an officer abusing the *Mishmi* and *Adi* boys in one of the training centres by stereotyping them as beef-eaters, snake-eaters and monkey-eaters (Elwin, 1959: 252).

This deep-rooted sense of superiority among those at the helm of affairs is nothing but the sense of superiority of the non-tribal in the Indian social fabric, placing people in social categories of high and low order. The state carries with it a sociological sense of discrimination and it becomes more evident in the divisions of labour adapted by the state. Elwin gives the example of the appointment of someone as 'sweeper', which suits this hierarchical Indian social order, while such a concept is alien to the tribal ethos (Elwin, 1959: 253).[5] Nehru's un-negotiated difference between the nationalist–statist discourses and the tribal subject was thus negotiated by Elwin by going through the silences of the nationalist-statist discourse, as well as the situation of such discourses in the life-world of the tribal communities. Elwin's negotiation illuminated the incommensurable spaces between the two, with the greater incorporation of the tribal context within the nationalist-statist framework. But this only illustrates the gradual absence of the tribals as subjects within the frame, which leads to an attenuation of the subject in nationalist-statist discourse. It was this that had made Elwin restate some of Nehru's pronouncements with a re-interpretative direction.

A re-interpretive position taken by Elwin not only negotiates between the state and the tribal communities, but brings about a 'fusion of horizons'. Elwin's idea was that a blending of modern technology with subjective and moral demands of people is the only way to make them capable of choosing their own path of development. In order to make such choices more significant, the path of development should establish their right to choose as a 'universal right', as it is a product of blending their ideas and choices with what the humankind in general conceived as the 'right to development'. According to Elwin, if the choices of tribes for their self-development are accepted, they will be the most universal of all such choices made by other sections of mankind (Ibid.: 208).

This blending or synthesis in terms of right to choose is the most daunting problem for applying the statist policies effectively. Elwin conceived tribal culture as a domain of some indispensable values and qualities that cannot be tampered with in the process of making the state agenda successful. So he developed an idea of tribal culture, which is living and not static. He wished that all the vital aspects of tribal culture flourish in a state of freedom. Elwin gave an ecological-cultural interpretation to this sense of freedom, inherent in the structure of tribal communities. Elwin tolerated this inherent sense of freedom within the political structure of the tribal communities. He argued that indirect rule—as an expression of our respect for the tribal institutions and our faith in the good sense, justice and fundamental humanity of the tribal people—would yield more desirable results than direct intervention (Elwin, 1959: 169). His reinterpreted vision of the tribal life-world represents the community in freedom. He stresses the crucial ties of the tribal community to the land as a foundation of a sense of security and freedom from fear. As a policy objective he considered tribal right over land and its assured possession as a lasting road to peace (Ibid.: 66).

Land becomes the metaphor of interlacing the tribal and the life-world. Land also inscribes the community in a relationship with other elements of the tribal 'form of life', compounded with the indirect approach of the state, to give priority to the tribal ethos. Elwin's metaphor of land situates not only a location, but a site for making the nation without the direct intervention of the state. Attachment to the land as an inseparable vantage acts as the motive for the tribals to belong to a culture and a place. It transcends narrow notions of owning land as an asset and imbibes a greater economy of life. The metaphor of land calls forth all those integral linkages that make the community, culture and state cohere in a historic combination. In case tribals' land becomes the primary site of dispossession and cultural disorientation, Elwin explores an inner passion of the tribal mind towards its umbilical connection with land as a location of community and life.

The Colonized and the Insights of Literature

Elwin's engagement with writing the tribal culture as a text, composed and woven with interconnected genres, metaphors, traditions and canons produces an intercultural discourse that joins patterns of ethnography and literature. He initiates a play of figures and discourses in the work of situating the tribals in a space of nation, state and community. His reconstructive and reinterpretive narrative produces a different space for the tribals to negotiate their cultural location. Elwin positions himself as an author-reader of the work of tribals and textualizes it in an alternative mode. His reading displaces the blind spots of some canonical texts that image colonized subjects and produces insights for decolonization. Elwin's concern is universal decolonization of tribal communities, who are canonically effaced in the texture of colonial discourse. Although other colonized, who are engaged in a struggle for recognition, can appear with their voices either as obedient or defiant subjects in the colonial text, the tribes remain voiceless signifiers. This concern sets its own canons for ethnography, to decolonize the human subjects and to represent humans in their existential plight. This calls for the task of decolonizing ethnography, which in its disciplinary fabric hitherto represented tribals as colonized subjects. So the task set by Elwin is far more edifying as it calls for not only giving a hermeneutical twist of revealing the colonial modes of production of ethnography, but also for rewriting of the tribal identity by turning it from voiceless signifiers to signifieds in their own right. This is accomplished through decolonization of their figure as available in genres other than ethnography. Elwin situates figures of literary discourse within the field of ethnographic reproduction by way of unpacking the colonial figures in both the genres of literature and ethnography and then by situating such genres in the Indian social and political context.

Elwin re-reads Shakespeare's *Tempest,* from an ethnographer's perspective, looking at the uncolonized Caliban. He distinguishes those Shakespearean artefacts that remain exterior to colonized subjects and colonial modes of textualization. Elwin reads those artefacts and their strands in the figure of the colonized subject. The colonization of Caliban (con)figures the modes of production of the colonized subject and its textualization, and refigures a self-conscious Caliban critical of images that are 'given' onto him. The images such as 'vile race', the product of witchcraft, 'a freckled whelp hag-born', (Elwin, 1959: 33)[6] attributed to Caliban by the civilized is self-consciously known by Caliban (Ibid.: 34). Elwin draws the universal analogy for colonization from the plot of the text. He locates the colonial master-slave relationship in the relationship between Prospero and Caliban. Elwin identifies how colonial masters transfer their vices onto Caliban; how the inferiority injected in Caliban produces a subject to be colonized and many other such clues for a reading strategy that aim at decolonizing the text. Elwin's decolonizing reading of Shakespeare identifies the presence of the authorial voice itself as an agency of decolonization, which obviously is a re-interpretive step. Elwin endorses Shakespeare's view that although primitive man is not much good, contact with civilization can only make him worse (Ibid.: 34). This is an ethnographic rendering of the Shakespearean text that locates the clues for decolonization. Elwin especially identifies the mode of colonial power in turning Caliban into a man of its own self-image, an acculturated convert who leads a life styled after the colonizer, but he highlights the moment of self-conscious recognition by the native of how he is colonized. Elwin redeploys this self-conscious moment as the crucial ethnographic pointer that distinguishes the moments of colonization and retrieval of the self of the colonized. Elwin further distinguishes an authorial ploy from the ruse of colonial power operative in the text and redeems this 'eye' of the text as the exposition of the native self-recovered from the text. This *retrieval* mode of reading in which the native is relocated as a self-conscious human subject forms the alternative canon in Elwin's ethnography.

In a metaphoric reading of Shakespeare, Elwin gives a symp-tomatic characterization of the relationship between the colonizer and the native, which is a one way traffic of immorality from the colonizer to the colonized. But the important strategy is to separate the world of the native and the world after the colonization of the native. Elwin commented that just like Caliban had been wronged—his ear for music, his command over poetry and his sense of sublime are all spoilt by the presence of representatives of civilized world—the tribal people of the North-Eastern frontier are undergoing the same plight. He also points out that it is because of the vilifying impact of Prospero and his civilized followers that Caliban takes to drink and turns treacherous to his master. The tribes of the North-Eastern frontier also would turn the same way unless the vile habits of civilization are not contained at the right earnest (Ibid.: 35).

Apart from this demarcation of the world, what is significant at the deeper level is the kind of meanings attached to the trans-formation of the natives. Taking to drink and turning treacherous are all the gambit of colonial power within which norms and values about 'good' and 'evil' are connected even by the self-conscious native. One of the paradoxes for a self-conscious native is that colonization produces a cognitive frame, in which vices flowing from such subordination become visible to the colonized who embodies it, but such vices are determined by the colonizer's criterion of value. Unless colonized, the native is not supposed to stumble upon such a realization. Caught within the nexus of colonization, a native is therefore dispossessed of his own criterion of value and his visions are shaped by the dominant ideological framework of the colonial power. Elwin reveals this image of the native during colonial domination and leaves open this question— whether the transference of colonial value gives rise to a sublation of the self that dissolves the location of the native in this or that world.

Elwin's reading of Milton's *Paradise Lost,* where the original sin of Adam is commonly interpreted as a metaphor of the gradual decline and fall of civilization, is locked in a contradiction. Elwin's reading credits Milton for descriptions such as 'The first Couple were of noble shape erect and tall, God-like erect. With native honour clad, in naked misty' (Ibid.: 35), as Milton's affinity for the native, and reinterprets the general understanding of the fall of Adam as decline, as the ethnocentric bias of civilization that locates the cause of its decline in original sin. Elwin's important ethnographic clue here is an unravelling of the deep-rooted bias against the natives as an unconscious narrative subterfuge of civilization. Elwin identifies this unravelling in Milton's deliberations on nativism.

This kind of alternative sources of canons for ethnography generates a double strategy in Elwin: firstly, a persistent critique of the Enlightenment and civilization for representing the tribals as drowned in sins and vices and, secondly, a reinterpreted body of culture that resists devaluation of tribal culture by taking back tribals to the sources of civilized norms. This double strategy sublimates explicit goals like regeneration of tribal culture or a return to the sources into the body of reinterpreted ethnographic representation. Such reinterpretation removes the artefacts of colonization and domination from the structure of the text. This requires a thorough-going and constant critique of dominant forms and ideologies within ethnography, which Elwin carries through his writings.

One such metaphor of critique is 'primitivism' for Elwin (Ibid.: 42–43), which he criticizes as an essentializing mode of representation. Elwin cites the cases as vulgarity accompanied in such representations, especially in the photographic mode. By imposing the notion of 'primitive' on the tribals, the civilized world turns them into objects of derision and pity, which for Elwin is a modern-day version of colonial domination, or perhaps the worst depreciation of the self-image of the tribals. The image of 'Noble Savage' is also a homologous version of primitivism that holds an image of pristine simplicity, beauty and joy of the tribals in the modern cultural space. This is an idealized version of primitivism, as available in the representations of tribes in the writings of Aphra Behn (1640–89), Denis Diderot (1713–84) and other writers. Aphra lived for a time in Surinam, an experience that inspired her first novel, *Oroonoko, or The Royal Slave* (1688), which Elwin alludes to as a novel that extols the virtues of being native, one who refuses to be civilized and needs no government to rule him. Of course, Elwin refuted Behn's idea that the native needs no external government and can enjoy all the raptures of free love. Elwin particularly feels odd about the eighteenth century travelogues of Captain Cook (1728–80) and others who had presented the image of the Noble Savage in their encounter with the natives. For Elwin, such representation casts the humans of flesh and blood into an imaginary type. Elwin identifies the eighteenth century French writer Diderot as a critique of such images of the native given by the European writers, travellers and explorers. Diderot's restoration of the native as 'Natural Man' was appreciated by Elwin, as he could also find a host of other supportive writing in the writers of the day, such as Johnson and Rousseau. Elwin identifies this strand of critique of primitivism and the celebration of 'Natural Man' as one of the routes of his critique of Enlightenment and European colonialism. But it is to be noted that Elwin goes with the dominant mode of Western ethnography, by not gendering the notion of Man, as he is silent about the 'Natural Woman' who just does not figure in his ethnographic imagination. The denial of women's subjectivity in the name of natural man, goes on to reproduce the subjugated status of tribal woman in the context of NEFA. Despite this shortcoming, Elwin builds up a humanistic canon of ethnography with a limited cultural critique of Western colonialist literature and ethnography. He identifies the stereotypical approach of the missionary and imperialist by stating that primitive man seemed to exemplify the ancient doctrine of original sin to the missionary and colonialist. However, it was above all necessary that he should be saved (Ibid.: 40).

Elwin identifies the stereotypical colonial imagination of natives as the sinners who committed original sin, which gave a fillip to their saviour motif. Elwin intends to develop a critique of such stereotypes and motifs by reading through a relatively modern novelist like Dickens. For Elwin, Dickens' scepticism about the Noble Savage was a reverse condemnation of the native that negates both the idealized 'noble' and the 'savage' in the native and projects the image of a native as wild and barbaric, typical of the European mind. Elwin quoted Dickens' statement that reads, 'His [the native's] virtues are a fable, his happiness is a delusion; his nobility, a nonsense' (Ibid.: 41). What Elwin intends to show is how Dickens had suffered from multiple layers of distortions produced from juxtaposition of images and counter images of natives in Western writings. In reading Dickens, Elwin hints at how Western writing on natives imbricates a complex motif of domination by juxtaposing images like 'Savage' and 'Noble Savage', and its demystification by way of reiterating the image of an essential cruelty and barbarity in them. One also needs to remember that the Western ethnographic imagination undergoes a sea change from Captain Cook's time to Dickens' time. During Cook's time, it was just the beginning of the empire and hence the image of the native was still not wholly evil; while in Dickens' time the empire had, by then, collapsed the distinction between the 'savage' and the 'noble savage'. It had evolved its own brand of hybrid connotations of tribes and natives, displacing its earlier characterizations. But it could never yield them a place that is equal to the Western human being. The original idea of civilizing the savage still operated with thicker descriptions of the societies already colonized. Elwin's strategy of re-reading such genres teases the construction of imaginary identities in natives by the West and introduces a modest therapy by way of whacking up fetishized textualization.

The therapeutic mode of Elwin's ethnography gives rise to a protocol of reading. The protocol is to situate an author in the text by way of mapping the images that the text bears of the natives. This calls for an unpacking of the layers of meanings, images and metaphors to disclose how the text favours a representation of the native that decimates him. Elwin located those dominant motifs like sentiments, pathos and desire of the West for knowing the natives in their bare existence. The natives became the subjects of the

Western discourse of condescension, sentiment and pathos, which enveloped them in an authoritative-possessive mould. Elwin identifies how such a presumptive authority on the natives becomes the canon, weaving the sympathy of the dominant for the pathology of native life. Elwin corrects this complacency of the dominant by gerrymandering the strings of dominance that weave the common universal motif in the representations of natives in various genres of writing. Elwin locates a self-conscious correction of the Western sense of authority in the attitude toward the native, by which, all that produces domination is chastened. Elwin represented the corrected position of the West, in contrast with a preceding and prior disposition of colonization, which looked upon the tribes as noble and good and tried to devise all possible means of doing good to them without affecting their nobility and goodness. This humanized way of looking upon the tribes also found its unanimous support in poets and artists who further deepened the perception of nobility and goodness in them. This is a correction of the distorted picture of the tribes constructed by reformers, clergies and uplifters who wanted to act as harbingers of civilization to them. The civilization that they had brought in remained insensitive to virtues of tribes, which found a sublime stature in many an art forms (Ibid.: 44).

Elwin criticizes the dominant motif of discovering and representing the tribe as a primordial human entity in forms of Western discourses. Even though such a primordial double of the civilized serves simultaneously as a conceptual artefact for restitution of the forgotten history of the West and an enlivening source of meaning, it serves the greater purpose of legitimizing the domination of the West. Elwin, therefore, uncouples the question of the development of the native from the genres of representation. He especially locates those metaphors that represent the natives as subordinated and whose conditions are alleviated by the West. He distinguishes between the canons of domination through condescension and canons of viewing them as respectable human beings. He considered the canons of domination as unselfconscious modes of Western representation of the tribal, while he distinguished the canons of viewing them as respectable human beings as an ethical imperative, with its unconditional commitment to the good of the native communities. This is how Elwin brings a context of working with the natives, by participating in their form of life, which can act as an imperative of building up a nation.

Incorporating Wisdom in Ethnography

Canons of ethnography and canons of nationalism merge in Elwin's reinterpreted ethical imperatives, commanding a move from mute and passive representation of the native to a live and active following of the native footprints. Elwin favours an uncontaminated and un-predisposed entry in the world of the native by merging one's authorial voice with/in the voice of the native. Elwin places the exteriority of nationalist discourse in the ethnographic interior of the native narrative, in order to bridge the incommensurable terrain of state policies and tribal self-development. To accomplish this task he invites heterogeneous genres of writing to interpenetrate and overlap each other, bringing on a displacement of the law of genre to do away with the forms of representation and thus producing a language of negotiation between the differentiated languages of state, nation and the Native.

Broadly speaking, Elwin follows two modes of ethnographic representation: literal and figural. In both the modes, his narrativization or presentation of the narrative caters those concepts and meta-phors that characteristically twinkle in their native gaze. In the literal mode, narrativization acts as the mostly applied technique in setting out a genre or intermixture between genres. Elwin classified genres in narratives of literal representation in classes such as 'fixture' and 'myth' despite their commonly poised tendency to merge onto the native life-world. The line drawn between such genres is not mutually exclusive to each other, rather as cultural expressions they are open to each other.

The fictional representation of some of the live imaginations of the natives of NEFA are textualized in the narratives of *A New Book of Tribal Fiction*. The fictionalization is exemplified in the creation of many images, referring to certain objects and meanings created within the languages of the tribes. In describing such images, Elwin traces the making of fiction. For example in an *Adi* story 'How Spiders Taught Men to Weave', the narrative runs:

There were two brothers who were Wiyus [spirits below the Supreme Deity] but had the form of men. When Sedi-Botte [the Great
Spirit of the World] died, the whole world was covered with water,
and the brothers had nowhere to live. While they were wondering
in despair what to do, an eagle flew to their help. They jumped into
the air and clung to him and he carried them into the sky, and when
the water dried brought them down again to earth.

There they built themselves a little hut, but they were cold and
naked, for they had no cloth. One day however, Spider wove her
web across a corner of their house and they said, 'If we could make
something like this, we would have clothes for the day and covering
for the night'. First of all, therefore, imitating spider, they made mats
of leaves, but when they saw the fine weaving of the web they were
not satisfied. But one day when they were out hunting, they found
some cotton plants and brought them home, though they did not
know what to do with them. Then another day, as they hunted, they
came to the place where Sedi-Botte had died. They made a spindle
and loom from his bones, and when they returned home they begin
[*sic*] to spin and weave their cotton, and soon had clothes to wear
(Elwin, 1991: 43).

The fictional element of this narrative arises in the disappearance
of the ethnographer as a recorder of the narration, as also the
disappearance of the 'real' teller of the story into an abstract
experiential tale in which the subjects of the experience are constructed. The experience itself is also constructed as an imagination
of the relationship of learning. The whole narrative produces the
subject effect of a culturally situated reader/writer/narrator emerging with a reflexive self. Just as the spider weaves the web, the
tale also weaves this experience of weaving like a spider, as if
without such a spider the intricate patterns revealed in the imagination would never be clear and distinct. Weaving as a metaphor
gives an extended field of meaning, registering how a community
weaves its imagination in coherence with an act of weaving the
cloth. The 'fictional element' of this tale arises because of the initial
flight of imagination from the world of objects to the world of
spirits inhabited by the *Wiyu* and *Sedi-Botte*. The Wiyus who
assume human form and the Wiyus of the Earth are put in a certain
relationship within the fictional frame of the tale. Later again the
relationship gets transformed into a primordial one from which the

creation begins once again. The tale brings out its ingredients of images and figures at a site of meaning and knowledge that can be commonly interpreted through the symbols it uses.

In the literal mode, myths join the familiar and the narrative events in a splendid revelation of meanings considered essential to the form of life of a community. Elwin locates a reservoir of desires, wishes and beliefs of specific symbolic origin in the myths of NEFA. Elwin studies and presents such myths by going through their motifs, and one of the remarkable motifs is that of the 'trickster'. He shows that the tricksters are created in order to satisfy those wishes of the community that have not yet been fulfilled, and how the penalties and punishments awarded to the tricksters for the tricks they play satisfy the wish of the community to punish the tricky wrong-doers. Tricksters as characters represent the susceptibility of the community to unwarranted mishaps in life committed by unknown forces—activities that bring out the folk psychology of fear and recriminations as available in the myth. Contrastingly, tricksters are invested with an immense power to create a world or a community. By situating the community in the motifs of myths, Elwin like an anthropologist unravels the self-conscious acts of self/community-making in tribal and indigenous thought.[7] A distinction between fiction and myth in Elwin's ethnography lies in their performative roles. Fiction performs a role of bridging the world of magic and the empirical, which is the main basis of the literal mode of ethnography. In the case of myths, motifs play the role of representing something pivotal for the community. As a literal mode, myths transmit that kind of knowledge which is specifically necessary to explain questions of the eschatological and cosmological kind. Myths are literal   configurations of cosmological and eschatological events narrated through the presence of certain figures, as we have seen, like a trickster taking part as an agent to make thing happens. Myths assume a temporal permanence by way of producing a strong belief in what they communicate, and thereby become stable/fixed markers of communicatively arrived at truths, by involving various families, classes and generations. They often redraw those memories that are congealed in the formation of beliefs that construe the community, and in that sense myths regenerate the past. Fiction does not require a regeneration of the past or essential beliefs of the community, but needs to create or weave some elements of culture, to give rise to a plot or narrative for everybody's consumption. Myths bring in a greater temporalized sense of belonging, while fiction brings in a sense of living in some plots and narratives (Elwin, 1953: xxiii). Both myths and fiction bear a kind of native realism, but with a difference in kind and degree.

The generic distinction between the two does not blur the possibility of their intermixture, rather, they call for an overlapping of boundaries. Fiction often assumes the form of a myth and vice-versa. Elwin's distinction between fiction and myths highlights tribal creativity and imagination (Ibid.: xxi). In recording both myths and fiction, he apprehended that they reflect something that would soon disappear and such marks of creativity are necessary for locating culture within a definite time and space. Elwin considers them as 'records' (Ibid.: 47) that illuminate the hard lives of the people of hills (Ibid.: xxiv). The convergence between canons of such ethnographic writing and canons of nationalism lies in the representation of cultural specificity embedded in the instances of culture. The nation arises in the specific cultural item, such as literality of the fiction, as without this the community cannot be thought or spoken of. Such cultural items bridge the gap between the space of the community and the space of the nation. Even though the latter exceeds the bounds of the former, the space of the nation needs to inscribe the cultural space of the community, and the space of the community needs to perform the role of a narrative substratum for the nation. The cultural space, acting as a substratum for the narrative constitution of the community, contributes to shape the national identity. The nation has to represent those images and symbols of the community around which its solidarity is conceived. Elwin's ethnography is a theoretic-narrative space of representation that enacts the canons of making the nation.

The tribal mode of representation acts as a symbolic structure that distributes meanings within the community and those meanings also get contextualized within the community. The specific tribal element is preserved in terms of in-group reference to the meanings that are contained in the representation. How such literal modes are an enactment of the desires of the community needs to be addressed and taken into account for a programme of national reconstruction.

This, as has been discussed, is exemplified in Elwin's texts. In *A Philosophy for NEFA* (1959), the stories of unbearable suffering of a woman and a man on being bitten by a snake and a bear, and their subsequent ailments, provide an example of an ethnographic pathos. Elwin's presentation of the picture of a 'charm hung before a house after a sacrifice to avert disease' provides an ethnographic profile of indigenous ways of thinking of cures for diseases (Elwin, 1959: 90–91). The launching of a healthcare delivery system by setting up hospitals and dispensaries are meant to provide medical services to the people. Elwin cites examples of many doctors who identified themselves with the tribals and calls it a 'success' (Ibid.: 92). For Elwin, remaining committed to the ethos of the tribals remains the hallmark of national reconstruction.

Elwin moves into the task of figural representation of the native life, in order to make it visible to the nation. Figurality is an intermixture of photography, narrative and celebration of the specific native characteristics and values. Elwin's narrative of the figural often describes a performance. Elwin remembers how Father Krick, who went into an expedition among the 'Abors' (now called Adis) in 1893, was greeted by them with a ceremonial arch and the natives had performed rituals to ensure his well-being. Elwin quoted Father Krick stating that as he reached the foothill, two of the youngest from a group of 18 young men covered his body with leaves in order to protect him from all diabolical influences. This exorcist act was followed by Father Krick's passing through an arch made of bows and arrows placed in a threatening position. This was meant to exorcise the more stubborn spirits. Father Krick was simply amazed to watch such rituals of which he was a subject, but at the same time he appreciated the concern of the tribesmen for his health and well-being (Elwin, 1991: 43).

The description given by Father Krick produces a text of the native images in an 'architectural' form, in which canonic motifs of ethnography are presented, offering assumptions about good and evil embedded in the community. But Elwin contends, 'The fearsome architecture today has lost some of its picturesque' and describes that the spiked fences and gates, with imitation arrows or realistic bamboo stakes are erected, and the head or body of a fowl, dog or monkey is hung up on it to deter the mischievous spirits (Ibid.: 43). Such architecture institutes a space of ritual performance with a motif of mobilizing the images and figures of gratification of certain kinds of desires. It manifests the structuring of the fear of death and withdrawal from everyday practices of livelihood. What we are concerned about here is the play of form to make the interior of the native life-world visible. The visibility produced in architecture is the vision of a haunted structure, created for ritualistic practices of the native that simultaneously produces strangeness and fear, both of which transgress the visibility of the architecture. The ethnographic basis of the community is reproduced in ritual architectures. Such a discourse creates a nexus among various elements of culture by being located in an original act of representation, as indicated in the experience of exorcism by Father Krick. The experience of Father Krick as a traveller indicated the showing of a ritual space in the space of the community, and this displacement is the mark of the inviolable exterior of the community. The figural representation of the community in such structured experiences is an appropriation of the outside, which it conceals within its constitution.

The figural mode of representation produces a fund of images drawn from native creation. Elwin presents a number of such images such as 'representing a woman with expothalamic goitre' (Elwin, 1959: 89) that aestheticize the face of woman with goitre and give a totality to representations. It manifests a queer phenomenon that gets idealized in the act of artistic representation, acquiring the potential of speaking of the native community in its peculiar distress. Similarly a figure of the '*Wancho* girl at her loom' (Ibid.: 60), represents a moment of performance of one of the most necessary acts of production that speaks of the most tenacious enterprise of women. This mode of representation is figurative, because of the possibility of a communication that transcends the specific contexts of the figure and speaks of the community. In a way different from architecture, such figures bring out that which is internal to the community into explicit visibility to occupy the exterior, to enter the chain of symbolic exchange that takes place between such figures, in delimiting the relationship of a native community with its Others. The figurative shines in a distinct manifestation of an internal character to the Others. In terms of canons, this is an exploration of ethnography in which the internal and core aspects of culture are made visible through its representations as represented by the community. The canon is a doubling of self-representation in an openly visible space that sites the community to the Other. The nation as a site of symbolic exchange accommodates such figures of self-representation, rejuvenating the native figures in a self-illuminating form. The nation-space plays an alternation between the visible and invisible—the native figures are absent, non-visible. The absence of the native calls for figures that evoke a sense of estranged attention, a spectacle of curiosity that returns with a sense of fulfilment in the representation of native figurers. Such figures immediately stand out and can be distinguished from other figures. For example, the native mark of women with goitre represents a face, a face that makes itself seen without being seen by the other; while the figure of the woman with the loom makes itself seen as a subject of vision in the nation-space.

What Elwin inaugurates is a framework of state policy, formation of nation and canons of ethnography, to intermix and evolve into a reinterpreted world of native-nation conjunction. His repeated intermixture of genres, interplay of distinctive categories, and a weaving of Nehru's statements in his ethnographic interpretations are a kind of repetition that produces an alternative domain of meanings in ethnography, which refuse a closed reading. This presents a textual field of an ever unfolding interplay of meanings in native images that does not succumb to a dominant image of nation.

ANTHROPOLOGY OF HEALING

Elwin enters the field of disjunction between the native and the nation by way of evolving a reinterpretive position of structuring a nation-from-below that gives rise to a mechanism of mediation with the state through native institutions. He does this by a delicate mingling of the canons of ethnography with the canons of nationalism. But Elwin does not reproduce those silences of Nehru's discourse that speaks of the native not in its own language but produces a representation in the language of state and nation. Being aware of the already existing disjunctions between such standardized languages and criterion of morals (Elwin, 1959: 51–52), as just discussed, developed a language of nationalism constituted by figures, images and institutions of the native acting as a substratum for the ethnographic interpretation of nation.

Elwin's philosophical anthropology follows a subtle principle of correction of cases of misrepresentation and misrecognition by the nation. He cites the example of a museum collection of life-size models of NEFA people with 'ferocious countenance' and 'pitch black' outfits that produces a voyeuristic image of natives, which could produce a sense of being ridiculed and dehumanized. Elwin notes the reaction of a group of Adi people seeing such voyeuristic images of themselves (1959: 143), and expresses deep agony in finding how other dominant communities have produced a stereotype of native culture in such a dehumanizing form, the force of which alienates the tribals and annihilates their culture. He identifies a similar counter response among the tribals who get extremely scared and befuddled in realizing how they are 'looked down upon' and 'despised'. How anything 'tribal' becomes an object of queer sensationalism is exemplified by Elwin: 'I remember a comic strip about somebody's cure for constipation, in which the hero was a corpulent and constipated Naga Chief who was always cutting of [sic] his neighbour's heads, until he took the magic remedy which eased his bowels' (Ibid.: 143). This kind of advertisement ascribing culturally connected markers of superiority/inferiority is a perverted form of representation by which a law-like principle is enacted. In the process of determination of the cultural value of a commodity, the rule is to establish the superior value of a commodity by way of ascribing lower values to the 'uncommoditified' cultural items. Elwin's concern here goes even deeper to locate a process of detribalization/culturation, by which loss of culture of the tribal community becomes a means for attaining higher cultural values for the already commoditified, civilized and non-tribal cultures. It is through the removal of the tribal self-image on which the self-image of civilized communities is built. Such a contrapuntal reading through mixed genres of ethnography gives Elwin the edge to locate the difference produced in representing tribals from others within the nation.

Elwin aims at 'correcting' such distortions and removal of the human image. He recites Nehru's catch phrase, 'A Touch of Healing', to spell out the approach to 'correct' such distortions.

His therapy is the evolution of certain moral imperatives from a pragmatic point of view. Elwin's exploratory mode of ethnography combines a myriad of anthropological, administrative and scientific discussions to set a sense of 'corporate responsibility' (1959: 143). He derives some canons of this responsibility from the tenets of Nehruvian Panchsheel towards the tribal and the indigenous people, which, as discussed earlier, delegated certain responsibilities to the state to preserve the traditions of the native and the indigenous form of life. Elwin explored various possible dimensions of such a self-delegated responsibility. He endorsed Nehru in explaining the guiding principle of that philosophy, which is that first and foremost it is a philosophy based upon the recognition of human personality because that is the fundamental conception and covers all the rest (Ibid.: 173). This recognition of human personality is found in Elwin's ideas on correction. He envisages a state that does not have a system of penalization, but evolves a system of rehabilitation of those who violated the norms of tribal society. He criticized the British system of jail administration and the treatment of offenders as criminals not only from a humanist's position but also from a position of neutralizing the administration from taking coercive action. Elwin contested the idea of a penal state in general, and the role of law enforcement in the context of the tribal areas of the North-East. He unequivocally said, 'In other parts of tribal India nothing has been more destructive of the high and simple standards of the tribesmen and their belief in human nature than their relations with the courts and lawyers' (Ibid.: 169). In another specific reference to the penal system of the state, he warned that locking the tribesman inside the prison is something that is completely alien to their culture and their sense of independence; but the danger is that such incarceration brings them in touch with 'hardened criminals', which changes their fundamentally innocent outlook on life for the worse (Ibid.: 176).

Elwin touches upon the inner debility of human nature produced out of the deeper level repression, of which the state is the external agency, and he extols the fundamental innocence of tribal nature that remains a qualitative exception. It not only reinstates a primal vision of uncontaminated tribal life-form, but also combines with it the possibility of retaining an area of sanctity within the modern state system so far as the tribal mode of life is concerned. He sees the system of punishment and imprisonment prevailing within a modern state as perpetuating a repression of human psyche and developing a sense of guilt. Elwin considers the construction of the tribal world as the development of a tradition that continues the idea of the free human spirit, mostly represented in the fiction, song, dance and other forms of expression. Elwin holds that the activities of a number of spirits, eschatological good and evil determined by supernatural forces, the cult of propitiation of vital forces of nature, have an effect that is both redemptive and works as a deterrent for the tribal communities. Some examples can be cited here. Elwin talked about the norm of 'multiple restitution' for settling disputes or punishing crimes. Elwin cited the proceedings of a murder case at Kameng district of NEFA. Before the case was opened for deliberation, a cow was sacrificed for a *Puffe* ceremony (a sacrament of peace and amity) that is meant to ensure peace and destroy hatred. The amount of compensation payable to the family of the murdered was carefully computed. For the murder itself, a male and a female slave were demanded. But this being disallowed, three mithuns were given instead of the man and two mithuns for the woman. Then, three sacred bells were given for the victim's head, heart and buttocks respectively, a dao for his ribs, a valuable bead for his eyes, and mithuns and sacred bells to various relations to make up for the fact that they could not enjoy his company any longer. For a second Puffe at the close of the proceedings, another sacrificial mithun had to be given away by the accused. Finally, an iron tripod was given to the village priest to drive away any evil spirit that might trouble the participants in the case (Elwin, 1959: 166).

This kind of native reasoning pervades all other spheres of life. In an illuminating discussion on the native concept of disease and healing, Elwin contends that the tribal idea of cause of disease is something 'spiritual'; hence he argued that what is spiritually caused must be spiritually cured, and this is the main reason why the tribals prefer to go their own doctors rather than to physicians with modern qualifications (Ibid.: 178). This mode of reasoning among the natives, according to Elwin, should be taken in the 'right attitude' (Ibid.: 179), which he elaborated in the theory that God answered the priest's prayer by making the pill more efficacious: the physician is the instrument through which divine compassion works. The priest will pray for him, the physician will give him a pill (Elwin, 1959: 178).

What Elwin indicated here is not a mere peaceful coexistence of the 'modern' with the 'native', but a greater possibility of rejuvenation of the free human spirit through an act of simultaneous prayer and application of medicine that acts as the spiritualizing factor in modern applications in the tribal context. Elwin locates a striking difference between the modern and the native, from the attitudinal disparity that crops up in interacting with the tribal mores of life which raises the question, 'Is there any way out of this dilemma?' Elwin explores an ethnographic answer to this question that reinterprets certain nationalist positions taken by Nehru, and extends it to evolve a way of symbiosis as suggested by Nehru.

Elwin and the Reinterpretation of Nehru

Elwin reinterpreted the Nehruvian position in terms of certain aims, spelling out a guideline of action in *A Philosophy for NEFA* (1959), which has been discussed at some length. Elwin intended to join the native institutions constructed upon customary laws with the state-institutions. The policy framework that he evolved is a delicate mixture between the ethnographer's empathy for the natives and the nationalist commitment for 'development' according to their own genius, even though such a proposal could be spelt only in terms of certain aims or goals. As we saw, Elwin often moved out of bridging these two extents of the imperative and explored the potential of development for the cultural resources and indigenous institutions. He explored a concept of democracy in tribal context that takes into account the functioning of tribal institutions as non-state actors, of which his book *Democracy in NEFA* (1965) is an example. Elwin commended that the traditional tribal institutions like tribal councils have great potentialities. These institutions are supported by social and religious sanctions and are expressions of co-operative and communal temperament. He opined that such institutions can not only support the law and order machinery of the state, but can work as agencies of development and progress (Elwin, 1965: 49).

This kind of recommendation puts into play the local traditions of tribals in ensuring that democracy starts from such ground level institutions that are built around the signifying practices of the native community and networks are created to retain these. Elwin considered such institutions and signifying practices of the native societies as an integral component of democracy, which would thereby re-centre a statist-nationalist conception of democracy in ethnocentric contexts. The crux issue here is to chart out the graduation of such native institutions into institutions of state.

His elaborate discussion of the functioning of tribal councils all over India and the NEFA is an example of his ethnographic representation of alternative layers of democracy beyond the functioning of the state, and he construes an autonomous sphere of operation of such councils. The *Monpa Tsorgens*, who are elected as the chiefs of well-structured village councils, are vested with all the civil, juridical and ritual powers. The *Aka* village council, called *Mele*, functions through a *gaonburah* or village head. The *Apa Tani Buliango* are even more decentralized, in which there is no centralized authority 'but village affairs are managed in a somewhat informal manner by a council of clan representatives (*buliang*)' (Elwin, 1965: 81).

The Nishi institution, called *Gingdungs,* have the specific feature to act as a go-between in the relationship among various clans and families. Even though Gingdungs do not hold any statutory power, they still play the role of negotiator in resolving conflict situations. Another important institution that Elwin notes is the *Kebang* (assembly of representatives of traditional institutions) of the Siang Frontier Division, which in his opinion is well organized and it acts as a repository of traditional laws and customs. *Ramos* and *Pailibos*, two small closely allied tribal groups living in the north-west of the Siang Frontier Division, do not have a pre-elected village chief. The leading man of the neighbourhood derives his authority 'from his character and knowledge of local custom' to claim the position of the chieftain, who can summon *Keba* (local village council) on an ad hoc basis. This is a matter of ethnographic interest, as the criterion of selecting such a wise person is totally internal to the tribe, and the investing of authority on such a person presupposes his sound knowledge of tradition. Therefore, a person recognized as a village chief by the government may not be a person fulfilling the internal criterion of the community (Elwin, 1965: 112). Elwin also gives an example of an inter-village dispute, in which the propriety over a particular shrub is traditionally decided by the ritual performance related to its extraction. The dispute centred not on the location of the shrub in a particular village, but the alleged violation of the ritual norms by the villagers of the village where the shrub grew. The complaint came from the villagers of a neighbouring village, after a fight among the two parties ended in a fiasco. Elwin narrated that the matter was referred to a village head, who decided that the Tagur people should pay compensation and persuaded both sides to make peace (Ibid.: 113). Thus, the whole dispute centred on certain life-world norms ascribed the status of 'truth', a violation of which precipitates the dispute. One can see here that native disputes do not focus on for variety individual interests, but on norms fundamental to the form of life of a community. Native institutions act as self-critical observers which evolve means to correct aberrations occurring within the community. In the case of tribal institutions, norms are an integral part of the life-world that is required to be preserved in order to retain the shape of the community. Nehru's commitment to retain the tribal form of life without tampering with it in the process of administration is a realization of the crucial significance of the tribal signifying practices. Nehruvian nationalism celebrated the sprightly dimensions of such signifying practices. He was quoted by Elwin:

> Tribal culture leads to a way of life which particularly makes the people rejoice in song and dance. Our mentors who go to them frown at their ways and tell them to desist from them in the name of reform. The result is that they lose somewhat that joy in life which they possess in abundant measure and gain little else in its place. They become joyless and devitalized, dull and insipid. Surely that is a wrong approach (Ibid.: 265).

In the context of independence, Elwin had formulated a questionnaire that inscribed the criteria of tribal development. He calls this questionnaire a touchstone. The questionnaire has several questions, such as whether the particular scheme helps the tribe grow in their own genius and tradition; or it would result into a copy of ourselves. Further, Elwin specifically raises the question whether the outcome of a developmental scheme would uproot the tribes from their social and natural environment and whether the programmes are grossly presumptuous about the merit of the thoughts that are imposed on them. Particular caution, according to Elwin, needed to be exercised in matters of possibilities of acculturation, destruction of their self-reliance and then burdening them with too many projects styled in the way official reports and the press found good. The question of ensuring the ultimate good is the most important thing for Elwin, as tribes are often deprived of the good at the cost of welfare and benefits. With this war against external impositions and decisions on behalf of the tribes, Elwin is equally weary about finding out whether the Nehurvian project of integrating the tribes with the rest of India is successfully carried out by ensuring the path of self-development for the tribes. The last item in his 10-point questionnaire presents that worry. In other words, Elwin's questionnaire brings a self-questioning through iteration, assuming the form of questioning the performative context, in which the nationalist discourse applies itself. The modes of self-interrogation assume the voice of internal criticism within the discourse of nationalism and this is a statist appropriation of the voice of the Other within the ambit of nationalist discourse. The return of the question to itself signifies a simultaneous inclusion and exclusion within nationalist discourse (Elwin, 1965: 285–86).

Elwin's ethnographic representation of the life-world of indigenous communities of the North-East, and Nehru's pronouncement of policy towards the tribals and the indigenous people, fall in the abyss between nationalist imperatives and statist prerogatives. While Elwin inclines towards situating Nehru in the cultural and ethnic contexts and prepares grounds for an indigenous rooting of Nehru, the latter's flight towards a universal humanist empathy for the elemental aspects of tribal life take two different directions. Elwin conflates ethnocentrism with Nehruvian nationalism, while Nehru conflates the nationalist vision of accommodation of communities, with the statist agenda for their development. Elwin's mode of grounding the nationalist discourse takes more and more an 'internal-realist' position, in which he locates 'nation' in the tribal mode of life, by extending the horizons of tribal life to the discourse of democratization, initiated by the post-colonial nation-state. Elwin stretches the limits of the life-world to make it fulfil the agenda of the state, thereby leaving open the possibility of a greater adaptation by the state to the tribal situation. The resources of this greater adaptation are drawn from the constructions of the world among the tribals. But the constraint of locating the nation within the site of tribal culture repetitively brings back the Nehruvian nationalist discourse of responsibility towards the tribals, and this is how the 'nation' is made visible to the tribals. The Nehruvian pronouncements of responsibility as a performative act makes tribals the subjects of the nation but Elwin's reiteration in the cultural context indigenizes the nation. The line between 'state', 'nation' and 'tribe' is blurred in the interior of such discursive grounding of nation and state in the tribe. Elwin's concern is to retain the tribal identity in the process of emerging into a nation, but the threat of the statist appropriation of tribal identity turns him inwards to ground the 'nation' and 'state' in the context of native life. The question of tribals becoming subjects of the nation becomes relevant in the way 'nation' becomes 'tribal'. This is how Elwin develops a discourse of the ethnocentric nation-from-below that emanates through the mores of tribal life.[8]

The images of the natives in terms of their rituals, taboos and shamans in Elwin's books represent a rejuvenating mode of tribalism that displaces the voyeur produced out of such native images in the nationalist discourse. This is done in order to use the field of native images against dominant national images and make the latter negotiate with the native ones. Elwin further displaces the colonizing appropriation of native images in drawing the canons of ethnography and upholds a decolonized life-world of the native. His strategy is to ground the nation in the native life-world, for which Nehru too strove in his Panchsheel. In both cases, the tribals remain a 'site' that requires re-invocation, not for its own sake, but to make the nation possible in an area of impossibility.

Notes

1. Juxtaposition as a method of reading could be used to compare and contrast select authors.
2. Refers to Nehru's Panchsheel Principles.
3. Elwin speaks of a deep-rooted sense of superiority among the persons interested in working in the tribal areas.

4. Elwin speaks of detribalization.
5. Elwin gives the example of Kabui Nagas.
6. Elwin quotes these lines from *The Tempest*.
7. Elwin situates community in the myth by way of detailing how community reproduces its 'unconscious' in the structure of the myth. Elwin's representation of the myth brings out the self-conscious act of making the community, as he redescribes the narration of the native informant in such a manner that the native can see himself in such narrative with a substantive demystification of the myth.
8. Elwin's proposal for an administration under the Government of India oriented to goals of preserving the tribal life-world is explained throughout his book, *A Philosophy for NEFA*. The need for having a tribal state is particularly advocated in nationalist terms in his *Philosophy* (1959: 8, 286–87).

4

Insurgency as Counter-Hegemonic Struggle in North-East India

Insurgency signifies a moment of rupture or disruption that generates a counter discourse to the already experienced milieu of subjection, alienation and compulsion. It articulates a sense of dispossession and betrayal tinged with the pathos of coercion and violence. As an experience of negativity it constitutes attempts of uprising and insurrection in order to counterblast the dominant symbolic order. The dominant order justifies the political and social conditions that sustain layers of disparities, which at the same time produces dissent and dismay over the micro perceptions of distorted self-image (Das, 1993: 1–3).[1] A question that we can ask here is: How does insurgency produce a participatory discourse of emancipation and salvation? In other words, what is the positive and euphoric dimension of insurgency? Does it nurture a vision of promise and hope beyond the aura of dominant discourses? In the case of North-East India, insurgency is a mix of a wounded attachment and a healing touch, a discourse of difference that helps the alienated communities to take them away from tackling the alienating symbols and images. It adopts a politics of combat and resistance to the ongoing discourse of subjugation and derives its sustenance from rupturing the dominant images. Though there is no such nodal point of radical rupture from the dominant images that cuts off a free and liberated home, an ever replenished effect to manoeuvre and struggle in an enemy terrain keeps insurgency alive. The language of insurgency reflects upon the dominant cultural symbols and contrasts it with the home grown cultural symbols in order to reclaim the autonomy of such indigenous cultural symbols.

The fact of clash and intertwinement between the dominant cultural symbols and indigenous symbols produces a dialectic of appropriation and expropriation that generates a politics of 'Otherization', a conflict of authenticity, ownership and legitimacy over these symbols. Therefore, insurgency in North-East India constitutes and defines its own positive core in terms of its own symbolic that produces empathy and passion in securing and representing an ethnic identity in a space of autonomy.

THEMATIC OF INSURGENCY

The thematic of insurgency in the North-East is the recovery of a lost terrain, and the reconstruction of a legitimate and autonomous identity. This thematic of insurgency is, in fact, a counter-thematic to the dominant national imagery of the celebration of 'nationhood'. But the fulfilment of this thematic assumes a long drawn vision of emergence into something radically new—a new nation-form that shall mobilize all the fragments of the 'insurgents' community to a natural teleological resolution. But this thematic of insurgency assumes a backseat as it dissipates into the whirlpool of the problematic generated and accented by dominant national imagery. Various insurgency movements of the North-East, such as Naga, Mizo and Assamese national struggles, have identified the 'Indian state' as their common enemy and undercut the claim of Indian national identity. In contrast, they assert the illegitimacy of the claim of nationhood of India and present a differentiated interior to point out the impossibility of 'fusion' or melting-pot imagery. Once the claim of nationhood is problematized, the idea of an Indian nation-state stultifies over its head to become a state with a unified nationhood.

This problematization is initiated by the dominant national discourse. The effect of the dominant national symbols is so alienating and exclusionary that groups of people from the North-East are separated off it to a distinct cultural and symbolic position. The dominant symbols such as Hindi-Hindu-Brahminical orientation of the Indian state (Kaviraj, 1994: 115–129) and its linguistic preferences constructs an exterior where the smaller identities who are without any leverage are to emplaced. The extension of state institutions to the peripheries and to include smaller groups of people is meant to legitimize the apparatus of the state. But the hierarchical nature of such an operation by the Indian state does not produce an even space of intermingling and interaction, rather it produces a differentiating structure of identities that clamour for recognition and redistribution. Therefore, this process of nationhood is another name for structural discrimination and differentiation to exercise power over various identities and to different degrees.

This ensues upon the problematization of the life-experiences of smaller identities as well as their position within the Indian identity. The pervasive differences between aboriginal and indigenous language and culture (Chattopadhaya and Bhadra, 2001: 33, 39)[2], on the one hand, and a language and culture standardized in the canons of 'Indian culture' on the other, constitute the sphere of negativity within the dominant image of the Indian nation. The experiences go like this: the language which a smaller community 'owns' is not a recognized language, the culture to which they belong is tribal or 'pre-modern' and, therefore, the unhappy feeling of being excluded haunts these smaller groups like the Naga and Mizo nationality. Even for a group like the Assamese nationality, the distortion produced by a national developmental process creates a chasm that de-historicizes the memory of being included into an Indian nation (Butola, 1996: 358–68). It turns out to be a struggle for the recognition of their distinct habitat and culture mixed with a struggle against maladies of nationhood for the Assamese nation. The persistent demand for ownership of Assam's natural resources by the people of Assam and a distinct notion of citizenship are examples of questioning the authority of the Indian nation-state, vis-à-vis an assertion of their own distinctive identity.

The problematization is further sharpened by the processes of appropriation and accommodation by the Indian state. The preferential treatment given to some Scheduled Tribes by the Indian state produces a dual consciousness of being an Indian national mixed with a distinctive sense of their own identity without bridging the already existing gap of recognition and redistribution. Although there are special schedules in the Constitution for the recognition of smaller similar tribes, but it has not been possible to accommodate of all such tribes within these provisions. Rather, the instrumental processes of accommodation of these smaller communities within the legitimate constitutional framework of the Indian nation-state generates a process of bargaining and persuasion that leads them to a kind of slow loss of their distinctiveness by being enfolded within the ambit of Indian nationhood. This kind of accommodation leads to silencing through persuasion by the Indian state which merely manages their consent but cannot ideologically usurp their positions. This kind of silencing of the accommodated nationalities has been practiced by the Indian state as a leaf out of the policies towards settlers and migrants pursued by the nation-states of Europe and America. This whole process is also viewed as a process of 'ethnicide' of or 'culturicide' within the dominant national symbolic order (Pakem, 1995).

CONCEPTUAL ISSUES

One can distinguish certain conceptual issues at this point of our discussion. One such conceptual issue could be the separateness of 'state' and 'nation' in the Indian context. The imagination of a common, central, ideological, moral edifice of the Indian nation-state derives its sustenance from the supposed interior of an unbroken and integrated Indian national identity. Such an imagination generates a problematique of claims and counter-claims. For example, the claim of Hindutva forces of a 'Bharat' that replaces the supposed foreign connotation of 'India' and gives primacy to a continuous and perennial Hindu identity inhabiting the territory of Bharat, in contrast to the claim of India as multi-national, presents a 'One versus Many' paradigm of Indian identity. Both these sides presume an already formed nation-from-above in order to anchor their claims, assuming a linear and continuous history of India or Bharat. This kind of construction of an Indian national identity is an elite-nationalist construction that also assumes a strong ideological centre of state power. Such a centre bases itself upon a unitary national identity. For example, the Hindutva argument for one nation and one culture bases itself against an other in Muslims. It shows that a unitary construction of national identity needs to assume the presence of an Other against whom the national identity should unite its diverse components into a single and common core. This is recognition of the Other as an enemy, foreign and different. Therefore, the Other is to be excluded from any imagination of national identity. Contrastingly, a view from below does not start with an already constituted nation to which a small community belongs, but begins from an already inhabited cultural location that does not recognize a unitary national identity, and also does not fail to recognize an Other outside itself. Narratives of submission of such smaller communities within a larger frame of power blurs the perception of an uncontaminated life-world of a tribe or a community. We can reconstruct this blurred vision of a life-world by taking into account how they are recognized as the Other, that is, by the dominant national identity, and then supplement it with their own self-defining narratives. Next, we can juxtapose the two sides without any presupposed linkages with networks of power.

The claim of Naga nationhood, undercutting the superiority of Indian nationhood, traces itself back to a locale that establishes its distinctiveness. The play of primary tribal and secondary pan-tribal identity with a shared communicative context of habitat and identity contains within itself the recognition of its smaller factions by 'their internal Other' in order to emerge into an unified identity that occupies a larger space. In the case of Mizo identity, a narrative reconstruction of the linkages existent among various small clans is conducted in order to emerge into a larger whole of the Zo family. This process of ethnic formation imbues a sense of unity in a cumulative way in order to reinforce certain shared cultural traits to present a consolidated block of identity in the face of collaboration and conflict with a larger dominant identity. Here again, an ethnic identity undergoes an experience of internal differentiation mixed with the positive will of retaining a distinctive cultural core.

These processes of ethnic formation never move beyond 'their self-defined interior' and, therefore, respond to the processes of subjugation by consolidating their own interior. The field of forces exerting pressures from various directions create a number of distortions and these prompt resistance and opposition from within an ethnic formation. What we would like to point out here is that such a self-enclosed nation, in terms of ethnic constitution, can never remain unaffected within an imposing structure of nationhood nor can a loose confederation of such smaller ethno-nations emerge into a *singly* constituted ideological core. Rather, the imposition of such a core vigorously affects the soft core of such ethno-nations.

Therefore, what can be pointed out here is that the institution of an imaginary nation after the departure of the British from India had strengthened the hegemony of advanced nationalities in an already emerged core of ideological structure that has percolated through the institution of the post-colonial Indian state. If a nation-state marks such a space of domination, then the new public sphere within such a nation shall become hierarchic and, therefore, bundle up various distinct communities in an indistinct way. This mode of appropriation constructs its symbols out of various communities in a representational mode, that is, it ensures a symbolic representation of such communities without assigning them an autonomous role of action. It assigns an agency role only at the surface of the representation to hold out the spectre of a nation-state (Biswas, 1996: 163–64).[7] An agonistic reaction of such representation produces an inverted representation of the nation—a nation bereft of a cohesive force. This mode of extracting representation heavily weans out the claims of a national identity to an experience of bottomlessness and, therefore, forces various identities to recoil back to their self-defined interior. Even in recent attempts of forging a common European identity, one could observe that various nations of Europe are clamouring to retain their own national identity as they have a history of consolidation over the last few centuries. The Indian national identity, being of recent origin, is facing internal resistance from local and smaller ethnic identities who fear loss of their own identity due to inclusion within the pan-Indian national identity. The question that we raise here is: how to knit together or integrate various smaller nationalities within a pan-national adhesive core? Does a pre-existent ideological hegemony contribute to the process of integration at a pan-national level? These questions need to be elaborated and answered on the basis of a nation-from-below perspective.

NATIONS-FROM-BELOW

A nation-from-below perspective counters a federation of autonomous nations assembled in a nation-space. This nation-space of relationship between self and Other(s) is not dictated by an ideological centre. It resembles the situation of a pre-national space, preceeding the emergence of a modern nation-state, but it also exhibits a flexible nation form in which entry and exit are not determined by any compulsion. Therefore, the nation-from-below is neither a vertical hierarchy nor a horizontal stringing together of various identities, but an autonomous social space, neither containing nor displacing any identity. Therefore, a nation from below is the free and undisturbed existence of an identity, however small it may be, and is not affected by any external pulls and pushes. What a nation-from-above does is to obstruct this kind of a free-space for ethnic identities and turns it into a field of forces numbing the clumping together of multiplicity of identities in an imposed cohesion (see also Chapter 3).

Given this kind of a distinction one can characterize the Indian nation as a nation-from-above, a nation built up by the state. We, thus, characterize India as a 'state-nation', an inverted form of nationhood in which the birth of a state acted as a precursor to the formation of a nation. The state took up the project of building up the nation and this particular phenomenon can be related to the onset of modernity as a colonial project and its structural continuity in the state-built nation. The force of the strong nationalist faith, of an emergence into Indian nationhood and the birth of citizens of the nation, disorients an identity rooted in its culturally formed context and de-contextualizes it in the form of a colourless common identity. It is this religion of asserting a high spirit of nationalism which heightens the Indian identity by sacrificing culturally rooted identities. The discourse of nationalism had assumed a self-styled legitimacy in terms of forming a national modern state and appropriated various identities in its fold without recognizing their autonomous existences.

In the post-colonial phase of the Indian state, nationhood, the national modern discourse, took three distinct turns: (*i*) it mobilized factors such as language, caste and religion, etc., in order to evolve a homogeneous nation-space; (*ii*) it evolved certain institutional mechanisms in order to ensure the normative and regulative capacity of the Indian state; and (*iii*) it inspired an ideology of mixing up various distinct markers to churn out a new identity. All such components kept on intruding into the agency of an identity in order to give it the desired shape, but this project of the state-nation suffered setbacks of irreparable dimensions. The multiple political contest, in various stages of holding power, engendered a reciprocal and reverse consolidation of various blocs that led to internecine conflicts. This kind of consolidation of various interest blocs under the patronage of the state-nation proved to be self-subversive as it produced more instability by way of neutralizing such blocs into a unified notion of Indian identity. The normative and ideological dimension of such a state-sponsored mobilization was never accomplished; instead, it yielded the exact reverse of mutually conflicting identities refusing to come to terms with each other.

This project of state-nation and its consequent state of disorder leaves open the space of alternative articulation of an identity which often overcomes the constraints posed by an imposing state-nation, but very often succumbs to the quagmire of utopic satisfaction of its own ends. Therefore, the situation turns out to be queer from both the ends, with the potential of an ethnic identity in making its own world that seeks its gratification within the state-nation, which gives rise to various forms of alignments and divorce. What this whole process does not include is the ongoing discourse of renewal of one's own 'self' to negotiate it in terms of the constantly and continuously emergent social identities. This residue of the discourse of interaction between these identities and the state-nation generates its own mode of presentation and fashions their self with a pedagogy of its own. This pedagogy of the nascent self of the social identities is what constitutes the autonomous historicity of the identities that does not draw its content from an impersonal social history. Rather, it—the nascent self—carves out its own narrative dimension of representing itself, which is again a distinctive enterprise unaffected by any extraneous forces. If state and nation are conceptually separated in the context of India, one can readily grapple with the activities of the state that produces a number of disruptions. The ideology of the state is to manoeuvre, manipulate and manage the consent of civil society in order to subsume the populace and various other institutions under its authority. This mode of functioning of the state makes it comparatively more or less aggressive, harder or softer, towards a chosen situation. Whenever the normative validity of the nation-from-above is contested by various identities together it is interpreted as an undermining of the authority of the Indian state, which then applies its force to put down such assertions of the various identities. Therefore, the situation can be called as a fight against the Indian state that interrogates the interior of the Indian identity.

The question that we ask here: once such a fight has started do the fighting identities that are in conflict become successful in giving rise to an alternative identity that distinguishes itself from the subsumed ones? What the state realizes is a consolidation of the subsumed identities which are achieved by such a fight against the state. Does one then infer that the fight against the state in its most generalized form gives rise to consolidated identities? The situation seems to corroborate this kind of a claim. There occurs a sharp polarization among various identities, each occupying a position within the mappings of the struggle, in evolving into a definite language and claim of their own.

In a post-colonial situation, such claims are already affected and shaped within by the emergent civil and political institutions and, therefore, assume an institutional form. During this period of emergence, the state exercises much greater power through institutional means to normalize and discipline the resurgent ethnic groups. The obvious response is greater organized resistance from these ethnic communities. Therefore, the state also turns increasingly to a mechanics of control and suppression through its coercive organs and separates itself from its ideological persuasion of winning over such communities with the force of law and persuasion. The state literally attempts at making the insurgent ethnic community surrender itself. Such a motivation of the state in order to preserve a totalistic identity is also resisted vehemently by an ethnic community fighting against the state (Lefort, 1988: 9–20).[3]

One can conceptualize the situation in terms of two processes: firstly, the subsumption of ethnic groups under the unified Indian national identity; and secondly, appropriation of such identities by the Indian state. The contra processes are also correspondingly dual: firstly, cutting out a separate identity-space for each ethnic homogeneous group; and, secondly, ensuring freedom for such groups within the state, of course by trying to create a state that does not interrupt the freedom of such identities. On a close analysis one can diagnose mutually contrary possibilities in the agenda of the state-nation: what the nation aims at is subverted by the state and vice-versa, portraying a strange marriage of the normative and the coercive. This is the inherent contradiction within the Indian state—the national formation. But this contradiction is managed by the Indian state-nation by granting the upper hand to the designs of the state which aims at appropriating various identities by imbibing or drawing them into the dominant ruling ideologies. This process of the state empties out the normative appeal of nationalism into some kind of overpowering political and social identity that secures a place for ethnic communities within the state. Therefore, there is gradual erosion of the normative ideal of emerging into a nation in the hands of the state that establishes its ideological domination. As discussed earlier, one can also observe that the inverted project of building of a nation-from-above remains as a state-sponsored project that tries to popularize the nation by projecting a dominant symbolic construction of nationalism, while, in contrast, ethnic identities fashion themselves in parallel by initiating a project of building a nation-from-below in which the symbols of the state-nation are necessarily counterposed. It assumes the freedom to express its voice by not aligning itself to the state-sponsored project and any intervention of the state in their freedom of exclusion is strategically contested. One can raise a question: do these ethnic identities produce the image of a state that ensures their free self-assertion? Definitely so, as this becomes a necessary outcome of their struggle for autonomy. They carve out a space for acting themselves, as an autonomous identity, combining both the elements of 'state' and 'nation' in a free state of existence. This gives rise to powerful imageries of a nation- state-from-below in the form of a free homeland that institutes the cultural symbols of the community. The recent emergence of East Timor from Indonesia, the lasting struggle of Palestinians over the Gaza Strip and the attainment of near autonomy of Tamils in Northern Sri Lanka present such combinations of 'state' and 'nation' in a stage of struggle against dominance. Although such combinations vary widely from context to context, still a continuity of struggle for autonomy could be identified that tries to achieve freedom articulated in a mix of cultural, political and economic terms.

Cultural Politics of the Nation-from-Below

A nation-from-below gives rise to a special type of homogeneous social identity that articulates itself by condensing the elements of its cultural life. It is homogeneous not because of mobilization of certain constituent features such as language, caste and culture, but because of sufficiently close-knit participation and sharing of specific ways of life. This is a state of living in which normative and ideological control and restraint is derived from the close knit structure of cultural life. This kind of a lived homogeneity engenders a discourse-community, which is structurally independent and retains its autonomous moorings of life. One can ask the question: can the project of the state-nation mobilize such an inner core of the ethnic life? The answer assumes both the possibilities of such a life being disrupted by the instruments of the state and also carries the possibility of creating an alternative ethnic-state with far greater autonomy. Given the structure of the currently existing Indian state-nation, this kind of freely construed state-nation imagery does not find a place within the ruse of power. It is just emerging from within the quasi-federal structure of the Indian state as could be seen in creation of Uttaranchal, Jharkhand and Chhatisgarh. Although they are present within the Indian union and claim a strong Indian identity in contrast to many of the North-East Indian identities (who claim to be accidentally Indian today), these new states represent aspirations of ethnic groups that claim to be original settlers in those states. In case of the North-East, the ethnic aspiration is driven towards a level of autonomy and independence by going a step further from what carving out of an ethno-based state within the Indian union can fulfil. The reason is the cultural distinctiveness of many of the North-Eastern ethnic communities, who have never seen themselves as part of the Indian culture and civilization. This could be understood better by distinguishing the claims of Nagas and Santhals of Chhotanagpur plateau. The latter claim to be merely aboriginal or adivasis who settled here before the Aryans but who were later driven by *dikus* or outsiders from their homeland. Yet they did not get totally dissociated from dikus and settled in places contiguous to the territorial domain of these invaders. As a result, there were cultural intrusions of these invading communities in their *Adivasi* life-world. Contrastingly, in case of the Nagas, they have never been subjugated or driven out by any such invading communities. Therefore, their claim of nationhood assumes having been outside the control and authority of the Indian nation-state, which stepped in by default only after the British left India. As such, their claim of national identity is wider than claims of Adivasis of Chattisgarh or Jharkhand. In the case of a community like the Assamese of North-East India, who have been part of the Indian ethos, their resistance is directed against the post-colonial Indian state that does not recognize the possibility of distinct cultural and political rights of ethnic communities. Therefore, articulation of ethnic and nationality rights by the North-Eastern communities assumes the duality of we/they and such other antagonistic terms, primarily because of the strategies of containment of their struggle for rights by the Indian state. The reproduction of these identities within the space of the state-nation contains an element of freedom assumed by their constitution that remains unaccomplished. Therefore, the state only uses its strategies of containing the aspirations of freedom of such identities without being able to develop a sense of belonging in them. Instead, what it develops is a sense of alienation that is deeply stuck in the psyche of such ethnic communities bound by the tentacles of the state. This freezes the self-definition of the ethnic community, while any resistance by it is illegitimized.

The struggle between the nationalist ethos and the ethnic community assumes the form of chalking out strategies of victory and subversion, and it turns out to be a struggle between the forces that seek to win the support of such ethnic groups by populist measures and by subordinating them to the structures of domination. This resistance draws its support from an already existing core of ethnic-cultural life with an added component of a spirited affirmation of their identity. This is an activated state of affirmation that blends together various distinctions of body and mind, instinct and consciousness, fear and hope in order to develop into a structure of resistance and an artefact of counter-imagination. The ethnic community attains a form of subjectivity in which judgements are dependent upon the singular characteristics of their identity and it is this kind of dependence that resists the attempt to fuse it within a large whole. It also gives rise to an uncontrolled nationalistic enthusiasm that leads to a cultural reawakening.

The homogeneous ethnic community constructs its own counter-discourse and generates certain truths that are contesting by nature. This is what can be termed as the capacity to make their world such that it can not be intruded upon or obstructed by the mechanism of the state-nation. It keeps on getting constituted in a state of tension and disruption without any wearing out of its creative energy.

Interpolating this situation in terms of history, one can observe the history of the post-colonial Indian state that exhibits an insurmountable ambivalence in which the will to nationhood cannot operate autonomously without being sponsored by the ruling hegemony of the state. At the same time it leaves open the ways of construction of an alternative world by knitting together myths, legends and values in a strategic way and consolidate such constructions in the form of struggle against the state.[4] Such a struggle gives moral and normative support to the counter-discourse of an ethnic identity. This kind of contemporary movement of history also illuminates the need of order and coherence in one's view of oneself. The distortion and fracture of a self-image produced by the state-nation renegotiates the ethnic self in a newer politico-institutional frame and, as discussed earlier, it maximizes its self-realizing potential through a course of counter-discourse. It generates a string of paradoxes: the development of a state-nation leaving aside its own marginal Others; the political and ideological grounding of ethnic identities into an alien social space, etc., giving rise to steady and persistently transgressive counter-discourses.

THE CASE OF NAGA INSURGENCY

The case of Naga insurgency in the context of North-East India is the earliest expression of ethno-national moorings. The early efforts of colonization which took place by subsuming them under the Indian state had continued by way of different kinds of manoeuvres till today and have correspondingly generated a sense of alienation and dismay. In the process a section of Naga elites had come to power, but this only substantiated the claim of the Naga struggle that the Indian state somehow had wanted to accommodate them within its constitutional framework. It is worthwhile to remember that as early as in 1929 the Naga Club (a political platform of unified occupied Nagas) submitted a memorandum to the visiting Simon Commission of British India in Kohima, demanding that the Nagas be left alone and free as they were before being conquered by the British empire. In 1941, Sir Robert Reid, the then Governor of Assam province, saw a possibility of creating a nation comprising of the areas inhabited by the Naga tribes belonging to Mongloid race who were neither Indian nor Burmese. Sir Reginald Coupland, a British constitutional expert, reviewed Reid's proposal and suggested that the Nagas be included within a colony, later known as the Crown Colony Plan. The freedom loving Nagas refused to accept the Crown colony as their demand was nothing short of independence. In 1946, the Naga National Council (NNC), a political platform of Nagas outside British jurisdiction as well as of territories occupied by the British, was formed. This served as an all-Naga political institution, which directly undertook the guardianship of a unified independent Nagaland before and after British India. Determined not to be further occupied and ruled by any other nations, the Nagas declared themselves independent on 14 August 1947.[5] The legitimacy of this mandatory act by the NNC is upheld by every Naga nationalist till date, although establishment of an elected Government in Nagaland throws up a challenge to such claims of sovereignty. The two states of the Republic of free India and Burma (now Myanmar) choose to follow the legacy of the British colonial policy. This history of Naga claim of independence and their subjugation provides a background articulation to the culture of insurgency as a mode of resistance offered to the Indian state that prolongs the colonial experience of the past. It invokes the 'life' of freedom that contextualizes itself in the idea that Nagas be left alone and free as they were before. But these words do not invoke the image of a Naga past, which is portrayed as that of internecine tribal warfare, brutality and barbarity; it abhors and disowns such a 'past' and reconstructs a past with the agency to remain free. It is this 'memory of identity' and 'identity of the memory' that shapes the Naga political consciousness. It brings back the memory of the past order to identify it with the present resistance to the currents of dominant discourse. The method of juxtaposing the past with the present is the narrative employment of a nostalgic experience (Ugresic, 1998: 229–30). But this kind of narrativization of every bit of thought and experience in the case of Naga insurgency suffers the crude repression of the Indian state as they are not allowed to speak. This presents the suppressive design of the Indian state-nation that represses and strangulates the voice of an emergent minority nation. It muffles and drowns such marginal narratives in the monotone of its legitimizing discourse, what Clifford Geertz (1993) called as the 'Integrative Revolution' in the context of Indonesia. The same is accomplished in the Indian context by a two-way process of suppressing the voice of a resurgent minority and by creating a class of collaborating elite within them. This process of suppressing the counter-discourse, fixed with the creation of a collaborating elite, does not fully satisfy the national aspiration but yields to a section of them an important place that serves the purpose of neutralizing national aspirations. The discontent stemming out of non-recognition of nationhood are channelized through a developing struggle for governmental power that mixes up the repressive and the democratic; it engineers a social division within the ranks of an aspiring nation. It makes the process of re-negotiation of one's selfhood all the more difficult by holding a spectre of national representation mixed with the disgruntlement of ungratified national identity.

It generates a strange sensation of pain and pleasure, hope and fear, through which the state produces the aspirations of the nation in an already laid down channel and staves off the agonies borne out of the encumbered ethnic self by giving vent to its simmering discontent of non-freedom. Geertz explained that a sort of parapolitics of clashing public identities and quickening ethnocentric aspirations emerge alongside of, and interact with, the usual politics of party and parliament, cabinet and bureaucracy, or monarchy and army (Geertz, 1993: 23–25).[6] He considers this parapolitical sphere as only an extension of a state-sponsored discursive field in which some social issues that seek resolution appear more vehemently than others, and around which there is a bitter power struggle. One response would be to include the entire arena of insurgency into this parapolitical sphere so that the spheres of civil society also get divided in terms of its allegiance to both the Indian state and an emergent national aspiration. In other words, the spheres of resolving the issues of social and civil concern get inextricably linked with the processes of state suppression and mediation of a colonized elite. This produces shocks and ruptures in any mode of quiet settlement of issues. In the context of Nagaland, some issues of social and civil concern are usually identified by various kinds of state discourses and public discourses, and these are discussed within the parapolitical sphere. For example, issues such as killing of people, drugs, corruption, extortion, human rights, peace, and so on, are brought over and over into the parapolitical sphere. All this intends to what Geertz called 'normalization' of an insurgent national aspiration. This is the space which is legitimately occupied by the state to spread its messages of nationhood through public performance of state rituals. Other partners and counterparts interact with the state in the parapolitical sphere to influence its rationalization process. But through such an artificially constructed sphere, the Indian state largely exercises its hegemony and earns the consent of civil society. Although such a process of integrative revolution is part of normalization carried out by a state in ex-colonies, the same could be carried out in a place or region inhabited by a dissenting ethnic group. Especially in case of insurgency-based dissent, the state would vigorously embark upon such a process of normalization in the parapolitical sphere as part of its strategy of containment of resistance and dissent.

Imageries of Naga National Struggle

The construction of insurgency within the Naga national struggle holds out the imagery of a free terrain of 'Kachin' through which the guerrilla militia was organized under the leadership of the NNC. 'Kachin' was an open terrain linking China, Burma and India through which military emissaries could enter any of these regions. During the 1960s, Kachin was ruled by the Kachin Independent Army, which was trying to free Kachin from Burma. The NNC guerrillas were allowed by them, after much hesitation, to cross Kachin and go over to Yunan province of China. The time spent by the NNC militia in China forms the most important experience of their training. The exposure of their volunteers to Chinese armed training was also important in terms of political direction. The Naga armed struggle got an instilling of Maoist line of thinking that inspired the nascent nationality spirit seeded within the Naga movement towards the right to self-determination. The Chinese authorities decided to train the NNC volunteers after much hesitation, as they were not very sure of NNC's political orientation. As NNC could dare to reach Yunan and tried to impress the Chinese leadership of the validity of their cause, the best option for the Chinese leadership was to provide them minimal military training without any commitment, political or otherwise. Most importantly, China refused to provide them with arms and shelter beyond the period of training. Therefore, the much-touted idea that China was interested in planting fissiparous forces within Nagaland does not hold much water. In fact, the Chinese refusal to provide any logisitic support forced the NNC leadership to go for Pakistan's support soon after their return from China. In realpolitik, China was not so interested in even propagating communism within Naga nationalist fighters as they were aware of sensitive bilateral concerns and did not find the Naga cause good enough for China's political and strategic interests. But for NNC, exposure to China and the latter's refusal to help them in any significant manner resulted in a change in the course of the struggle. NNC had to broaden the horizon of Naga national struggle to the international level in which it had to establish its relevance. What is also striking here is the transposition of the homeland imagery from the territory of Nagaland to Kachin and to Yunan province of China, an extension of their territorial imagination to shift international alliances. The struggle for the Naga homeland drew its emotional and imaginative resources from territories such as Kachin and China, which on the one hand means a deterritorialization into an 'alien' land and on the other involves a romantic exile in the minds of insurgent communities. As a national struggle, NNC's sojourn to Kachin and China dislocated the boundary of the nation, extended it to a new horizon of hope and heroism. From the perspective of guerrilla warfare waged by the NNC, the stirring of popular imagination through acts of fugitive guerrillas had been a long believed strategy of mobilizing popular support. The territories of exile and sojourn became the integral part of the imagery of national freedom.

The news of the arrival of 500-odd Chinese-trained guerrillas generated a lot of alarm and worry. The Baptist Churches of Nagaland came out in the open to criticize the influence of China, since they feared that instilling of Communism in Naga minds would have a disastrous impact. It cautioned the youth not to fall prey to Chinese ideology. Also, it was publicized adversely that the NNC was thinking of surrendering its thought, action and homeland to China. All this propaganda culminated into a rebuff against the Chinese influence on the Naga national struggle. This brought out the fragile interior of the construction of Naga national identity based upon two layers of consciousness: firstly, that of belonging to a tribe; and, secondly, that of belonging to a pan-tribal identity. An ideology that professes an identity beyond the Naga national identity makes one relinquish the tribal identity. This limited idea of a national identity among the NNC did not permit the Nagas to accept any broader framework of struggle, as that affects both the layers of tribal and pan-tribal consciousness. The tribal identity presents itself as the 'given' and the pan-tribal identity structures itself around the 'totality' of a common territory, myth, history, etc. There are groupings, sub-groupings and integration between these two levels as well as intra-level combinations and re-combinations. The claims of a pan-tribal identity are shaped by various factors such as contiguity and migration and, most importantly, by the onset of 'modernity'. Modern institutions, in spite of being internally inchoate, could bring together these various tribes into a common fold. This most often produces a pan-tribal identity deemed to be national in its conscious articulation and assertion. Christianity and the control of a modern nation-state are the two most significant factors that have contributed to the making of Naga identity at a pan-tribal level that centres around nationalism based on cultural affinity. But the same factors are responsible for

Nagas not choosing any secular ideology for the struggle. Nagas, therefore, battled against the Indian state based on strategic alliances. In the context of opposition to the Chinese line of struggle against the Indian nation-state, one can read how the opposition from the Church blunts the ideological horizon of an 'extended exile national imagery' to re-centre it on the concept of a 'Naga Nation' bereft of an exterior. This ideological benumbing by the Church of the much talked about Maoist influence on NNC takes it away from the path of Maoist mobilization of the Nagas. This also shows the structural linkage between 'colonial modernity' and supervention of Christianity upon the discourse of the nation. Moreover, as the articulation of Christianity directs towards the formation of a Naga national identity, the post-colonial state discourse of the Indian nation augured through Christianity jibes well with the roots of colonial modernity. The points of difference and distinction between Nagas *qua* Christians, Nagas *qua* Nagas and Nagas *qua* Indians are blurred and blended with each other due to the colonial roots of modernity leading to a pan-tribal national formation, and tribal and non-tribal Indian formation. The historical possibility of an alternative discourse based on the Maoist line of class struggle could have instead separated the various shades within the articulation of the Naga national discourse in terms of identification of hegemonic blocs and counter-hegemonic forces.

Viewed from another angle, the making of the Naga nation as a generic one, with respect to the project of nation building by the Indian state, followed the same pattern of nation-from-above. The Naga nation was constituted at a plane of acceptance of certain 'common' characteristics such as Christianity or a lingua franca. Further articulation against a dominant Indian identity got weakened because of its inclusion within an already formed interior of colonial modernity. The colonial administration of the British created separation of the North-East frontier from the heartland of India, but the colonial modernity that dawned upon the Nagas created the aspiration of emerging into a separate and free nation. It became a contestable subject with the strategic withdrawal of the British leading to an automatic handover of Naga territory to the Indian state. Naga resistance at that moment of handover was an independent move of the Nagas without any mediation of the British, busy in packing up from India.

Therefore, this was a moment of assertion of the Nagas, which was ethno-national-modern in character and was directed against an appropriation within Indian national-modern identity. Repeatedly the NNC asserted the status of Nagas as a separate nation but the Indo-Naga agreement of 1947, between the NNC leaders and Sir Akbar Hydari, the then Governor of undivided Assam, made them to enter into a negotiated settlement within the framework of the Indian state-nation. The creation of the Naga Federal Government in 1956 against the provisions of draconian laws imposed on Nagaland also demonstrated the possibility of Naga unity against the torture, repression and brutalities of the Indian state. The compulsion of the Nagas to wage an armed struggle against the Indian state arose due to the latter's continuous deviation from keeping its promises and simultaneous mobilization of the army to discipline the Nagas forcibly and to make them surrender under the control of the Indian state. This was a continuation of British policy of repression and persuasion of the Nagas to fall in line and give up their demand for independence. But through the successful conduct of the 1951 plebiscite for independence and the subsequent formation of the Naga Federal Government in 1956, the Nagas had aptly demonstrated their determination to self-rule and their rejection of the authority of the Indian state. Therefore, they fought back the attempts to manoeuvre their political end of independence from the Indian state and stringently resisted the efforts to suppress them by direct coercion.

The strategy of the Naga national movement became the continuation of the struggle from the 'underground' and the state also looked upon them as 'hostiles' and 'insurgents'. There were massive counter-insurgency operations since 1954 that led to widespread killing and bloodshed. The worst happened in villages like Yangpang, Chingmei and Chemong, and the NNC held the army responsible for massacres, burning of villages, rape and all other forms of destruction. There were soon counter-offensives launched by the Naga underground; a few remarkable instances of such a counter-offensive were the capture of 78 Indian armed police as captives and the bringing down an Indian air force plane by Naga activists. What all these events signified was the perpetuation of a spate of reciprocal violence on each other and the more it turned macabre, the wider was the rift between the two sides. The urge for freedom from India became the sharpest point of mobilization for the Nagas, while the preservation of the territory and authority became the key purpose for the Indian state. The attempt of the Indian state to grant 'statehood' within the ambit of the Constitution of India could result into a greater concentration of armed struggle between the two sides. What went on as talks for peace in between and attempts to arrive at an agreement with respect to statehood turned out to be another round of manoeuvre and political experimentation only to fall apart in the subsequent escalation of armed struggle. The situation called for another round of negotiation for 'ceasefire' and this time the Baptist Church leaders and political parties were instrumental in arriving at a ceasefire agreement in 1964. But the agreement could not have been actualized because the Nagas once more felt that it was detrimental to the claim of 'sovereignty' and wholesome disarmament of the Nagas by the Indian state would incapacitate them to a large extent. Therefore, only proposals of giving Nagas the fullest possible autonomy were mooted without its actualization. But as nothing could be settled, so the history of disbanding the Naga Federal Government and the Naga Army repeated itself once again in 1972. Meanwhile, the ranks of NNC had suffered a split and there was an emergence of the Revolutionary Government of Nagaland under the leadership of Sumi Nagas, who later surrendered. The Federal Government of Nagaland and the Naga National Council did not surrender to the state and continued negotiations with the government. With the failure to arrive at a negotiated settlement, the ceasefire ended and once again, there were raids and killings by the Indian army of the members of both the organizations. It seemed that the Naga national movement and the armed struggle of resistance had lost its efficacy because of the divisions within. As a result they had entered into an agreement with the Government of India in 1978 to end the armed struggle against the Indian state and accepted the rule of the Indian Constitution. What followed was President's Rule, from 1978 to 1980.

One can read in this whole story a strategy of 'combat and retreat' in the struggle between the India state and the Naga national groups. But what we call deviance from the Maoist point was that the line of struggle that Naga national groups followed led the movement to a defeat at the hands of the Indian state. The deviance lay in the failure of carrying out a protracted armed struggle by mobilizing the masses. Another interesting angle to the cause of the defeat could be that a Maoist line of struggle did not really suit the ground reality of mobilizing various tribes within the Naga nation, the reason being the demand of the Maoist type of organization in surrendering primary identity of belonging to this or that tribe within Nagas for the sake of unity. Such a necessity commanded by Maoist type of organization contributed to political differences within the ranks and established the dominance of one tribe over others. Because of such contradictions within the main Maoist ideological line, the struggle for self-determination and sovereignty by the outfits of the Naga national movement lacked the power of waging a revolutionary ideological struggle against the Indian state. Left at that, the whole domain of struggle centred around the popular aspiration of remaining independent after the withdrawal of the British. 'Independence' in this context only meant the temporal continuation of a native identity located in their habitat, but such an anachronistic stasis of the Naga mind was already broken by colonial intervention and the subsequent organization of various Naga tribes into pan-tribal associations. But the status of independence as a desire was effaced, and such desire operated at the level of an aesthetic of self-reconstruction as a response to the offensive of the Indian state. The formation of a Naga militia and its underground operations have kept alive the sensibility of that desire of independence, to rewrite the biography of the nation by a re-engagement with past imagery and its present contours. This is especially seen in the role of countering the dominant Indian symbols by way of reflexive postures, which, in order to reaffirm their self-defined nationhood, has always kept the Nagas in a state of livewire tension. Therefore, one can name it as a defiant nationalism that always produced a subject with a reconstructive narrativization of an experience of struggle. The desire of such self-reconstructive and defiant nationalism invoked the trope of 'independence' despite its stasis ignoring the temporal shifts. The sublimation of such a desire attained its depth through pain, suffering and victories in the struggle against the Indian state-nation. It is the common cause of the struggle that catalyzed the attempt to transcend the confinements of individual tribal boundary to emerge into a kind of solidarity that lies beyond the closed communitarianism of a liberal statehood. This solidarity in social bonding through the signifier of the identity called 'Naga' was engaged in a search for intersecting histories.

Phenomenolgy of Naga Struggle

The whole Naga experience of struggle can be described in terms of an experience of denegation—defiance constituted their affirmation. This can be referred to as the process of transgressing whatever had bound them or constrained them, the enforced boundary of the Indian state, the authority of the state, and so on. Such acts of transgression constituted the trajectory of guerrilla warfare of the Nagas. This can be further described as a manifestation of the martial being of the Nagas, a transition from colonial ethnographic description of a diverse cultural plurality to a modern solidarity. The transition is not directed towards an already emerged positive unified core, rather it maintained a difference within, only to give it the name of solidarity, which symbolized an attempt to develop a nation contra to the 'Indian' nation. The martial being transforms into becoming a consolidated Naga national identity that simultaneously transgresses the normative unity of the Indian nation and transcends its own inherent differences through this act of martial transgression. The moments of manoeuvre came at the moment of conducting 'peace talks' with the Indian state and several times such 'politics without bloodshed' taught them how to position themselves contra to the Indian state.

There have been 'wars of positions' 'during such moments of manoeuvre' by the Naga national movement. In its campaign for freedom, the Naga national movement intended to achieve the political ends through persuading the ruling government. It persuaded the British government to ensure that they were left to themselves and later persuaded Mahatma Gandhi and the Indian state on similar counts. Such means of persuasion were chosen to suit the established modes of voicing protests and opinions, such as the 1951 'plebiscite'. The adoption of such a mode of public mobilization created consolidated and opinionated blocs of resistance, which could not be restrained by the state. On the part of the state, the strategies of containment of the Nagas through agreements acted as points of hypocrisy of the state. The Indian state could neither provide an acceptable alternative to what it pledged, nor an ideological or political fulcrum which the Naga people could put their trust in. Therefore, the Indian state had to follow a policy of capitulation from its own stand and suppress the resentment produced by such capitulation. A hegemonic state could not only have won significant ideological victory but could also have brought them under self-discipline. India being a state-nation and deriving the ideological and moral resources of statehood from a supposedly constructed nationhood could not but fail in including the Nagas within that definition of 'nationhood', as Nagas had differentiated themselves from an Indian identity. A case in point is the LTTE struggle for independence in the Northern Peninsula of Sri Lanka which invokes the difference between Sinhalese and Tamils. But one has to remember that Sinhalese nationalism, in contrast to Indian nationalism, is more homogeneous in character. Therefore, politics of difference by Tamil militants becomes easily understandable as the line is black and white. Construction of a state-nation in case of India does not assume such a centred concept of nation except that it follows an axis of caste, religion and tradition. Such an axis either endears or distances some of the communities based upon cultural ties and linguistic affiliations. In doing so, the Indian state distances itself historically from communities of North-Eastern states that are historically not so closely linked with the major cultural and linguistic groups of the Indian mainland. Even then the line is not clearly black and white in the case of Nagas versus Indians because the latter is neither a monolithic entity like the Sinhalese in Sri Lanka, nor is Indian nationalism synonymous with nationalism of any particular linguistic or religious group. Therefore, the politics of difference that the Naga struggle invokes is an ideological critique of mainstream Indian culture that acts as the basis of formation of the nation from above, ignoring a large number of tribes and other minorities from the axis of caste, religion and tradition. Although Indian nationalism does not succeed in building up a unitary concept of nationhood, still the facade of every community belonging to a common Indian identity produces deep dissents within. The reason is that communities are expected to accept the idea of common culture and nationhood without any recognition of their specificities. If some of the communities are dominant in terms of cultural and religious influence along with a place in the scheme of power, the space occupied by these cultures is comparatively larger within the mainstream Indian national identity than allowed for cultures which are different. As a result, cultures which are different are yielded little space and have to follow the value systems of the dominant cultural groups. This assignment of a subordinate position to the culturally different communities in general, and specifically to those from the North-Eastern states, assumes a cultural superiority, an arrogance of the mainstream. North-Eastern communities refuse to accept an Indian national identity as a by-product of cultural mainstreaming. Rather, they want a non-coercive acceptance of their due place within the Indian nationhood with recognition of the difference.

The maintenance of a unitary idea of national identity by the Indian state, with cultural boundaries drawn not only within the space of the state but also within what is considered as culturally Indian, results in a politics of manoeuvring smaller identities. For example, when the Nagas had mooted the proposals of the Peace Mission in 1964, it reflected contradictions and parleys between the state and the Nagas. Consider the following from point number 12 of the Peace Mission proposals:

> Some appropriate meeting point has to be found, where the aims and ideals of the Nagaland Federal Government can be achieved, at the same time making it possible for the Government of India to accept those within the framework of the political settlement to be mutually agreed upon.[7]

One can read here the fullest appraisal of Naga Federal Government's aims and aspirations and their conflict with the perspectives of the Indian state, while the suggested mode of political settlement, to be mutually agreed upon, at least does not show the dominance of state perspective. The success of Naga manoeuvre lay in talking about the framework of a political settlement to be mutually agreed upon. An examination of the role of the Indian state for shifting its position, from considering the case of Naga people for self-determination after 10 years of the Hydari agreement to a further continuation of the rule of the Indian state over the Nagas, had endowed the Naga national movement with an enhanced legitimacy. This was believed to be one instance of infidelity of the Indian state towards the Nagas based on which the Naga insurgents took up arms. This was accompanied also with the 'war of positions'. As against the position of the Indian state to grant rights such as autonomy within the Indian Constitution, the Nagas demanded the right to self-determination from the Indian State through secession. Also, as against the position of the Indian state to establish legitimate forms of governance, the Nagas established a separate Naga Federal Government with its wings such as the Naga army. Such manoeuvres and war of positions represented the popular will against the Indian state in Nagaland and the Naga national movement had articulated itself against the manoeuvres of the Indian state. The excesses committed by the state acted as justification for insurgent counter-violence. Everything that the state should have as its machinery—for example, civil, police and administrative—the insurgents contested by building up parallel counterparts. Matching the state in every respect, through popular mobilizations and its ideological articulation as 'nationalist', was what produced the inner strength of such postioning by the Nagas.

The movement sustained itself by mobilizing popular imageries constructed through the wide play of symbols such as the tale of glory attached to a place like Khonoma, which stood as a perennial symbol of resistance for the Nagas. Calling themselves as 'valiant soldiers' against an 'enemy' army, the movement aroused folk passion to recall the memories of victory and resistance that had constituted the public memory of various groups of tribe at various locations. Locations such as Yangpang, Chingmei and Chemong were remembered for the atrocities of the Indian army. Every person who laid his or her life in the battle against the Indian army was treated as a 'hero' of the national struggle and popular passion was aroused on every such occasion. At every stage of guerrilla warfare and imposition of prohibitory orders by the state, the transmission of news about events of casualties produced sensations in the minds of Naga people and the immediate reactions went in favour of the guerrilla fighters, and there was a spontaneous resistance built up in the public. Guerrillas operating from outside the boundary of the state particularly impressed the public. Their mobilizations enthralled the public with a lot of speculations. What we would like to conclude here is that insurgency produced a structure of responses from the public, and that is how the Nagas could combat the offensive of the state launched at the level of ideology. The level of sensitivity attached to such insurgent acts also made the Indian state paranoid and threat perceptions of the state were also correspondingly very high. Therefore, one can say that the war of positions between the Naga national movement and the Indian state also decided the intensity of armed struggle. Further, the manoeuvres adopted in 'Peace Talks' by both the sides created sharp ideological divides between them and both spoke in non-negotiable terms.

During the failure of the 1964 ceasefire, the Indian state refused to accept any claim of sovereignty from the Nagas, while the Nagas refused to accept any subsidiary status within the Indian state. The Nagas were haunted through and through by a feeling of being subordinated by the Indian state and the state became the symbol of domination, and with such a construction of the 'dominant' in the Indian state it became impossible to settle anything within the framework of the Indian Constitution. Therefore, peace accords that were arrived at were condemned to be instruments of treason. Treaties meant undermining of the independent state of the Naga nation and acceptance of the dominance of India. For the Indian state it meant a victory over Naga rebels. It meant success in calming down the Nagas within the mantle of the state. One can read here a conflict between state-nation and nation; for the former an acceptance of its institutional and constitutional authority by a nation or a collective is the be-all and end-all, while for the latter, recognition as a 'nation' is the most desired end and, if not accomplished, every other benefit or gain is futile. Therefore, the strategy of the Indian state became the invention of means by which the rebels could be made to surrender and it is superfluous to say that the state gained success in these efforts. The agenda of the state remains to settle with any perceived threat or rebellion and to bring back the rebels into the mainstream.

Refiguring The Naga Nationalist Struggle

The turning point in Naga nationalist politics remain the year 1975. The defeat of 1975 inaugurated a new era of nationalist struggle. There was a re-emergence of the nationalist struggle from within the ranks of the NNC which opposed any compromise with the

Indian state. Isak Chisi Swu and Th. Muivah led the initial resentment against the submission of NNC which later got crystallized into the formation of a new national organization called the National Socialist Council of Nagaland (NSCN). This crystallization occurred through a revisionary narrativization of a contingent past; it redrew the battle lines and created a new ideological edifice. The redrawn manifesto of the NSCN was based upon an ideological critique of 'Phizoism', described as reckless nepotism, 'familism' and capitalist egoism, and it condemned total capitulation. The statement of the NSCN from Oking on 3 January 1984 can be read as a 'text' of reconstruction. The text reads:

> Our Naga people know for sure that their future is only in the socialism of the National Socialist Council. The reactionary traitors have felt the impact of this irresistible wave on the people. They are in dread as their dooms draw fast closer upon them and finding no other way out from their doom, they ceaselessly devise means for the extenuation of their high treason in one and thousand ways... How could there be unity between the dead and the living, between darkness and light, between rust and steel, between the reactionary traitors and revolutionary politics, between capitalist egoism and socialistic altruism, between the treacherous A.Z. Phizo's tribalism and the Socialism of NSCN?[8]

One can read here the overtones of the Maoist critique of reactionaries from the descriptions of tribalism, egoism, etc., and upholding of socialist altruism and socialism. It is interesting to note that by the time NSCN had framed such a critique, Deng Xiaoping had become supreme in China and Maoism was discounted. Of course, much later after its establishment, NSCN had also undergone mutation and had definitely moved away from a rigid Maoist line of thought. What remains interesting here is the framing of a derivative discourse of nationalism and socialism with an indigenous idiom to differentiate between lines of struggle: Phizoist versus Socialist. The statement depicts the attempts of Phizo to once again raise the hue and cry for a 'unity' in order to recover some of his lost ground. But the NSCN pointed out that the Phizoean syndrome of compromise with the Indian state and their utterances such as 'whoever would oppose A.Z. Phizo and the Shillong Accord shall be totally crushed' were detrimental to any unity. Further, it had been pointed out, Phizo's tribalism had a motto—'Angamis and Chakesangs are to be united as they are more reliable than others'— which stood for vertical division within Naga nationalism and bade goodbye to it in the name of primordial loyalties. Therefore, NSCN exposed the divisive politics of Phizo in the name of an apparent appeal for unity, listing some paradoxes of the Phizoean brand of politics for his vituperative appeal to exterminate the 'communists' such as Isak and Muivah by the 'Christ Soldiers'. The NSCN sorted out this blame of sliding into communism by referring to their pledge of struggle for a Christian Nation which would have a socialist economy and, therefore, made their ideological framework much more open and wider than narrow subscription to Maoism and socialism. It blended the Maoist line of ideological struggle against the enemies with the aims of socialism and centred the whole discourse on the 'people' who are the sovereign rulers and subjects of a free Naga nation. The idea was to protect the spirit of sovereign people by referring to a 'Nagaland for Christ' which inspired faith in re-making a decolonized Nagaland in which the will of God shall work. The NSCN statement had clearly drawn the battle lines between 'capitulationists' and defenders of nationalism by shifting the burden of 'false consciousness' of the struggle between the Angamis versus the rest of the Naga people or between communities versus Christians. Instead, it drew the line clearer by dispelling the false consciousness of being led towards sovereignty by some leaders, by exposing them as collaborators to the manoeuvres of the Indian state. In respect of the NSCN position toward the Indian state, the statement decries any subsidiary terms of settlement, rather moots the idea of an 'honourable solution'.

The reconfiguration of the whole terrain of relationship with the Indian state by the NSCN came in terms of disclosing the betrayal of the promise repeatedly made by its leaders like Gandhi and Nehru. Further, the intrusion of Indian military and Indian culture gave the NSCN the mandate to accept death fearlessly for the just cause of freeing the nation rather than to compromise. The mandate was indigenization of the national-socialist discourses in terms of retaining a distinct Christian identity. The NSCN manifesto reads: 'The failure of the Christian leaders to grasp the way evil forces work and their failure to face them in the way they should, has, indeed, placed Nagaland on the most serious trail.'[9]

The distinct political purpose of being united in a common Christian faith remained not only as a mark of difference with the perceived Hindu world-view of India but also an ideological and spiritual mantle to bring together various Naga tribes. It occurs as the main ideological plank of NSCN. In the course of struggle, this enables what *Shepoumaramth Regional Church Bulletin 1994–95* called 'God has chosen Nagaland for his glory'. It said:

> The kingdom of Nagaland for Christ is very precious. Whoever commit themselves not wholeheartedly to Christ will perish and they will not see this Kingdom. The Naga nation is no longer, the smallest, it is now the largest. Nagaland's Kingdom is not only our alone but also belongs to God. Faith will rule over the whole earth, not gun and man power. Those who oppose this nation will oppose himself. Nagaland is a heavy stone for the Indian and the Burmese, all who lift it shall grievously hurt themselves and still they will come together against it....At the same time it is not only the fault of India but also Nagas. We have been suffering for many years, going against God. God's children cannot divided and time has come to become united as a bundle of five sticks...Nagas are travelling in two boats trying to fulfil the pleasure of the world and to please God. Our Church becomes the centre of Politics....God has chosen Naga nation as the second Israel. Nagaland will be transformed to a new Jerusalem, and all nations will marvel seeing this small nation. National Workers will no more be hiding in the jungles. The educated pro-Indian of the Nagas like Sanballat and Tobiah are against the sovereignty movement....The Land of the Naga is purchased by the blood of the innocent youth. Their bones are not yet decayed, and blood not yet divided. Those who died in the jungle for the nation are still shouting for Nagaland's sovereignty, and God hears these crying.[10]

This long peep through an exegesis of the 'Nagaland for Christ' reveals a deep sense of commitment, confidence and faith in the Naga attachment to Christ. The slogan 'Nagaland for Christ' describes the most moving and the most fearful experience of struggle and sublimates it in an awakened invocation of Christ. It bears a mark of apocalypse, an arousal and an emergence to sovereignty, which needs to be recovered from its contemporary loss.

One has to ask this question: can nationalism and Christianity go together with socialism in one ideological framework? It won't be a digression to repeat that Nagas as Christians simultaneously became a part of the process of formation of 'nation' in India, as Christianity was a marker of colonial modernity. It is through Christianity that the Nagas underwent a transformation. The nature of colonial modernity was such that it brought various communities under one administrative umbrella and, therefore, under a unified framework of the colonial state. In the case of the Nagas, Christianity operated as a parallel nation-building force linking them with the turns and twists of colonial history. If the anchorage of modernity had ensured the process of nation-building, then Christianity among Nagas also complemented that process by making them the subjects of that modernity and burdened them to carry on with the process of nation-building. Even their explicit de-linking from the rest of India and the absence of an anti-colonial struggle in a fashion similar to that which was going on in other parts of India produced a difference with the process of nation-building. However, they could not withdraw from modernity and the nation-building process within the colonial state but remained of a nature that forced them to be subject to all such spillovers of colonialism. The difference lay in the fact that the making of Nagas as a community did not share the consciousness of being an Indian. This difference is asserted in the form of claiming a separate national identity by way of a narrative of unity through Christianity away from the state of India created out of isolated provinces by the colonizers. The landscape of colonial polity conjoined them with the Indian state and the chronology of colonial retreat did not automatically provide them the slip into the wherewithal of a separate state, but had already placed them within the ambit of the Indian state. With a different consciousness, the encounter of the Nagas with colonialism was more pedagogic than of disillusionment and the rupture of that steady state with the withdrawal of British colonizers became a shocking episode in their collective memory. The Nagas were the uncolonized people awakened to a sense of distinctness that produced an estrangement for them within the political boundary of the new state-nation.

The Nagas' inclusion into the Indian state brought in the spectre of a different identity, different from the self-defined territory of the Naga identity and took them into another dominant discourse within which Nagas as a social category were much less substantial. They became something other than what they were in a new national whole written by the state of India, of which they were never a part but made a part. The communitarian ethos of Naga identity was broken through this feat of induction and, therefore, the colonized Nagas had to speak in a language of difference that reinstates a sense of self within a terrain of dominance. The liberation of the Nagas into the Indian state was a forced transformation that did not match with whatever aspirations of freedom it generated in them.

The peculiar coexistence of socialism, nationalism and Christianity could be answered in terms of a process of indigenization that progressed through concrete experiences of struggles of the Naga. The Maoist socialist orientation of the NSCN as a plan of the post-Phizo nationalist struggle and a sure weapon against capitulationism could have been contextualized only in a religious way, the way that makes all the Nagas committed to a distinct practice of life and also that which makes them distinct from other Indians. Pieces of discourse such as 'Nagaland's kingdom is not only ours alone but also belongs to God' generates a symptomatic crusade for its restitution, a movement of return from a supposedly ideological exterior of Maoism, socialism and nationalism. The iconic presentation of Nagaland as the 'Kingdom of God' is a symbolic re-enactment of the battle of Christ for redeeming Jerusalem, a move out of the dominant symbol of the Indian-state-nation. The nationalist aspiration of the Nagas expressed in the form of fighting back the appropriationist Indian state acquires the form of a symbolic battle against the dominant Indian symbols, and gets translated into guerrilla warfare against the state that heightened the release of the imagary of Naga national existence as a counter-hegemonic ideological discourse. The process of indigenization through invocation of religiosity was a practical necessity as it could only provide a popular front against the dominant symbols and, therefore, the strategic use of Christianity as the rallying point for different Naga tribes could sustain the spirit of defence and struggle against domination by the Indian state. Further, the indigenization of socialism and nationalism was driven towards an independent Naga identity that could be sustained only through the aspirations shared among its various components through the bridge of Christianity. There is another interlinked process of indigenization of 'Christianity' by turning it into a gospel of 'peace', 'sovereignty', represented in the slogan 'Nagaland for Christ'. Also one can read here the emergence of Naga national consciousness as an interface between Christianity and nationalism, despite its fuzzy relationship. The incorporation of socialism also presents a desire for self-determination, freedom from oppression and exploitation. It is a qualitative transformation of the Nagas from their discrete state of existence; it reconfigured a kind of 'recognition' from within the internally separated history of specific tribal and local characteristics.

The discourse of the NSCN combined the contours of all such variant processes of 'modernity' as a clustering of images through nationalist aspirations that was developed in response to colonialism and Indian nationalism. The appeal of Christianity in shelving away the various kinds of 'spirits' worshiped by Nagas had disciplined the sacred imagination of the community by evaluating the sundered and shadowy past as 'pre-modern'. This impact of redefining the community as 'Christians' made it an artefact of national imagination. The 'national' imagination described in the NSCN manifesto made a significant departure from the Phizoist figure of nation as familial and as an imagined tribal and kinship structure and reoriented it to a universal imagination by presenting it as 'Christian' instead of 'tribal'. Through Christianity the NSCN developed a positive view of nationalism based upon political bonds and solidarity among the various Naga tribes. The Nagas located in various parts of the North-East, especially Nagas of Manipur and Nagaland, established a broad linkage through the renewed ideological campaigns of the NSCN. This discourse of unity centred around an understanding of the virtues of Christianity. It described various virtues of 'Christianity' as 'nation-building' factors, such as the crusade for recovering the lost land for Christ. Christianity serves here as a rationalizing factor to sharpen the contrast with mainstream Indian culture. Therefore, Christianity acts as an instrument of unity and struggle and moves beyond the narrow confines of church services. The role of churches in spreading the message of Naga nationalist struggles through gospel and gatherings turned religious occasions as not just places of worship and prayer but as moments of battle cries. The whole paradigm of Christianity is changed here from salvation to liberation. This is again in contrast to affinities of kinship, intra-tribal feuds and localism that are seemingly too narrowly built upon older primordial loyalties to ground a generous concept of nation. The analogy to a world religion such as 'Christianity' serves to better convey an image of the nation which is open and ever cosmopolitan in its horizons. It rejoices a mixture of various distinct tribal groups into a nation. This euphemistic, hilarious and carnivalistic inside of NSCN's ideology turns 'charismatic' when it rejoices a socialist line of struggle. This important twist in NSCN's ideology is crucial in leading a multiplicity to a historical imagination of unity. It is not only a displacement into an imagined exterior for home-coming, but it is the messianic imagery of resolution in which Naga soldiers come back home defeating the enemy in the course of a protracted guerrilla warfare.

Above the affinities of emergence into a new Christian identity, the struggle of the various Naga tribes for their common political destiny through life and death seem to have a greater impact than merely belonging to a common cultural, religious and ethnic 'core'. Seemingly, dying for ones own country acquires a political grandeur, attains a charismatic valour and enters an element of iconic ultimacy in the national struggle. It involves dramatic sentiments and passions en route to battle and this sense of belonging to a 'community of life and death' serves the historical purpose of organizing the community as a sovereign polity ready for war. In case of the NSCN, it could generate such a preparedness for war from the continuity of the history of disarmament of Nagas by the Britishers and later by Indian army enforcements. It is during such occasions of war that the nation is imagined embodying ultimate values. Every instance of death and killing heightens this image of the nation as a field of struggle and the instances of army brutalities are interpreted in a fateful connotation. The response of the Indian state through counter-insurgency operations in order to save its territorial integrity also heightens the sense of disenchantment towards Indian nationalism, comes as the other horn of the dialectic, thus strengthening the hue for the Naga Nation. The more the Indian state acquires the monopoly of retaining the univocal and precise national identity, the more it affirms through coercion, and the space for contestation in terms of national identities gets sharpened further. The weight of nationalist aspirations of smaller communities turns heavy to such an extent that the spark cannot be extinguished. Thus, the war for nationalism gets transferred from 'imaginary' to 'real' with its fragments of the subversive symbolism. Construction of a nation around the subversive symbolism of guerrilla warfare eludes the symptomatic differences within the texture of the 'nation'. The split of the NSCN into NSCN (I-M) and NSCN (Khaplang) in 1988 and the subsequent bloody fratricidal war between them is symptomatic of an internally differentiated nature of the nationalist struggle. As such, an affirmation of nationalism based upon an affirmation of a self-defined core of a tribe or a community cannot last; there is no golden way to contain it within the whole of a nation. The latent pluralities drawn together by a consensual articulation of nation re-affirms itself through internal differences and self-definitions. Put in another way, the 'differences' between constituent units within the 'whole' is a phenomenon within a hierarchy, in which 'small units came to be defined by being bearers of special marks'. But this analogy of hierarchy perhaps cannot explain the homogeneous, non-hegemonic and non-hierarchic imaginary of nation in the Naga context. NSCN's fervent call for unity based on common national interest and transcendence of narrow primordial tribal loyalties, therefore, had to face a contest from within. The critique intends to overcome the differences within the Naga nation, but it cropped up as a symptom of an un-integrated core of the 'nation'. The NSCN's plea for unity has a structural component in terms of a position within the organizational structure and an ideological component in terms of a common national interest, both of which are intertwined in the 'whole' of ideology. Both these components are organically linked with each other and the difference is inscribed in such a way that any one of the components creates rupture in the other. This mode of structurization of NSCN produces a national identity that is internally united on both components, but the split within NSCN was based on certain political-ideological differences. The Khaplang faction came out alleging capitulation on the part of Isak and Muivah (I-M), and the rift grew into a clash of interests as well. It was mostly the Hemi Nagas and the Nagas located in eastern Nagaland bordering Burma who became the followers of Khaplang, while the rest of the tribes remained with the I-M faction. The Zeliangrong Nagas took a different stand for attaining Zeliangrong state comprising of the localities inhabited by Zemi, Liangmei and Rongmei tribes.

The Maoist line of struggle of the NSCN (I-M) delves into such contradictions within the Naga identity. Based upon its strength to fight the Indian state and the rival faction, NSCN (I-M) retained its command on the majority of Naga tribes. There is an inevitable clash over the leadership of the national struggle in ideological and moral terms. There is a struggle between the 'correct' and the 'incorrect'. The more acute the struggle between the two, the sharper is the division within. The explanation for this phenomenon could be the assertion of a more fundamental identity below the national identity and such assertions are based upon tribal consciousness. It generates a conflict of power within the projected 'nation'. The pan-tribal national consciousness brought by modernity exposes its fragile and unmingled interior that expresses the actual tribal consciousness. In this sense, the nation-from-below returns to the concrete tribal and community consciousness to expose that nationalism in its ultimate manifestation is an exhibition of its core of multiple loyalties and multiple identities that clamour for self-recognition. In case of mobilizations against the dominant state-nation, it presents 'a view from below'. So removal of the veil under which forces of disparate nation clash and struggle remains the pedagogy of such mobilizations. Given this possibility, the Naga movement not only presents fissures below, but such fissures also produce a distinct strand within the broad framework of the movement. A distinct assertion of tribal or community characteristics represents the tendency of remaining independent and sovereign. Nations-from-below, therefore, subvert the unitary logic of national identity and transform it into discrete entities with distinct markers, which is a demystification of nationalist mythology. Therefore, mobilizations of a counter-hegemonic nature are inherently unstable and revealing as they unveil the layers of identities from their condensation into the 'whole'.

The subversive interior of Naga insurgency are the experiences of suppression by the state. It exhibits the targets on both the sides. For the state any Naga is suspect, and it assumes draconian laws to contain and flush out insurgency. The presence of the state as

'Panoptican' in which it views insurgency as anti-national and controls it by force is felt in Nagaland and Manipur. The repression of the state and its punitive operations are a horrendous distortion of the fabric of social life. Attacks and counter-attacks by both sides inflicted on each other leads to a large number of casualties. Ambushes by the NSCN on the Indian army and the deaths resulting from encounters with the army produce sensations that involve the populace. The NSCN made allegations about the most criminal and devilish strategies adopted by the government, which are the so-called psychological warfare and the counter-insurgency operations launched against the Naga people.[11]

A state of siege was laid upon public life by the state and its organs. Most often people are caught between in the crossfire, particularly when the commoners respond to empathize or repulse the events of killings and arrests. There is a general silencing of the 'public'. Commands and propaganda from both the sides, therefore, shape the opinion of the silent majority. The deep national sentiments of the Naga people are often stirred by such events like deaths in encounter; sometimes there is a lurking fear and a pathological tension prevails in the populace, which take them neither here nor there. The context produced out of the insurgent versus the state battle is subversive.

Between Subversions of the State and the Self

The subversive symbolism of insurgency is structured in memory, pain and hope. The discourses of the state-nation also employ a particular proportion of all such states of feelings as part of a discourse of containment. Gandhiji's utterance that India would not force Nagaland to join India generates 'hope', while Morarji Desai's, 'I will exterminate the rebel Nagas' generates a kind of fear from the state. A proportionate mixture of all these states of feeling are deliberately linked to the goal of domination. The Nagas are subsumed in the dyadic and narcissistic construction of 'Indian nationhood', which is paternalistic and excludes any desire for freedom. Mahatma Gandhi's affirmation 'India has bled for her own freedom. Is she going to deprive others of their freedom?' is an instance of transference of the Naga desire for freedom, but transferred into the site of the state, it crosses the boundary of that desire by its assumed inclusion within the fold of the state. The desire of the Nagas operates as the 'political unconscious'[12] of the state discourse that operates as subversive within the narrative of the 'nation'. The Nagas, as a people, recognize their desire for freedom as true, but that desire only perpetuates its absence and, therefore, the Nagas' self-revolve around a non-self identity. It rather stoically construes a self which represents freedom from political suppression, and which is displaced to various disparate and diasporic entities simultaneously.

The subversive symbolism of insurgency undercuts the monologue of state interpretations. The Indian state considered the claim of Naga nationhood as illegitimate and, therefore, directed its discourse towards subsumption and dissolution of the Naga claim. The Manifesto of the NSCN aims at subverting India's attempt to subsume the Naga nation; as it says:

> The world is for the monster and not for the people. This view represents the mentality of the lower nature of man, especially when taken over by an aberration. It makes the existence of human society meaningless...The strong make might their resort. They are more easily prone to the use of force in settling problems. They are able to do much harm and can even annihilate many of the weak and win battles; but it is perseverance and the act of undaunted confrontation with eventuality of death for the truth that one knows that win the war in the long run.[13]

This futuristic and moralistic vision about possibilities within the struggle is neither fantastic nor fanatic. But it is the will or determination to gradually dispel the overarching strength of the hegemony of the Indian state. Again this is more attached to the Maoist line of protracted warfare. Just as LTTE is trying to defeat the Sinhalese-dominated Lankan state, the NSCN (I-M) is committed to overcome the undermining policies of the Indian state. Although ex-colonial states like India and Sri Lanka have emerged out of a struggle against colonialism by asserting a liberated conception of national identity, they seem to be the worst perpetrators of violence on any claim of national self-determination. One can locate a predominance of territorial interest over recognition of national rights. Such an abstract notion of 'national interest' by a supposedly democratic state marks an increasing centralization of national rights in the hands of a few dominant nationalities with the exclusion of others from the space of the state and culture. To recover its self-identity from the already appropriated space of the nation and state, the NSCN followed a policy of war without bloodshed, in terms of historical resistance, mixed with preparedness for war. Isak, in particular, makes it clear that attempts at establishing peace are in no way a submission to intimidation by the Indian state, nor could it be a sell out of the idea of freedom in return of 'development packages' of the state. He sees peace 'in terms of freedom' which is the inalienable 'possession for a people, great or downtrodden'. Freedom is the entangled objective of peace in the context of realization of the Naga nation and Isak Swu's repeated caution that peace can not be bought or can not be attained by throwing of the weight of political strength simultaneously expresses the resistance to any manoeuvre, as well as a determination to fulfil the yearning for freedom. Swu argued, 'Thank God we are able to break gradually the sphere of Indian influence. The issue is no longer in the shade; India can no longer run down, as she did in the past, the reality of the Nagas.'[14] He further said, 'On our part, we believe in political solution ever since the very inception of the problem. And we do not permit this point of sincerity to be questioned on whatever pretext. At the same time we won't have any policy from the Indian government that flies off at a tangent.'[15]

Therefore, one can see here a simultaneous resistance to the forces of repression and an affirmation of an acceptable solution through understanding. This double-voiced mode of discourse of the NSCN subverts the monologue of law and order. It clearly brings out the issues in a holistic way and desires their resolution. It assumes a potency to reduce any conflict and opens up the discourse for reconciliation. It contests the claim of superiority and authority of the Indian state expressed through forcible domination and replaces it with the objective of a political solution. At the level of an attempt of reconciliation by the Indian state, there is no subversion, but what it subverts is the attempt to dominate. The subversive aspect of the NSCN discourse centres itself around on events such as 'capitulation by enemies within', attempts to silence the national movement by the state and the melancholy of atrocities and brutalities. The subversive symbolism does not express offensive affronts, but merely charts out a counter-attack. The approach is not to intimidate the state, but to produce subversion in its function in the political sphere, which is to send the message across that their voice be heard. This kind of pre-emption devises the strategies of insurgency and especially the fight against repression of the state assumes a guerrilla form. The theory of 'protracted warfare' is an interpretive strategy of sending messages of rebellion through acts of violence and disturbance, but all these never ensure a decisive victory over the enemy. Therefore, the subversive symbolism of insurgency is constituted more by way of vigilance, calculations, memories of horror and desperation. In the case of Naga national struggle, the same was not formed by a passion to kill. Such pre-emption is more fortuitous than mere speculative victories in the course of their 'protracted warfare'. The approach of the state to repress this whole process of subversion and secure its functioning leads to a determined and targeted extermination, on both sides, by the state and the insurgents, with an already legitimized interpretation.

Localizing Insurgency

Insurgency in North-East India generates struggle over domination and control of terrain among various 'nation-aspiring' groups from below such as the clashes between Naga and Kuki, and Kuki and Paite. Without going into the nitty-gritties of the massacres and evictions one can identify the struggle for dominance between the NSCN and the Kuki National Army (KNA). It was largely a struggle for enduring the hold maintaining the status quo of the two warring organizations over each other in the hills of Manipur, especially in the districts of Ukhrul and Senapati. The struggle centred around the notion of areas under dominance by way of subjugation of the other community to make them supporters of insurgency. The taxation of Kukis by Nagas and Kuki resistance to it generated this bitter and bloody struggle. The logic of such struggle can be explained in diasporic terms. The settlement of Kukis within areas predominantly inhabited by Nagas and the habitation of Nagas within Kuki-dominated areas provided the backdrop of mutual *lebenserum*. The creation of mutual distrust among them resulted from acts like taxation and consequent apprehension of being subordinated by the other side. The clash is of a localized character as it intended to establish the superiority and command of one over the other. The demand for Naga homeland can not be accepted by Kukis. As a response, the KNA has demanded their own homeland. Both met at cross-purposes, as neither of them can extol the presence of the other side. This marks the rise of a 'stimulus-response' structure of feeling between such contiguous nations. The claim for a Naga nation was responded to with the claim for a Kuki nation, both mutually exclusive and yet not being able to segregate themselves from each other. This exclusionary and self-determining portrait of 'nations-from-below' seething in internal clashes turns self-subversive. Hegemony of the state did not become an issue here, but an imagined dominance of the other community sensitized the localities in which both the communities live contiguously. We interpret this sensitivity in terms of an intersection of diaspora, between Nagas and Kukis, which an exclusionary variety of nationalism cannot accommodate. These clashes could have been evaded and there could have been solidarity between the two. Looked at from another point of view, the penetration of the NSCN (I-M) influence over other tribes belonging to Kuki-Chin group and the carrying out of the NSCN (I-M) writ by Hmar, Paite and others infuriated the KNA and ultimately it turned out to be a struggle for supremacy between the two organizations. The intervention of the state could not resolve these issues—of whose organization shall reign and which area shall be under whose influence—but merely led to further repression of the national movements of Nagas and Kukis.

A worse follow-up is the continuation of such clashes in different forms. It is interesting to note that even within Nagaland, the Kuki language is taught at the primary level and sometimes works as a link language between various Naga tribes. So there is an already existing relationship of mutual dependence between Nagas and Kukis. But in this relationship there is an implicit sense of superiority involved, as Kukis think that Nagas could be their brethren and are hitherto one with them. Nagas as an aspiring national identity would assert their difference from/with Kukis and hence the imagined ties between the two would be tenuous. The consciousness of the Kukis that Nagas are almost a part of them and the Naga consciousness of a difference are also contributing factors to the conflict. The continuation of this conflict over difference between Kuki and Paite, caused by the latter's deviation from their erstwhile allegiance to the Kukis and their hobnobbing with the NSCN (I-M), was a dismal consequence of the rift between Kukis and Nagas. The Paites, as alleged by the Kukis, joined the Zomi Revolutionary Army and the Zomi Reunification Organization, which was largely viewed by them as a shift of allegiance and created a split within the Kuki-Chin group. Again, both these Zomi organizations were treated by Kukis to be followers of the NSCN (I-M). The declaration made by Phun-zathan Tonsing, the Paite chief of Manipur Congress, that 'The Paites are not Kukis' intensified the violence between Kuki and Paite.[16] Therefore, it is clear that the definition of ethnic boundaries and its alteration, being over-determined by contingencies of life, create contradictions within an aspirant nation. Kukis, trying to preserve a unified Kuki-Chin identity in a state like Manipur, perceived the above stated declaration of Tonsing as a violation of their national identity. Such a perception of the loss of identity triggered violence against the offending tribes such as Paites. This kind of constant shift of the boundaries of an identity and breaks within it not only produces ruptures, but it also manifests itself through clashes and conflicts.

The fractures within a defined interior of an identity seemingly become the moving factors for 'nations', a cultivated image of which, in certain non-negotiable terms such as inalienable right of habitat and sovereignty, in a converse way exhibits the strands within a larger identity. Such fissures release an emergent mode of self-definition by fracturing a presumed common core. The rise of incommensurability and resistance to the dominant marks the potential of stability within the construction of a nation or an identity. Insurgency manifested in the form of redefining boundaries and reconfiguring identities becomes the moving force of a nation-from-below. Such mobilizations are participatory and are based upon the ethos of a community life with a play of power relations within the stable interior of a nation. There is an amount of uncertainty and unpredictability in such mobilizations as it goes against a stable interior. The affirmation of a smaller identity as different does not confer any stability by itself, but it challenges the stable core within which it was intended, and it ensures an exit from that static position to a struggle for recognition. When the internal Other of such an emergent identity reacts to it violently, the affirmation of its difference becomes evident and its expulsion from the already enfolded bond turns volatile.

This clash of identities, such as between Naga and Kuki, mobilizes the whole habitat of various identities that were referred around the generic signifiers. The colonial policy of bringing together disparate groups of people through certain interventions, such as settlement, propagation of a common language and the creation of a uniformity through abolition of practices obstructive to normalizing such identities, mobilized signifiers like 'Naga' or 'Kuki' as names for some groups of people. Basically, what such interventions intended was the production of certain identifiable uniform communities in order to negotiate power for them. The spread of Christianity further sustained this process of homogenization within tribes to emerge into pan-tribal entities. But this process of forming identities could not automatically demarcate and distinguish the boundaries between such generic denominations of clusters of people. What it exhibited was the possibility of constructing an identity based on some shared signifiers oriented through power-relations. Therefore, it required a different kind of negotiation, a negotiation that takes into account a collective form identified as a community to decide upon various contingent needs.

If this process of mobilization of smaller identities could be called as 'colonial modernity' because it initiated a process of clustering and setting it in a set of relations with other such clusters, the lines of difference and distinction were pretty well mediated by the colonizers. The withdrawal of the colonizer brought in the possibility of an independent mobilization and renegotiation of boundaries between parties in which access and exit could be negotiated in the in-between space. Therefore, what the colonizers initiated, that is, the process of making an identity and an active negotiation between them, acquired a greater propensity in post-colonial India to emerge into a sense of autonomy and free negotiability. The limits imposed on such free negotiation, both by the generic bounds of the community or by the state, are subjected to interrogation and violation in order to involve them in a free space. There is a self-conscious articulation involved in such acts of interiorization/ exteriorization in relation to some other identity. Claims over identity appear as contesting claims in relation to some other identities. The post-colonial Indian modernity generates a greater swing in laying bare the cores of larger wholes or groups of identities, the compulsion of which drags the state to involve into a mode of negotiation by which the state mediates between such identities. Apart from the state, the identities themselves negotiate between themselves. As discussed earlier, the claims of such identities as nations are shaped by their sharing of a national ethos, by positioning themselves as equals against some communities within or without. This process of negotiation gives them the fillip to claim the status of 'nation'. Had there not been an image of nation, the claim for separate nationhood could not have mirrored the rise of such smaller nations. The processes of negotiation make the emergence of identities 'political' in character. As, for example, in the case of the Naga-Kuki clash, the mediation for peace by the leader of the Church and the state exercises a normative force that bind such identities to a definite behaviour. In the case of Kuki-Paite clashes, the attempts of negotiation by the Kuki National Army and the Zomi Revolutionary Army with other mediators could at least bring some respite.

Back to the Parapolitical

What such negotiations bring about is a deciding role of the parapolitical upon the conflicting identities. The parapolitical sphere exercises a definite normative power upon these identities to negotiate the 'rift' between them. The role of the state in the parapolitical is the least, as it cannot settle the terms of conciliation between the conflicting identities. This is evident in the case of ceasefire with the NSCN (I-M) beginning from 1 August 1997 for three months. The ceasefire agreement was intended to chart out a peaceful settlement with NSCN (I-M) and a general solution to the Naga problem. The ceasefire between the Indian state and the NSCN (I-M) had evoked resentment among many other insurgent groups as they feared being marginalized. They also apprehended neglect to their cause by the state by giving singular importance to the NSCN (I-M). The Indo-Burma Revolutionary Front (IBRF) comprising of the NSCN (Khaplang), United Liberation Front of Assam (ULFA), Hynniewtrep National Liberation Counil, Karbi National Volunteers, People's Revolutionary Party of Kngleipak, United National Liberation Front, National Liberation Front of Tripura and others, demanded confinement of ceasefire between NSCN (I-M) and the Indian state only within Nagaland. It also pointed out the idological confusion of NSCN (I-M) over the issue of sovereignty. Again, the ceasefire declared between the NSCN (I-M) and the Indian state was termed by the NSCN (Khaplang) as 'treacherous to the Naga people'. These contradicting positions within the parapolitical set in another field of struggle to resolve contentious issues through negotiations. Another example of such a conflicting position within the parapolitical is the stand of the Kuki Inpui, the apex Kuki body, to sever its relationship with United Naga Council (UNC), which is also a part of the Naga Hoho. The organization resented the move by United Naga Council's decisions to demand the resignations of all Naga MPs and MLAs and also against UNC's initiative to extend the NSCN (I-M) ceasefire to the Naga-dominated areas of Manipur. One can see here the resentments from within on the issue of ceasefire as it ensures the hegemony of the Nagas over others. Such apprehension also directs their critique in general on the Indian state, which had brushed aside the interest of other communities in order to settle the Naga problem.

Hegemony and Dominance as Key Issues of Conflict

Therefore, one can read here the possibilities of multilayered conflict involving various communities and the state, which can be resolved through the sphere of the parapolitical. Based upon the perception of domination, the relationship among such parapolitical communities evolves. It keeps on changing its interior boundaries, and asserting its desire to remain outside the dominant influence. Parapolitical groups by their mediating role not only change the relationship of dominance, but emerge as a non-hegemonic space of discussion and dialogue. Through the parapoltical, the struggle against domination remains to be the source of affirmation of a collective in relation to its close Others. This process of emergence of identities negotiates in the parapolitical space in order to come out of the perceived hegemony of the state or their counterparts. Not only the splitting of Kuki as a generic identity into smaller groups such as Paite, but also splitting of Naga in various configurations such as Zeliangrong, Chakesang, etc., based upon geography and cultural affinity, can substantiate this process of moving out of hegemony. This is an internalization of the spirit of counter-dominance that grounds itself in the parapolitical activity through affirmation of a collective for its distinct place. It is also an unravelling of the repressed underside of a whole in which it seeks to recover its uninterrupted inner core. One should ask the question: does such a process of splitting a 'whole' negate the claim of nations such as the Naga? If it negates the possibility of something generic, then by the same token the possibility of acceptance of a larger national whole such as 'India' is negated. The strategy of the state to divide a generic identity into tribal distinctions strengthens the possibility of disempowerment of each divided and discrete piece of identity and it annihilates the core of 'national' identity. But the possibility of fighting the domination within a generic identity heightens the possibility of redeeming the repressed identity and extends the space for greater political negotiation. The militancy expressed in such moves to segregate brings out one of the main sources of insurgency in the region.

One example will help explain the situation better. Post-insurgency Mizoram witnessed the manifestation of Hmar identity as separate and distinct from Lusheis. The movement launched by Hmar People's Convention to affirm their due share of power and resources created recalcitrant resentment among Lusheis as it blamed the latter for their deprivation. The conflict took the form of a symbolic struggle in the form of Hmars asserting their linguistic distinction from the Mizo language and Lusheis denying the naming of an Autonomous Council comprising of the Hmar population in the Hmar tongue. This assertion of Hmar identity breaks out of a perceived hegemony and affirms an original core. Interestingly, within the Hmar community, the assertion distinguished between those Hmars who speak Mizo and those Hmars who speak their own tongue, and it was largely an assertion of the latter. Interestingly again, the Chirus, who are looked upon as a constituent of Hmars and considered just to be a 'clan' differentiate themselves from others within the Hmar community. Within the Hmar movement, the abandonment of the agenda of a greater Hmar autonomous state, comprising of areas in Assam, Manipur and Mizoram and its concentration only in Mizoram, created dissension and the Hmar Peoples' Conference got divided into various factions. This phenomenon of emergence of smaller identities from within an assumed common identity is a reaction to the binding processes of hegemonization, and this is how nations-from-below grow. One can term this process as ethno-nationalism contesting hegemonic identities by internalizing—paradoxically—the consciousness of being a 'nation' themselves, while they are bursting out of the interior of a common national core. One can term this process of bursting the core of a national whole as a mode of indigenization of 'nation' that sheers off the burden of being dominated and subsumed under a core.

Another most interesting feature of saving a supposedly national core from fracturing is the express reactions against 'separatism'. When such reactions are expressed, the struggle between the 'whole' and the 'part' assumes a politico-ideological form dragging the state into it. The state is called in primarily to protect the 'minority' from persecution and there is an articulation on the part of that minority in terms of its specificity and distinctiveness. The reaction of Mizos to Hmars and the reaction of Nagas to Zeliangrong are similar, and it is a travestying reaction to brush aside claims of difference. In such contests, the hegemony is constructed centring the generic identity, and the difference is construed centring the areas of subordination with reference to concrete histories as a resistance to the hegemonic articulation.

On the issue of uniting Naga areas together in a distinct political boundary, the response of other people of Manipur in terms of a fear of disintegration of the state evoked a patient response from NSCN (I-M) and their followers. The NSCN (I-M) did not press for their demand following the sentiments of the other sections of people. This mode of 'rationalization' for not breaking the existing political boundary expresses NSCN (I-M)'s regard for the concerns of the other peoples. Such regard gives a self-sustaining and fulfilling capacity to the desire for national sovereignty as it refuses to erect another barricade of hegemony to other people. It is also an adherence to the popular mandate through which the popularity of an organization remains high and the influence of the parapolitical decisions remains binding. In fact, the perceived threat of breaking of existing boundaries of the states of the region for the purpose of establishing Nagalim has always been a subject of much debate in Naga civil society. But then such 'rationality' for retaining a stable political boundary despite the need for distinct emergence in a community cannot be universalized. The specificity of the social contexts in which power relations are articulated determines how such a wish as not to intervene in other peoples rights is actualized.

In the case of Assam, the insurgency, post-Bodo Accord, reconfiguring the demand 'Divide Assam Fifty-Fifty' aimed at countering the perceived hegemony of the Assamese people by creating another centre of power. Such a perception developed through complete effacement of the aspirations of Bodos from the text of the Assam Accord and later in the failure to determine the areas of the Bodo Autonomous Council (BAC). After the signing of the Bodoland Autonomous Council Accord on 20 February 1993, there has been a struggle launched by several Bodo outfits attempting to establish the power of Bodos over areas identified within BAC. This meant flushing out of non-Bodos from the proposed BAC areas. This had lead to violent massacres in Bongaigaon where the slain were Bengali Muslims. The killing of large numbers of Santhals and Bengalis by militant Bodo organizations has created antagonism towards the Bodo Accord of 1993 among other communities living in BAC areas. The process of minority cleansing exhibits too strong disillusionment with the Bodo Accord and with the movement to create a separate Bodoland state. The approach of the Indian state is not to allow a separate state for Bodos. This repression of Bodo political desire by the state makes it possible that the Bodos would remain dominated under the Assamese hegemony. While Bodo movement directs its anger against other Indians, the possibility of being dominated remains a quiet truth, which at the same time turns the movement into an arrogant nationalism. The linkages between ULFA and Bodo outfits further sharpens their aspiration for separation from India which they camouflage under the issues of creation of a separate Bodo state. This spate of violent release of the repressed desire of the Bodos in acts of ethnic cleansing even neutralizes the parapolitical sphere. The fundamental thrust of Bodo affirmation against Assamese domination presents a conflict in power-structure in which the Bodos are represented as a token. The exclusion of the Bodos from the fold of caste-Hindu Assamese society not only drives them against Assamese hegemony but also turns them against other minorities living in BAC areas. Bodos reconstruct their 'history' through articulating their excluded position from Assamese society. The Bodos simultaneously rearticulate the necessity to reorient their language and literature, speed up economic development, social mobility and so on to strengthen the markers of their identity. This attempt of reconstruction affirms their linkage with the Sino-Tibeto-Burman group of languages, and severes them from the tendencies to use other dominant languages.[17]

The signing of the Bodoland Territorial Council Accord has further sharpened the resistance of the non-Bodos in Bodoland areas, as they fear total subjugation under the Bodos. They came together to form a united platform of all non-Bodo communities to oppose the Bharatiya Janata Party (BJP)-led central government's unilateral decision to create the Bodo Territorial Council with a meagre representation of these communities. Although the All Bodo Students Union (ABSU) and Bodo Liberation Tiger leadership have repeatedly assured protection of the interests of the minorities living within the Council areas, there are instances of radical groups within Bodo movements still continuing the line of aggression against the minorities. The National Democratic Front of Bodoland (NDFB) has maintained an ambivalent response towards the accord and hence the minorities felt insecure about its intentions. In addition, there is a crucial question regarding the control of funds by the Assam government, as the Centre cannot directly fund the proposed Council. Given all these weak outcomes of the settlement the situation has still remained volatile, despite a large section of Bodo militants remaining withdrawn from any tangible action programmes. Bandhs called by non-Bodo organizations largely passed off peacefully, while the Bodo outfits restrained themselves.

Redrawing Boundaries in Space and Time

In this process of redrawing and redefining the boundaries of communities, the clashes between the 'affiliative' and 'filiative' communities could be identified. An affiliative community such as 'Naga' contains filiative tribes within it in order to operate at both the levels simultaneously. The state can hold such a community by generating a certain degree of affiliative and filiative relations with it. The affiliative relation that the state generates is through an institutional positioning, for example, by the creation of a state or by signing an accord, which are the formal instruments towards establishing affiliative relations. But the state cannot create filiative relations that proceed only through inter-community relations.

Differences within an identity are negotiated at both affiliative and filiative levels. In the case of Kukis, coming out of the United Naga Council is a case of breaking an affiliative relationship and then subsequently siding with various non-Naga communities of Manipur; the community sought a wider affiliative relationship. In a rather different way, the Paites' affirmation as non-Kukis seeks to change its filiative relation with Kukis, by way of seeking an affiliative relationship with the Naga national movement. At the same time the NSCN (I-M) affirming the age-old brotherhood between Meiteis and Nagas is a distinct mobilization of both filiative and the affiliative. Such a mode of sharing a common objective by establishing different kinds of relationships is a play in the heterogeneous force field of the nation space. But through such play, the agency involved in a community acquires a place within a complex web of inner-community relationship mediated by the state as well as the communities themselves, to evolve into a structure of filiation and affiliation.

Regarding the Bodos, the struggle against the non-Bodos is a rupture of the filiative and the affiliative. Even as they reconstruct their affiliation to the Sino-Tibeto-Burman group of languages and reclaim their 'Kachari' past, such reconstructions cannot readily get recognition or affiliation from the state and the battle continues for affiliation. Looked at from another angle, P.S. Dutta's usage of overlapping between political boundary and the social boundary[18], and the consequent changes occurring in that could be another way of understanding this process of filiation and affiliation. Bodo dissatisfaction over delimitation of 'political boundary' of the BAC also brings into play the extension of 'political boundary'. The non-Bodo have already alleged that their non-Bodo areas have been included within the BAC and such an act shows the transgression of the Bodo 'social boundary' and extension of 'political boundary' beyond it. The case of the NSCN (I-M)'s demand for unification of Naga dominated areas under one political framework is an example of bringing disjunctive social boundaries under one political boundary. But then the social boundary of the Nagas cannot exclude other communities from within a shared social space even though this was what they intended—their political exclusion. On the other hand, the political boundary of Manipur restrains the Nagas from redrawing social boundaries for themselves. Therefore, the mutual play of political and social boundaries evolves into the determination of the 'self' in an insurgent mould. One can ask this question: does not insurgency intervene in such boundaries and relations? Definitely, it breaks the passivity of the settled markers of identity such as boundary and inter-community relations.

Rather, insurgency redraws such boundaries by crossing over the limits of community; it alters the nature of the political and social spaces. It also alters the flow of temporality by way of emergence of an identity that breaks the moment of identification between communities. It generates an in-between temporality in which the marker of an identity attains a new meaning. The emergence of NSCN (I-M) figures one kind of temporality through the proclaimed event of 'Nagaland for Christ'; the time gets signified through sacrifice and suffering by being elected by Christ. It ruptures the flow of the sense of time in which the Indian nation has emerged. The characterization and articulation by NSCN (I-M) assume a new mode of time, different from the mere clockwork, and the soldiers live in 'time', which is a moment of encounter with the state, an encounter between life and death. The change of space is even more evident. The space becomes a space for battle, a space that can not be controlled from the established echelons of power. This rupture in time and space along with changes in markers such as boundary and relation signify the 'shift' that insurgency inaugurates.

Fuzzy Markers of Identity as Sources of Counter-Hegemonic Struggle

'Nation-from-below' presents the state of several emergences without a restraint on their affirmation. It mobilizes specific instances of resemblance to cognize a 'whole' and sees itself as a part of it. This logic of the identity emerges within modernity in which there is blurring of consciousness of specific markers of identity within a 'whole', thereby making such identities analytically unstable. The rise of such inherently unstable and fuzzy identities within a 'whole' called 'nation' is a process of being enveloped within a definite institutional structure and, therefore, the communities in which people saw themselves as living were fuzzy compared to the community or the nation that is proposed now (Kaviraj, 1994).

Also, the presumed anonymity of living together within a nation and, in the context of India, the inheritance of a colonial state mobilizing those specific identities to the anonymity of nation-state is a process of erosion of those specifics. The immobilized signifiers of identity with which the consciousness of a community identifies itself at the bottom of a hierarchy are pulled out with force and that is how, within the limits posed by the state, the conditions of making of an identity are effectively altered. The alteration of those conditions such as recovery of one's older faith and rejection of policies of misrecognition operating from the bottom change the field of political discourse radically. Such changes in definitions and privileged interpretations given to an identity extend the space for its self-definition and it appears through a rupture or a disjunction in time and space. The biography of a nation, concealing the gaps between law-like succession of history and underdetermined ethnography of peoples, slips out in the rupture at the bottom and opens up the possibilities of its negation and resistance.

Insurgency directed to mobilize nations-from-below produces ruptures. The most fundamental rupture is an articulation in which it produces a disjunction in the narrative representation of the nation instituted by the state. In the case of Nagas, the mythologization of ancient knowledge about them in the Hindu texts, or their alignment during colonialism, are consciously reappropriated in the Naga discourse. Such reappropriation of their position from the interior of a narrative representation constitutes the 'nation'. This process of reversal of the dominant narrative operates as fundamental to the claim of 'nation'. Therefore, internalization of 'nation' is an attempt to countering the projection of the 'Other' as nation by appropriating what the other has projected and own it on ones own terms. This appears at the moment of disjunction with the dominant 'Other'. The articulation of nationhood in the case of the Nagas is an articulation in which they asserted their will to remain 'free'. India's appropriation of all that the colonial world had left behind dispossessed the material right of the Nagas, while their counter position on freedom empowered them politically. The insurgency movement mobilizes metaphors of freedom through establishment of a parallel government, constitution and army, which enact overpowering episodes to mobilize popular support. These metaphors of freedom have their disjunction from narratives of the dominant moving towards a symbolic reclamation of certain losses by mixing up degrees of fear and hope. Another important fact of insurgency is the transgression of the dominant norms, and, in case of insurgency in North-East India, it transgresses the borders of the nation and bases itself in a foreign land to rouse the hoi polloi to freedom, presenting the brutalities committed by the Indian state in the international forum to seek justice. Such act of transgression empowers the insurgents as a form of camouflaged 'foreign aggression' to thwart the perceived hegemony of the nation. The response of the state to such transgressions takes an all-encompassing form of 'proxy war', especially by terming it as anti-national and dangerous. Still, insurgency speaks through its muffled voices, presents writings that are 'banned' and incriminating, and tries to steal the attention of the public to the experiences of brutalities and pangs of an emerging nation-from-below. All that symbolically heightens the imagination of a free country, even though nobody knows what awaits at the end of the road.

The Emerging Vision of Independence

The insurgents possess a vision for the whole of the North-East that constitutes the future map of the region. The vision is that of an independent country. The state looks at this vision of 'independence' as a manoeuvre of the insurgency for attaining objectives such as progress, development and quality of life which the state does not ensure in public life. Especially the NSCN (I-M) ideology of emerging into a free Nagaland, which will be a land of the Christ, bears a sense of election in which Nagas are transformed into the agency of establishing God's will. In the vision of the NSCN, Nagaland should be free from what they called the vile influences of 'Indian culture'. In another context the words of Peoples' Revolutionary Party of Kangleipak (PREPAK) leader Meiraba Luwang affirm:

> It is the firm belief and reality that 'national liberation' is the common goal of all the revolutionary organizations in Manipur. In order to emancipate national liberation, the PREPAK has taken a firm decision to work unitedly with all other revolutionary organizations.[19]

With much greater clarity he has gone on to say, 'We are multi-ethnic people constituting a nation. Each and every community should strive for peaceful coexistence, cultural harmony and mutual understanding. We all are brothers and should be prepared to fight the common enemy, India' (Luwang, 1997: 18). Such a vision of a harmonized imagery of a nation built around the diversity of the North-East is further universalized in the discourse of ULFA. In its resolution for the formation of 'United Front' in struggle for liberation, it emphasized:

(*i*)   united front inside the motherland (unity of national liberation struggles of all of the indigenous nations and nationalities of Assam); and

(*ii*)   unity taking North-Eastern region as the base (for historical, geographical, political reasons). [20]

ULFA's vision of a united front coincides with PREPAK's vision and such joining together of the theme of sovereignty and independence provide a projected vision of liberation of dominated peoples. It shapes the self-image of the people in terms of being colonized and dispossessed of their own characteristics.

There is a propelling imagery of the homeland in insurgency in the North-East. Homeland is a construction that signifies a location, a territorial attachment, all of which are subordinated within the political boundary of the nation-state. Belonging to such a homeland transcends the presence of a community in an occurrent location. The transcendence comes through referring to dislocations and displacement of the community within a diaspora, which is imagined to be the barrier against the coming together of the segregated parts of the community. For example, Mizos in Mizoram feel for the people belonging to the Zo community in Burma, Tripura and Bangladesh. Garos in Meghalaya crave for continuing their kinship with the Garos of Bangladesh. Therefore, there are diasporic breaks across the physical space, and there is a further narrowing down of that space by political institutions. It provides an avenue for inter-community negotiations and limits everyone by the breaks in diaspora. The vision of a liberated North-East mobilizes this imaginary map of undisturbed linkage of communities within itself. This is exactly not what a national imagination looks but it is more of a sense of belonging to a common whole in an anonymous way, while the vision of liberation in North-East India represents a self-conscious diasporic continuity resulting into resentment against the breaks through presence of other groups and political boundaries. Therefore, the vision embodies a sense of 'lack' or 'loss' around which it articulates liberation. The sphere of invisibility of a part of the diaspora, of an inevitable disruption in kinship relations due to the socio-structural arrangement and political economy of the nation-state of India is conceived to be negation of the identity, a desire which gives flight to their imagination to produce fragments of memory that are culturally shared (Anderson, 1983: 22–36).[21]

Such collective memories are also disturbed by 'counter-memories'. In the case of Mizos, Lanldenga's memorandum to the prime minister of India in 1965 quoted Nehru describing the status of frontier states of North-East India as being governed by treaties, customs and usage without its regular inclusion within governance. This mobilization of 'truth' in the public discourse of authority is presentation of the unrepresented and there is an invocation of the memory of the ruler by Laldenga's memorandum. In the case of Nagas, the termination of the 10-year agreement with the Naga National Council is invoked to awaken the memory of a supposedly forgetful ruler, and such instances simultaneously operate as counter-memories to them. In guerrilla warfare against the Indian state, such memories and counter memories are displayed through bearing the transferred violence by the state on them for holding such memories. The state transfers its own authenticated memories of nationhood by way of repressing and relocating their memories and the victims create a web of 're-memory' of their past. There is reciprocation on the part of the oppressed communities of North-East India and the immanence of their consciousness in such reciprocation inscribes the fixed place assigned to them. This place is the place of an overdetermined other such as 'Nagas as Nagas'. The discourse of insurgency subverts such overdetermined categories of self-identity, say, 'Nagas as Nagas', by redefining themselves such as 'Nagaland for Christ', which forces the fate of non-reconigniation. In response to such non-recognition, the Nagas mobilize a counter-gaze and resist the nondescript status attributed to them. They describe this process of systematic annihilation of their self-presence, and in the language of NSCN manifesto, 'We rule out the illusion of serving Nagaland through peaceful means. It is arms and arms again that will save our Nation and endure freedom to the people'.[22]

The Indian state denies its 'otherness' and strives for the invisibility of its designs, driven by its own denial of 'others' and the resistance to such denial. Simultaneously, what Naga scholar M. Horam had noted that the self-deceptive perceptions of the Indian state such as 'Nagas are divided', 'they have been bought by us with money and wine', etc., reveal the conditions in which the hegemonic rule of India can continue. This over-determination by a hegemony is a mode of representation in which it sustains the deprecated image of the dominated, while it misrecognizes the impossibility of keeping Nagas under domination. This ambivalence of the Indian state imposing a structure, an order of things, which it inevitably is incapable of sustaining only demonstrates the objective conditions under which insurgency could grow to such a stage. The supervision conducted by the surveillance on the various 'rebel' groups of the North-East, which completely circumscribes them, is carried out by the police, intelligence and the army in an urban or rural space. It falls on everybody as their movements are controlled and their lives confined, patrolled and surveiled. Everyone is a suspect and subject to interrogation, raids, search and arrest, and this mode of functioning of the state elicits retaliation from insurgents. The state fully takes note of reactions to its preparedness from insurgents and tries to nab them in their moves to strike back. In the parapolitical, the populace makes a strategic choice to pursue the self-determined undertaking to resist such abnegations of its presence caught between the crossfire, and it alters its position in relation to the warring parties to design its own freedom. Given this kind of scenario, the liberating imagination of freedom moves primarily from 'repression' in order to recover its 'self'. The situation can be redescribed in terms of carving out a free space for identification and construction of discriminatory knowledges that depend on 'presence of difference' that provides a process of splitting and placing multiple/contradictory belief at the point of enunciation of subjectivities. This is a process relevant for the emergence of 'nations-from-below' which engage themselves in a process of 'splitting into multiple/contradictory belief' and keep on oscillating between positions. The collective or community of people in the North-East is located in an active space of ambivalence, in simultaneity with its multiple positions. In the course of a struggle, the redemptive imagery of freedom is an imagery to fulfil the desire to occupy simultaneous subject positions within and without the dominant space (Thiong'o, 1993: 27–28).[23]

Therefore, the adventure of insurgency into terrains of unfamiliar nationhood and international spaces, where they are de-recognized, often turns out to be a misadventure and the relief comes through negotiations with the state. The vision of a liberated North-East is such an image that negotiates between the empirical presence of the Indian state and its exiled consciousness of nationhood. It bears the simultaneous tendency of moving in and out of the defined terrains of power. It traverses the border between the defined limits of nation and the 'foreign', it bridges the gap between the state and the nation. Through such a positioning of itself in the in-between spaces, it subverts the regular and ordered political discourse of the state, which aims at stabilizing such moves.

Notes

1. This distorted self-image is conceived in terms of a colonial power, in this case the Indian state. For details see Parag Kumar Das, *Swadhinatar Prastab* (Pamphlet in Assamese), Guwahati: Seuj Sathirtha Prakashan, 1993, pp. 1–3.

2. Aboriginals are the original settlers of a place whose settlement dates prior to settlement of communities who are represented in history. In contrast the original settler's history and culture are usually suppressed under the regime of the later settlers. Also, aboriginals are appropriated as lower castes or tribes within the culture and society of later migrants. See Partha Chattopadhaya and Gautam Bhadra (ed.), *Nimnabarger Itihas* (in Bengali), Kolkata: Ananda Publishers, 2001, pp. 33, 39.

In contrast, indigenous peoples are those aboriginals who are not yet appropriated within a dominant culture and who maintain their marked socio-cultural difference with the settlers who came later than them, not only in terms of a distinct social structure and religion, but also crucially in asserting their difference. See the *International Working Group on Indigenous Peoples Yearbook, 1998*, Copenhagen: United Nations Publications, 1998.

3. The communities engaged in a struggle against the visible governance by the nation-state themselves constitute a space that the dominant discourse is unable to represent. This is the source of self-determination as opposed to official notion of sovereignty. For a detailed understanding refer to Claude Lefort, 'The Question of Democracy', in his *Democracy and Political Theory*, Cambridge, MA: MIT Press, 1988, pp. 9–20.

4. One such example of struggle is anti-merger movement by a large number of civil society organizations of Manipur led by the All Manipur Students' Union (AMSU). The movement bases itself on knitting together folklore, legend, myth and events that go to show how India legalised inclusion of Manipur into it. See M.C. Birla Meetei, 'Anti-Merger Movement', *N-E Sun*, 14 November, 1996, p. 6.

5. Brief Statement on Naga Struggle by Naga Students' Federation in All India Peoples' Resistance Forum International Seminar, 16–19 February, 1996, New Delhi.

6. Clifford Geertz explained this in his book, *The Interpretation of Cultures*, New York: Fontana, 1993, pp. 23–25.

7. Text of the Sixteen Point Proposals of the Peace Mission, 1964; see no.12.

8. Statement of the National Socialist Council of Nagaland, 3 January 1984.

9. *Manifesto of the National Socialist Council of Nagaland*, Oking: NSCN, 1987.

10. *Shepoumaramth Regional Church Bulletin* reprinted in *The Shepoumaramth in the Naga National Movement* (Shepoumaramth: Government of the People's Republic of Nagaland, 1995, pp. 225–28.

11. Manifesto. op.cit.

12. 'Political Unconscious' is coined in the sense of Freudian 'unconscious' that acts at the level of fear or obsession in lieu of a thoroughly rational determination of a perspective. To read in detail refer to Fredric Jameson, *The Novel as the Political Unconscious*, New York: Routledge, 1992.

13. *Manifesto*, op.cit.

14. Isak Chisi Swu's Speech, *NE-Sun*, 1–14 April, 1997, p. 9.

15. Isak Chisi Swu's Speech, op.cit.
16. Yumnam Rupacahandra, 'Kuki-Paite Clash' , *The NE-Sun*, 15–31 July 1997, p. 6.
17. Bodo Sahitya Sabha has affirmed about the non-Sanskritic origins of the Bodo language and identified with languages like Sonowal Kacahari and Garo as sister languages.
18. P.S. Dutta, in a personal conversation with Prasenjit Biswas in August 1994 made these points about construction of boundaries and the ever mobile structuration of the ethnic imagination.
19. 'We Discourage Communal Violence': Interview with Meiraba Luwang, *The NE-Sun*, 1–14 July 1997, p. 18.
20. Statement by ULFA at the All India Peoples' Resistance Forum's International Seminar, 16–19th February, 1996, New Delhi.
21. Benedict Anderson, *Imagined Communities*, London: Verso, Duke University Press, 1983, pp. 22–36 discusses such linking up of memories of living spaces and the experience of simultaneity in time.
22. *Manifesto*, op.cit. Simultaneous subject positions within and without of the dominant space is employed in analysing the strategies of ethnic mobilizations. One can refer to Pierre Nora's works on memory as the mobilizing factor; see Pierre Nora (ed.), *Realms of Memory: The Construction of the French Past, Vol.1 Conflicts and Divisions* (translated by) A. Goldhammer, New York: Columbia University Press.
23. Ngugi wa Thiong'o, *Moving the Centre: The Struggle for Cultural Freedoms*, Oxford: James Currey, 1993, pp. 27–8.

5

Shades of 'Colonialism'

Contextualizing United Liberation Front of Assam (ULFA)

Categories such as 'colonialism' assume a different meaning in the context of the claims of distinct nationalities and ethnic groups of North-East India. In a field of contest between nationalism and its counter-ideology, ULFA posits a dehistoricized presentation of the dominant national ideology in order to counter it with a parallel and contesting 'nationalism' (Das, 1983).[1] ULFA contextualizes itself between colonialism and nationalism and circumscribes the field with an affront against retrogressive colonialism, described as occupation by India (Mahanta, 1994b: 3–4).[2] ULFA declares:

All the political parties protect the agenda of India's occupation, covering up their inability to develop Assam as they had declared they would through their smoothly scripted manifestos. They never accused India of its colonial occupation, which is the root cause for the underdevelopment and overall plight of Assam. Occupation India has been wantonly draining away our resources, bending the economy of Assam on to its knees. Markets of Assam are flooded with the consumer goods from other parts of India, which are made of the raw materials drained from Assam. Demography has been crushed by the influx of illegal migrants. Nevertheless, the collaborator governments never open the Pandora's box of their master's because they know very well that there are no alternatives in the hands of the ill-fated people of Assam, but to choose from any one among them under compulsion, to fill the vacuum of Dispur after every alternative five-year-term.[3]

ULFA is a group that wishes to enter a new ideological fold. This clash of ideologies is its legitimizing rationale. It reverses the opposition between nationalism and colonialism by juxtaposing the two as 'colonial nationalism', from which it seeks to recover the 'nation' in its undistorted form. Therefore, the site of its struggle is the dominant fantasy of a 'nation' (Connor, 1994: 90–91)[4] which conceals its 'colonial inclusion' and suppression by an 'integrated pluralism' (Ibid.: 102) and reveals itself in blatant exploitation and oppression of nationalities within itself (Horowitz, 1983: 21–25). Thus, ULFA purports to liberate the Assamese nation from the yoke of Indian colonialism. It employs a reversal of the explicit modes of domination present in the ideology of nationalism, altering the category 'nationalism' to 'colonialism'. Ironically, the national identity of the Assamese in the ULFA discourse derives its ontology from the yoke of so-called Indian colonialism and seeks its liberation by its desecration (Bordoloi, 2001: 17–18). It is a mode of destabilizing the dominant ideology of nationalism and then reinvesting its conviction into a different nationalism in order to liberate the nation from colonialism.

DISCURSIVE STRATEGIES OF ULFA

The reinvestment of nationalism in a form of 'Right to Self-determination' in ULFA's discourse is a deconstruction of the dominant self-image of being an 'Indian'. ULFA's argument of Indian colonialism hinges upon the disclosure of the modus operandi of Indian capitalism, which operates through exploitation of the raw mineral and natural resources of Assam (Das, 1983). ULFA not only posits this drain of resources as a marker of colonialism, but it adds that the drain results into control of land and other resources in the hands of external forces, who are socially and culturally different. The drain, therefore, marks an end of one's own community right over land and all other resources. The draining of natural resources of Assam by other parts of the country means that the Indian state and its ruling elite create an internal periphery in Assam and the North-East, thereby achieving colonial control. In other parts of India the economy gains from such utilitarian activities of the Indian state and the market, as the state also invests, except in those areas which are peripheries and which are treated as zones of supply of resources. More recently, there have been a large number of such internal peripheries in every so-called prosperous state of the country that has borne the fruits of development. Such peripheries of development are a direct outcome of the center-periphery relationship within the game of development. Cases of Vidarbha, Chattisgarh, tribal belts of western Gujrat, Tehri-Garhwal and so on, reflect the universalization of peripheries in the backyard of development. It does not mean that peripheries and backyards of development shall develop if the state and markets go for greater extraction of untapped resources. When the so-called centres of development are experience a crunch of resources, they look for renewed extraction of natural and mineral resources in the peripheries. This is the reason why ULFA had recently cautioned the Government of India not to explore the river bed of Brahmaptura arguing that the Centre should not think that natural resources are unlimited in Assam, and that the Centre should desist from further depleting the already thinning resource base of Assam and India's North-East. In the case of Assam and the North-East, what adds to the woes is the suppression of popular movements and insurgencies by means of a repressive state apparatus as well as by means of maneuvering by the state in the field of culture and politics. This brute fact of exploitation by the Indian market and the state mixed with the operation of a constitutional process of legitimizing designs, such as illegal migration of people of other communities and the subsequent loss of the indigenous identity of Assam, are the evidences through which ULFA urges a resurgence of Assamese identity in a reconstructed mode. In case of Tripura too, the increasing gulf of cultural, political and economic difference between the tribals and the non-tribals is a reminder of how demographic minoritization of tribes could result in deprivation on the one hand and accumulation of power and resources on the other. What follows from such a skewed nature of development is that the tribes lose their minimal rights even though they are the original inhabitants before settlement by others. One could well say that the skewed nature of development and the repressive role of the Indian state create a colonizer-colonized relationship between indigenous and settling populations with the possibility of cultural and economic domination by settlers over the indigenous. As a response, the indigenous people strike back at the settlers, which of course results in cleansing of settler populations, most of who are again internal minorities in the tribal areas. To thwart such a diabolic situation of people versus people clashes, ULFA needed a re-assertion of an Assamese identity sensitive to the actual processes of domination and control by the Indian state machinery, which not only distorts the identity of the indigenous but turns them into instruments of violence against the minorities. ULFA, therefore, redefines Assamese identity in terms of a voluntary cultural and linguistic acceptance of Assamese language and culture. The marks of forced domination by the Indian state become the enunciative source (Chandra, 1992: 116–154) of Assamese identity. In a contemplative and retrospective identification of a historical past, the present marks of disruption are mobilized to shape the interior of the space occupied by memory. A rejection of such fractures and disruptions become the prime motivational factor towards liberation. This is how the self-conscious mobilization of the space of memory endorses its own marker of identity. Therefore, identity is drawn between the processes of the dominant and the memory spaces of the community, disjointed from each other by visible temporal and spatial gaps. An ULFA document, 'History of Assam' (n.d.), puts the responsibility on those who rule the Indian state. It states:

> They are conducting their cultural, economic and political repression under the cover of Indian constitution. With these rules and systems, the Indian government has closed all the doors to the solution of 'National Problem of Assam' establishing the right of self-determination of the indigenous peoples of Assam.

That means:

1. The right of national self-determination is not recognized in the Indian Constitution.

2. The Indian constitution and the other state systems are founded on the idea of 'one nation state' other than the character of 'multi-nation state'.

3. It does not empower any nation to adopt any eco-social and cultural planning or programme in its own motherland.

4. It does not entrust any power to the national peoples to determine the demarcation of the area where a specific nation lives unaccompanied.

5. The Constitution provides for a powerful centralized system (clauses 352, 353, 356, 360) to crush any movement organized by the national peoples to solve their problem by imposing 'emergency' without any consent of the people's representatives.

6. In Delhi, the President of India and the Governor in Assam is supreme in power; the people's power is neglected.

7. In Assam, they are enforcing different laws and acts that are discriminatory compared to rest of India (Illegal Migrants [Determination by Tribunals] Act 1983, Armed Forces Special Powers Act 1958, in Assam, Manipur, etc.).[5]

Apart from such mobilization of identifiers at the site of struggle against the dominant, one can settle with the uncanny characterization of the Indian state as 'colonial' provided it presents a strategy of problematization of the fixed ideology of the Indian state. The problematization by ULFA does not follow the classical political economy perspective of colonialism, rather, it tracks the course of subsumption of the community/nationality within the boundaries of the Indian state that conditions the compelling category of colonialism imposed from the other side. This is a cognition of one's own subjectivation within the dominant and it has nothing to do with the external political economy of such domination in the form of 'colonialism' (Bordoloi, 2001: 45–47). Thus, ULFA's perceptions of domination of its self and community is a self-conscious gazing back onto the force of subjection in which it sees itself as subjected by a dominant state. This is how ULFA's sees the Indian state as a colonizer. The political economy of such subjectivation of the community within which ULFA lives is of a kind in which ULFA cannot recover the already lost space; rather, it situates itself in that already dominated space in order to develop a form of struggle that takes it out of that space. This struggle assumes a form of articulation that resists domination in various spheres of life. In the field of economy, this resistance is much more subdued than other fields such as politics and culture, because in the former only a revolutionary class can resist it. ULFA can resist domination not in political economic terms, but in the pre-articulated positions within the community (Bordoloi, 2001: 46).

Positions such as resentment against illegal migration, deculturization and destruction of social ethos, the lived experience of all of which cumulatively put up an effective self-defence to domination that occurs in the sphere of economy. Looked at in another way, the formation of the middle class (Misra, 2000: 73) in the sphere of economy through the processes of a semi-feudal semi-colonial state neutralizes resistance to economic exploitation. Articulation at the super-structural level such as language and culture only symbolically restores these lost terrains that remain as the leitmotif of a cultural resistance to the dominant. Such a manoeuvre accentuates a greater crisis in the sphere of culture as it only prioritizes articulations centred on community and identity (Baruah, 1985: 200–01). Also, this engenders a dichotomy within the ULFA discourses, yielding to domination in the sphere of political economy while enacting resistance to such domination in the sphere of culture.

AMBIVALENCES WITHIN AND WITHOUT

This apparent ambivalence in the ULFA discourse is not even removed in its emphasis on establishing a sovereign, independent and 'socialist' state of Assam. This is because socialism merely liberates Assam from the yoke of the colonial economy of India, but does not go in for a 'dictatorship of the proletariat' as per classical Marxist formulation. ULFA merely identifies the 'peasantry' as an ally of advancing revolutionary classes and masses, the latter mostly constituted by middle class (Misra, 2000: 76–77)[6] and intelligentsia. Therefore, it opts for the mobilizational potential of peasantry as the means of liberation of the Assamese nationality. On the other hand, ULFA identifies its class enemy among the tea garden monopoly companies and traders and businessmen, manifested in their guerrilla mode of action against them. It considers such strata within Assamese nationality as an ally in the liberation struggle, who would have been otherwise enemies but for their being Assamese. The criterion of belonging to a culture, the forms of differentiation and the presence of the Other, all get obfuscated. ULFA can neither identify any communities as allies, nor do they do away with the presence of Others (Indians) in the construction of culture of the nationality. In effect, ULFA discourse on national self-determination is caught between the blinds of redefining an Assamese identity and settlement of the question of who is an outsider. Further, ULFA is ostensibly opposed to processes such as 'commoditification' of human relationships, vulgar consumerism, corruption, communalism, influx and a host of other subversions from within and without. It identifies various tribal and Aryan elements as foundational constituents of Assamese culture in order to make a unifying edifice of 'popular culture', which would be simultaneously revolutionary and communitarian in character. Tribal elements are represented by communities of Mongoloid, Tibeto-Mongoloid, Austric and Negritois origins who migrated from the eastern side of Assam. Aryan elements are represented by a small section of Brahmins who entered from the western side of Assam. ULFA's discourse of Assamese nationalism tries to accommodate the wide ranging and variegated cultural traits of such diverse communities of various ethnic and racial origins. On the one hand, the tribal elements such as language and culture of a large number of plain and hill tribes, and, on the other, the culture of syncretism adopted by prophets like Sankardeva and Ajan Fakir present a significantly multicultural and yet mutually non-antagonistic social base. As and when ULFA refers to 'people belonging to Assamese nationality', it encompasses this diversity within the fold of Assamese identity. Of course, ULFA defends these diverse non-antagonistic elements of Assamese culture by commending a historical process of assimilation that enriches Assamese language and culture. ULFA ensures that antagonistic political and social constructions on the basis of tribal, caste Hindu and Muslim identities are neutralized and resisted within the struggle for national liberation. For ULFA, Assamese identity stands as a united front at both cultural and political level. To accomplish this task of unity, ULFA invokes the peasant-agrarian social and economic base of

Assamese community that makes the diverse cultural elements blend together. This strategy of building up a national unity on the basis of social and economic support provide ULFA an easy access to cultural plurality and diversity without necessarily following the politically contesting claims of cultural identities. This accommodative character of ULFA's struggle extends the definition of Assamese identity to anyone who is ready to speak the language and accept the cultural festivals and rites that are assimilative by their very nature. For example, *Bihu* serves as the most important marker of cultural assimilation that unites tribes, caste Hindus, Muslims, adivasis tribals and all such diverse constituents of Assamese nationality. ULFA doesn't have to build up anything here, it already pre-exists as the cultural foundation of Assamese nationality assertion. What ULFA needed is a tactical mobilization of such fragments within culture. But it is also interesting to note that ULFA debunked any form of linguistic and religious communalism that can pit Assamese against the non-Assamese and Hindus against the Muslims. They consciously abandoned this path of unity till they found any antagonistic resistance from other linguistic communities. But other linguistic communities had certainly not subscribed to ULFA's ideology of Assamese nationalism, and in some cases considered it as opposed to their interests. They thought so as ULFA emphasized the priority of Assamese as a language in Assam over other languages, although this could be looked upon as an 'ideological error' inherent in the struggle for nationality rights. Although ULFA could garner a lot of support among the immigrant muslims, tribes and adivasis, it could not mobilize other major linguistic groups by its ideology.

These 'fragments' of ULFA's symptomatic resistance comprise of layers of ambivalence; the class allies and enemies are defined mostly by whether they belong within or without Assamese nationality, and thereby it represents the aspiration of the dominant comprador bourgeoisie within it.[7] As a consequence, ULFA stressed upon the 'Right of Self-determination' with reference to the distinct cultural linguistic identity of Assamese nationality. This blurring of distinction between ideologically different classes within nationality restrains ULFA from taking an oppositional position to the comprador bourgeoisie within and this sustains the structural processes that produce the latter too. Resistance revolves around the theme of presenting an 'essential' cultural core of Assamese nationality. Therefore, there is no precise determination of class allies and enemies within and without, but the only mode of determination of an enemy is decided by virtue of an apparent exploitative activity of an 'individual' or a group of monopoly houses. This whole selection mechanism is centred upon a distinction between Assamese/non-Assamese, national/foreign. Therefore, the whole discourse of ULFA is caught between a reflexive comprador bourgeoisie resentment and its devious links with discrete elements of dominant Indian nationhood. The terrain of cognition of ULFA for deciding the course of political action, therefore, remains 'nongeneric', rather, it focuses on the specific and the discrete that allows flexible positions within the culture of Assamese national identity (Satirth, 1996).

Class is diffused in the category of nationality and therefore colonialism in the ULFA discourse is an insignia for an opposition to pan-Indian nationalism. The relationship between colonialism and nationalism is set in contradiction in terms of liberation of oppressed nationalities (Chandra, 1992: 116–154). These oppressed nationalities appear as colonized in the sense of their dependence and suppression within a colonizing dominant ideology. The knowledge about such dominance comes through the visible and the perceived modes of oppression of a nationality (Ibid.: 134). There is a power of feeling this 'anonymous' (Hooghe, 1997: 27–43)[8] regime of oppression through the subjectivation of a nationality that gets articulated in the sense of being colonized. This gets further expressed in the experiences of marginalization and deprivation within the rule of the Indian state, but then the sublimation of such experiences take a 'nationality' route because of historicity (Misra, 2001)[9] of the modern formation of Assamese nationality. The agenda, therefore, becomes the liberation of Assamese nationality in order to simultaneously overcome its fragile interior and to consolidate the positions of various sections of the masses and subcultures within it. The agenda of 'secession' and 'independence' from the Indian state also forbear concerns for acquiring a stable identity/nationality in order to negotiate this identity on equal terms with other dominant factions of the Indian nation. Minimally, it seeks that the nationality is capable of withstanding the explicit moves to dominate it. As an auxiliary to such worries, the hold over productive forces, capital and political power is also a contingency, and to accomplish which total independence is necessary. However, the elitist Indian state refuses to listen; instead it intends to remove the specific nationality aspirations reflected by ULFA to facilitate a uniform regime of Indian capital and polity. Therefore, intending to resolve such aspirations within its framework, the Indian state inevitably drowns such worries into some neutral and universal criteria of development (Roy Burman, 1990: 25–29).[10] It aims at weakening the historical specificity of a nationality at its bottom in order to join it to a common national identity at the top, which leads to the dominance of the stronger sections of various nationalities upon others who are already kept behind (Phukon, 1985: 80–95). As discussed in earlier chapters, the more the Indian state tries to tighten its grip over such nationalities through several mediating/ persecuting processes, the more such nationalities attempt to subvert such subordinating moves and carve out a different space for themselves.

THE NATIONAL QUESTION

Ironically, those nationalities that historically were a part of anti-colonial struggle to liberate India from the yoke of the British Raj feel subdued and muted within the post-colonial Indian nation-state. Moreover, the assumption of greater authority over the Indian nation-state by certain dominant nationalities is directly opposed by the smaller nationalities, which is felt more acutely in the superstructure than in the structure itself. Various nationalities negotiate their desires through the superstructure, and the only mode of such negotiation is predominantly political. Therefore, such nationalities also politicize their aspirations by waging a political struggle against forms of domination. This limitation at the level of politics and at the level of superstructure produces greater 'structural crises', because it underdetermines the form of the structure.[11] Given this state of affairs, ULFA's assertion of aspirations of Assamese nationality appears as a structural phenomenon because it interrogates the very structure of the state in negotiating such aspirations. It identifies the structure of the state as 'colonial' because of its lopsided positioning of the dominant at the 'Centre'. ULFA's discourse of resistance not only resists the dominant but it refuses to accept conditions of the dominant to place itself under its supervision and normative control. From the perspective of the Indian state, there is a crisis of legitimization. It cannot give a discursive legitimacy to ULFA. The Indian state lacks a corresponding emancipatory principle (Sachdeva, 2000)[12]; it merely tries to produce such identities as citizens without recognizing the discursive reproduction of their imagination and specific cultural life. In its diffused public space, the state produces these identities as 'mass' or 'public', disorienting the space of their 'life world' contexts (Mukhim, 1996: 31).

This articulation of cultural modernity within the nation-space of the post-colonial Indian state abstracts various nationalities and their particular cultures into a common identity, articulated through a common genealogical and mythical narrative that tries to unify cultures. This mode of abstraction develops a 'superior' yardstick of value and culture arrived through a sequence of sacrifices to which cultures of various nationalities are assembled in vindication. Such variety or diversity appears to be the expression of what is abstracted out of it in the nation-space. This metaphysics of the Indian state melts the concrete content of various small and distinct cultures in such a way that such cultures appear only as a phenomenal form of what is abstract or metaphysical. This inversion from the 'particular' to the 'universal' by the state shapes the attitude towards those distinct cultures as a part of the great Indian mosaic. Their distinctions appear only as marked characteristics within the nation-space. This is how the 'ideological state apparatus' of the Indian state appropriates and negotiates between various nationalities. ULFA launches an ideological battle through this terrain of appropriation, identifying the grids. One very important grid is creation of a 'standard' by the dominant Indian discourse that places the nation above nationality (see Chapters 2 and 3). The same also puts national culture above the culture of nationality and this is nothing but what Amilcar Cabral (1970) has called conversion 'by the ideology of the nation'.

ULFA's struggle for the liberation of Assamese nationality urges the people, especially the elite and the intelligentsia, to dispel that superior standard and reaffirm the glory and dignity of Assamese culture. Cabral has called this recalling as 'reconversion' in the process of national liberation, which for our context shall only mean reawakening of one's own ethos after colonization brings in the stark experience of loss of a distinct national identity. Cabral's idea, that reconversion happens after the colonized elite realize that they are not autonomous, is a revival of an idea of nation that existed in the pre-colonial past. How reconversion happens could be understood from ULFA's argument that Assam lost its independence in 1826 after the Burmese aggression. The question posed by the Naga nationalists about how the long stretches of frontier, which were neither India nor Burma, could disappear into India and Burma after 1947 generates an idea of a homeland free from the rule of external powers. Such references to pre-colonial get imbricated within the idea of a national identity that precedes the current national identity of being an Indian. This happens primarily because Indian nationalism never emerged from the margins but it always conceived a mainstream as its ideological origin. In this context, Naga or Assamese nationalism, even if they wish to be a part of mainstream nationalism, cannot be because of historical differences. Cabral points out that regeneration of the idea of nation on the part of a colonized elite is conditioned by the mainstream nationalist ideology recognized by the colonial rulers. He further points out that contra mainstream notion of an independent and self-ruled homeland is imagined by one's own variety of nationalism. ULFA's self-reflexive gaze on itself as being a colonized nation inside the nation-space of India generates a spectre (Pakem, 1996)[13] of 'internal colonization' in terms of lived experience. The nature of 'internal colonization' is that of producing victims of nationality oppression within and parcelling out of resources from within. ULFA points out the difference of colonization of Assam and Assamese by the Indian state in terms of the nature of subjugation: Assam remains non-self-governing as it is both geographically separate and ethnically distinct from the country administering it.[14] ULFA does not consider the presence of Assamese nationality within the existing machinery of the Indian state as self-governing. The reason lies in its drawing of cultural and political boundary in terms of Assamese nationality rights. Further, the presence of other Indian communities in the state machinery signifies, for ULFA, a different national identity of the state. The Indian state, for ULFA, represents not the sovereign interest of

Assamese nationality, but exists only to establish hegemony of an Indian ruling class over Assam and Assamese. The *being* of the colonized sees itself here as enslaved in the chains of various legitimate political and economic processes. The hallmark of internal colonization is the creation of a comprador class which allies with the external ruling class, and it is controlled by that external ruling class, with a legitimately created state. The state gets structured in this way: (*i*) it monitors transactions between the 'national bourgeoisie' situated at the apex of its ruling machinery and the 'local/regional bourgeoisie' mediating the siphoning off of resources from below; (*ii*) at every level of such mediation the state extends its ruling machinery. As a result of this two-level operation, the state gets organized from the bottom through a nexus of its agencies and the stratum of bourgeoisie. Apart from this physical structuring of the state, it assumes the form of an organic ideology in which it subsumes its constituent allies. The ideology of the nation, thereby, percolates a sense of belonging, reverence and obligation at various levels of the structure. What is interesting to note is that this is happening in Assam but not in Nagaland. The reason lies in the crucial difference of pre-existent cultural contact between Assam and the Indian subcontinent, and Assam's participation in the anti-colonial struggle launched by the Congress. In case of Nagaland, there was no such mobilization during the course of the freedom struggle of India. Of course, in the case of Assam, its inclusion within independent India acts as a source of critical evaluation of what Assam and the Assamese gained from such inclusion. Contrastingly, the movement for integration of Manipur in India is looked upon by a large section of Meiteis as an acceptance of cultural and political hegemony of the Indian nationalism. But mere acceptance of Indian nationalist ideology is seen in no way an achievement of the rights of the community. Rather, it is linked with emergence of Vaishnavism that relegated the indigenous religion of Meiteis to the background by a process of Sanskritization. Rejection of the Sanskritized cultural traits is equated with rejection of Indian culture and, in effect, inclusion within India. In a very different way, the ideology of the nation, therefore, needs to hold together the disparate nationality interests through a nexus with various apparatuses of the state. The structure of the state plays a performative role in facilitating the investment of nationalist ideology at various levels, starting from macro communities to micro groups, families and individuals. What is 'nationalist' from the perspective of the Indian state is an attitude of conformism to this structure of the state. As Indian nationalism further presupposes a territorial integration, support to the structure of the state assumes a totalistic form as transcendence of nationalism from above and immanence of nationalism within. In the case of internal colonization, this mode of domination gives the Indian state an added component, that of a permanent supportive class from within a culturally homogeneous group. In the absence of such a permanently supportive class in a comparatively heterogeneous cultural context, the state could give such cultures some representation, or it could play up their differences in order to neutralize them all. The state and its supportive class operate as a shield that conceals the colonizing class, and they become an internal Other within the community. The creation and consolidation of such a class simultaneously provide a political and an economic agenda: the state remains within the Indian Union and this class operates as a monetized entity maintaining economic transactions between lower, middle and upper bourgeoisie.

ULFA's agenda of nationality liberation aims to suborn this ruling class, which becomes the site of contestation between the Indian state and itself. This class suffers from the pressures of both sides: its insecurities are capitalized in the struggle for liberating the nationality.

THE CLASS QUESTION

The strategies of the liberation struggle further determine which side the class chooses to align with.[15] If ULFA stresses more on their marginalization under the dominant state, this class would respond in sympathy. The nature of its sympathy to the nationality liberation is provisional and limited. The state's accommodative strategies disorient them from a belligerent posture and turn them into a submissive entity. The discourse of state nationalism in its ideological persuasion presents a democratic-liberal ethos with its policies of development and normative sanctions. It addresses the 'people' to rise above 'narrow' considerations of culture-specific identities and to participate in that broad democratic ethos by way of exercising their will and asserting their rights (Bordoloi, 2001). The state goes for an orchestrated campaign for mobilizations and the supportive class which holds official power acts as its instruments. Contrarily, the discourse of nationality liberation also focuses on its marginalizing role and exposes the silences of state discourses (Bhuyan, 1996). Such an enunciation formulates the position of the members of the nationality as muted and subjected and it encompasses various strata, rich and poor alike, within its discursive formation. In its goal for nationality mobilization, it appropriates sentiments and feeling in a large way to mobilize members having different experiences. As discussed earlier, regarding internal colonization, the struggle for national liberation presents both a critique and a purposive assimilation of the state-sponsored comprador bourgeoisie. ULFA's discourse identifies peasantry and the poor masses as the force of liberation which can entangle the middle class and traders as well. In a conscientious critique of the exploitative economy, it introduces a denouncement of state sponsored corruption and posits the prospect of a liberated nationality free from such malaise. Moreover, ULFA's discourse externalizes the causes of such malaise to an alien presence of the Indian state, more directly the presence of alien Indian officials, businessmen, and so on. It raises the question about the legitimacy of their right to stay within Assam. This is how ULFA negates the presence of the state (Ibid.: 154). An enumeration of the flow of cash and resource outside Assam in contrast to the proportional deprivation of the Assamese people in clear and numerical terms is made.

What ULFA's discourse offers is a passive and supportive mobilization of sympathy of these supposed followers of the Indian state, the comprador bourgeoisie inside the community.[16] It is at this juncture that ULFA distinguishes between nationalities—the people primarily belonging to Assamese nationality and those who do not. This becomes necessary in order to articulate the interest of Assamese nationality and address them to rise against colonialism. Two components in ULFA's discourse illuminates the spectre of internal colonization: firstly, the question of deprivation of nationality rights considered inherent such as right over land, resource, jobs, income, and so on[17]; secondly, the question of being subdued, dominated and marginalized by others in various spheres of life. In both the necessity to re-establish the right of the nationality is emphasized. Both these heighten the necessity of acquiring the status of nation, without which there would not be any guarantee to the rights of the nationality. The Assamese elite also instinctively joins the concerns expressed in ULFA's discourse in securing nationality rights, such as rights over resources and governance. The most sustaining factor in ULFA's discourse is its successful campaign about the disability of the Indian nation-state to fulfil any of these legitimate aspirations. ULFA shows how the Indian state benefits by subjecting Assam, especially by extracting petroleum and other natural resources, rights over which are taken away from the Assamese nationality by the Indian state.[18] Therefore, any developmental and infrastructural implementation by the Indian state is explained by ULFA as a means to facilitate its exploitation of resources and furthering the development of the market to give a boost to the already emerged consumerism. The nexus of contractor-officials-businessmen both from within and outside the Assamese nationality acts as the bedrock of this process. ULFA focuses on the process to explain the phenomena of colonization rather than on the actors in order to alienate the nexus that supports internal colonization within the nationality.

THE QUESTION OF EMANCIPATION

In ULFA's discourse, what attains primary importance is the role of the Indian state in colonizing Assamese nationality within its structure, instead of the supportive class that makes such colonization possible. On the question of who is the colonizer, ULFA identifies actors and agencies outside the nationality by being oblivious of internal colonizers, the internal Other. Further, ULFA's identification of the process and causes of colonization is quite abstract in the sense that it identifies only those actors, institutions and agencies which operate as 'external' factors.[19] The mode of identification of the external enemy is always through reversing the equation of the internal enemy with the external agencies such as the Indian state. ULFA identifies the process that is responsible for splitting Assamese nationality, which disorients it from its natural rights, but such identifications are meant to be dismantled only by launching an ideological and military offensive. Needless to say, this only forces the state to build a defensive mechanism to protect such people or institutions identified by ULFA. Therefore, ULFA's formulation about internal colonialism is only a sequel to showing that Assamese nationality is marginalized or disempowered by agencies of the state and the market, but it does not go to the extent of identifying the forces that work internally for supporting such marginalization. So, one can term ULFA's thesis as 'exocolonial' instead of 'endocolonial'.[20] This typically fits into that kind of mobilization in which the mobilized group targets something as the enemy. This exteriorization of the 'enemy' is a strategy of closing ranks within and marks an all encompassing battle cry against it. Such axiomatic construction of an enemy merely operates as the source of rationalization for ULFA's movement. At the political level, such an enemy can remain a permanent target, and the Indian state becomes such a target. The hegemony of the Indian state does not only come from the political level, but depends on production of an experience of subjugation. The Indian state assumes an authority that can never be friendly, but can only be an arbiter to negotiations of its hegemonic rule. Therefore, situated within the Indian state, ULFA experiences the colonial character of the state coming from without; while from within it generates a process of reconciliation and readjustment.

The state mobilizes the colonizing factors and forces with a strategy of giving rise to dissent and a consequent reconciliation. The persistence of such a contradictory and yet singular process through the state sets the terms of resistance within its political and social space. But the possibility of shaking the ideological and moral basis of the state arises out of de-legitimization of its dominant cultural symbols. Within the closed political and social space allowed by the Indian state, ULFA displaces the dominant cultural symbols by way of essentializing an Assamese nationhood that does not derive its moral sustenance from the Indian state-nation, but garners it through the characteristics represented in the whole corpus of the 'Assamese' narrative. The configuration of 'Assamese' in the discourse of ULFA signifies the economy of colonization by making it a generic name, a name that not only produces the domesticity of counter-politics but a space, a home against dominance.[21]

Notes

1. ULFA gives a sub-nationalist version of 'economic nationalism'. As an upholder the rights of smaller nationalities, it can give its own version of economic nationalism in terms of rights over economic surplus, and ownership over natural and cultural resources. See Parag Kumar Das, *Swadhinatar Prastab* (Pamphlet in Assamese) Guwahati: Seuj Sathirtha Prakashan, 1993.
2. Harin Mahanta, *Amar Hiyat Kiyo Jwaliche Jui?* (Pamphlet in Assamese), Jorhat: Seuj Satirtha Prakashan, 1994, pp. 3–4.
3. Press release by ULFA on the eve of 1991 Parliament and Assembly elections in Assam. See brief statement by ULFA in *The Assam Tribune* (Guwahati edition), 25 April 1991.
4. The dominant fantasy of nation is expressed in apparently allowing nationality rights without territorial sovereignty. This fantasy of the ethnonational movements is analyzed in Walker Connor, *Ethnonationalism: The Quest for Understanding,* New Jersy: Princeton University Press, 1994, pp. 90–91.
5. United Liberation Front of Assam, *History of Assam* (pamphlet), n.d.
6. Udayon Misra, "The Quest for Swadhin Asom" in *The Periphery Strikes Back,* Shimla: Indian Institute of Advanced Study, pp. 76–77, where Misra discusses the peasant origins of middle class and middle class led uprisings, culminating in a concept of *Swadhin Asom* (liberated Assam).
7. Middle class leadership in movements of Assamese nationality emerges as 'comprador' or 'middlemen' between colonial masters and peasant and tribal bases of social relations. This is discussed in Sachetan Satirth, 'The Nationality Question in the North-East' in AIPRF, *Symphony of Freedom: Papers on Nationality Question,* New Delhi: All India Peoples Resistance Forum, pp. 163–70.
8. The anonymous character of the regime of oppression is discussed in Liesbbet Hooghe, 'Nationalist Movements and Social Factors: A Theoretical Perspective', in John Coakley (ed.), *The Social Origins of Nationalism,* London: Sage Publications, 1997, pp. 27–43.
9. This historicity of formation of Assamese Nationality is discussed in Udayon Misra, *The Transformation of Assamese Identity: A Historical Survey,* Shillong: North East India History Association, 2001.
10. The neutral criterion of development is part of a statist discourse. See B.K. Roy Burman, 'Land and Forest Rights' in *Seminar,* no. 366, pp. 25–29.
11. The drowning of the voice of the nationality struggles under a homogeneous regime of capital is a part of the political economy of building an

overpowering and strong state that holds a will to dominate. This is what is the structural crisis created by the politics of development. See Rafiul Ahmed and Prasenjit Biswas, *Political Economy of Underdevelopment of North-East India*, Delhi: Akansha, 2004, pp. 105–8.

12. Except adopting a policy of liberalization, the Indian state is incapable of mitigating the woes of North-East India as a region. See Gulsan Sachdeva, *Economy of the North East: Policy, Present Conditions and Future Possibilities*, Delhi: Konark Press, 2000.

13. Spectre of internal colonization in terms of 'lived experience' could be understood from identity concerns. See B. Pakem, 'Inaugural Address' in M.M. Agrawal (ed.) *Ethnicity, Culture and Nationalism in North-East India*, Delhi: Indus, pp. 19.

14. ULFA, 'National Question in Assam', in AIPRF, *Symphony of Freedom: Papers on Nationality Question*, New Delhi: All India People's Resistance Forum, pp. 153.

15. ULFA, 'National Question in Assam', op.cit.

16. ULFA's appeal for Assamese nationalism found a sympathetic following among a section of Non-Resident Assamese (NRA) in America.

17. Memorandum submitted by ULFA to United Nations on 15 June 1991.

18. In a sense, ULFA joins that line of development thinking which suggests an alternative of 'non-extractive' and 'non-colonial' nature of resource exploration. See Mrinal Miri, 'Of Fusions, Alliances and Isolation' in *Grassroot Options,* bi-monthly published from Shillong, June–July, 1997, pp. 49–51.

19. Gail Omvedt, 'Social Movement and the Demand for Autonomy' (mimeo.), NERC Special Lecture series 3, ICSSR, North Eastern Regional Centre, Shillong, 1993. Omvedt argued that for a movement for autonomy needs to take care of 'shifting identities' that grow within the movement. Instead, ULFA's identification of only external enemies is an ethnonational syndrome that goes as a problem for any movement for independence or autonomy. See pp. 9–10, 14.

20. As ULFA identifies colonial forces as external to the national identity, so their thesis could be called 'exocolonial' as opposed to 'endocolonial' that identifies the colonizer within the nation. For further discussion see Anthony D. Smith, 'The Ethnic Sources of Nationalism' in *Survival*, vol. 35, no. 1, 1993, pp. 48–52.

21. Harin Mahanta's *Amar Hiyat Kiyo Jwaliche Jui?* (1994a) states:

Guns are the symbols of our pain. But it is you who forced us to take guns, if you give me an occasion to set our hands off from its triggers, we will be grateful to you forever (...).

The addressees here are the external colonizers.

6

Nations-From-Below

An Interpretation of Life and Politics

Nations-from-below are identities that attain their autonomous positions by way of inverting the claims of the dominant nation, that is, by claiming sovereignty, territory and institutional authority for themselves. This means launching a struggle against the machinery of the state that inducts smaller identities within its fold. A nation-from-below does not make a claim of statehood, as a nation-from-above does by establishing the primacy of the state in asserting its authenticity. The authenticity of a nation-from-below lies in its parallel counterclaim based on its own cultural distinctness and is not based on the power of the state.

The counter dominance struggle of the nation-from-below in the context of North-East India raises the issue of internal colonization, as asserted by ULFA and NSCN, by the Indian state. The North-Eastern Indian communities are, therefore, sensitive to cases of deprivation by way of privileging the non-ethnic people in matters of the state, who, in turn, make it an instrument of marginalizing the ethnic people. The resistance to such a process is another characteristic of an emergence from below which pre-empts the possible consequences of dominance of non-ethnic communities upon them (Fanon, 1963; Baruah, 1991: 4–9).[1]

In the process of the inclusion of the North-East within India, a host of reactive and rigid identities embroil themselves in conflict. The colonial state simultaneously pitted such identities against each other and negotiated between them in such a way that the legitimacy of colonialism was not questioned by such identities. One of the important nationalist strategies was to uncover this colonialist manoeuvre and to free the state from banking upon planned civil conflicts. The idea of nationalist resistance was to reconstruct a harmonious civil society by bridging its internal differences in order to put up a united front against the colonial state. The nationalist forces, therefore, had to resist simultaneously the politics of culture played by the colonial state and maintain a united civil society to thwart the hegemony of the colonial state. As far as resisting the colonial politics of culture was concerned, the nationalist line of action was effective, but in their attempt to reconstruct a united civil society they had to go along the already constituted markers of differences that existed. Therefore, nationalist discourse merely lined up such identities in a counter strategy of containment of the colonial power and orienting all its ideas of reconstruction of a harmony towards resistance to the colonial power. The cultural compulsion of the nationalist discourse to forge unity among contesting communities could not draw the latter towards evolving a unified civil society, but gave them a vague sense of unity against the imposing whole of the colonial power.

This process of constructing a civil society divided between communities on the one hand, and negotiating between these communities on the other, formed the agenda of the colonial state. The creation of Excluded Area, Partially Excluded Area and a system of voting based on religion, and so on, were mooted by the colonial power to reinforce the already existing primordial bound-aries between communities. In resisting these, the nationalist discourse of the Congress Party had to devise a strategy of bringing together religious minorities, tribal and dominant Hindu caste groups within its fold and design principles that took care of each of these interests. The Congress was interested in keeping these blocs together by a common agenda of struggle against the colonial power to be a part of the wider system of governance, and it faced resistance from all those who could visualize the consequent dominance. The elite nationalist project left out the possibility of affirming distinctive cultural claims on the part of the constituents of the nationalist whole.

Consequently, historiographic and politico-ethnographic constructions of the native spaces of the North-East could not attain a phenomenological validity in terms of being true to the distinct forms of life lived in material hardship. Hermeneutical elements in such constructions were never put to any test or authentication matching the intensity of these hardships. It was the hegemonic goal which prompted these constructions. A rebel consciousness in the ethnic formation was an obvious corollary of this subversion and dominance through governance. An unfortunate and promiscuous consequence was the power acquisition game among different ethnic groups that yielded inter-ethnic violence. The state, which had no control over this ethnic conflict, based its hegemony on such conflict. A play of the ethnic rebel consciousness can be read in certain actions of interrogation of the markers of the dominant metaphor of the Indian nation. The call for boycotting national days such as Republic Day and Independence Day by the militant outfits of the North-East is an attempt to subvert the dominant national imagery. The image of the nation as the Other projected by militant outfits brings out slogans such as 'we were never a part of India', and 'we want sovereignty'. The boycott is a rejection of the process of homogenization and dominance of the advanced communities (such as major Indian linguistic communities, upper castes, political and cultural elites, etc.), though the state assumes them to be subjects of consent. The native and indigenous (which mean the people who claim to be original settlers of a place, which in the context of North-East overlap with each other) sense of history endow these communities with a different sense of sovereignty and freedom, which cannot reconcile that sense of freedom with the rise of the post-colonial Indian state, and thereby problematizes both the claim of sovereignty and legitimacy of the Indian state. This problematization undercuts the normative bonds among communities as prescribed in the rules of the state, which by implication also means an opposition to the socially-rooted dominance on which the state bases itself. The ethnic criteria of autonomy, self-subsistence and sovereignty come as a reactive factor to the state's dismissal of these and fashion a different self-identity, which is opposed to the universal national identity upholding the legitimacy of the state. In the case of the North-East, construction of identities like Zo people spread beyond Indo-Myanmar borders, greater Naga homeland including Myanmarese Nagas or even construction of a Tai-Ahom nation, appropriate territory, history and sovereignty in a much more different way than the run-of-the-mill anti-colonial nationalist narratives of the 'Indian' kind. The direct opposition between the customarily rooted indigenous system of governance and the Indian state produces a sense of marginalization and apprehension among the native communities of the North-East (Elwin, 1959: 145).[2] This situation necessitates a multiple agenda of struggle against dominance that articulates sovereignty, equal rights, development, secession, and so on, in order to make a move apparently beyond the limits of the Indian state and nationalism.

To account for this articulation of a sense of difference in laying claims of sovereignty, territoriality and community linkages beyond the boundaries of India, one can clearly distinguish the official statist-nationalism from the ever emerging claims of independence and nationhood from native communities. The official statist-nationalism differs from ethnic-nationalism of various communities in a significant way as it debunks the claim of sovereignty of those communities on the ground of inviolability of the Indian Constitution and indivisibility of Indian territory. The claim of sovereignty of ethno-nations is based upon their distinct cultural ethos, which has never been a part of the sudden recrudescence of the nation-state from the colonial past. The decolonization that flows from the emergence of the nation-state creates a situation of reaffirming a self-identity by such communities in distinct terms and this they encounter their own allies and aliens, positioning them in a distinctive way, as discussed in earlier chapters. This reaffirmation problematizes the priority of the Indian state over their ethnic affiliations, and resets the ethnic and cultural domain as prior to the defined limits of the state. This mode of positioning of an ethnic community is a symbolic negation of the superiority and primacy of Indian nationhood, which positions a state above all claims of sovereignty and independence. Indian nationalism, in its statist form blocks the space for alternative claims of sovereignty and thereby produces resentment among the ethnic communities of North-East India.

THE POST-COLONIAL NEMESIS

What is contested in North-East India is both the forging of post-colonial nationalism by selective appropriation of cultural resources of native communities and the Indian state that administers such an appropriation and encodes it as development and democracy. But the contest centres around the visible dominance of the state created through socially rooted dominance of certain communities. These communities are those pan-Indian communities who have come from other parts of the country and the Indian subcontinent before and after 1947 and maintain a coherent ethnic, linguistic and cultural identity much different than the tribes and communities of North-East India. Economically speaking, these communities are part of the political-bureaucratic framework and hold larger shares of the surpluses. Such communities are considered aliens, outsiders or foreigners depending upon the context of struggle. Dominance of these communities is explained in terms of their status, power, wealth and attitude towards the indigenous communities. Although they exist as minorities, yet they are part of larger pan-Indian national identity because of their cultural affinity to communities living beyond the ethnic boundaries of indigenous peoples of the North-East. From a cultural point of view, these pan-Indian communities are engaged in various activities within North-East but do not assimilate themselves with the indigenous cultures of the region. A cultural arrogance separates the two sides to the extent that there is very little inter- and cross-cultural exchange and contact (Hazarika, 1994: 354).[3] This has led the ethnic communities to struggle against both the state and those dominant communities on whose behalf the state supposedly acts against the interests of the native communities. The past poll boycott call in Nagaland by the apex body of voluntary and village organizations of Nagaland could be interpreted as an example of this contest with the Indian state on the ground that elections are not acceptable unless a solution is arrived at with the militant organizations. Two layers of legitimacy are in conflict here: on the one hand, the authority of the Indian state is questioned by boycotting the legitimate means through which the state holds its authority, and on the other, claims of sovereign citizenship for an independent Naga nation is mooted by such an action. The nation-from-above, the nation which is already constituted and designated in the Indian state, is opposed by a nation-from-below against the perceived dominance that is forcing acquiescence upon it. Quite interestingly, the soft pedalling by the Indian state on the demand for carving out the Naga dominated areas from Manipur to create a greater Nagaland was contested by other communities of Manipur, who were against the vivisection as well as the subsequent dominance of the Nagas. Here, the resistance is directed against the creation of Naga dominance and, interestingly enough, the Zeliangrong Nagas had also opposed the move to separate Naga dominated areas as they perceived the threat of dominance from other Naga tribes. This many-voiced terrain of community mobilization against dominance creates a field of resistance for those who refuse to accommodate themselves within the monolith of statist nationalism. The burgeoning anti-integration movement in Manipur demanding pre-merger status also exhibits a move beyond the limits of statist-nationalism. The contestation against dominance is carried out at a deeper level, making possible the emergence of a group identity with counterposing claims of equivalent nationalist feelings. This emergence from below against a hierarchy of dominance structured by the state from above could be coined with a neologism: nations-from-below.

An interesting example of such an emergence is the configuration called Komhrem comprising five tribes of Manipur, namely, Kom, Chiru, Aimol, Koren and Purum, which had made itself visible by way of cultural resemblance. The coming together of all such tribes is propelled by their exclusion from dominant tribal formations, in this case Hmar and Kuki. A culturally positive assertion against a perceived sense of marginalization from the exterior creates resistance against cultural exclusion and cultural dominance. In their search for distinctness, the Hmars in Mizoram had created a narrative of cultural difference from Kukis and Mizos by referring to their distinct history and cultural memory. The clash between Nagas and Kukis brings into focus the contest over territory and a kind of unreconciled sense of victim consciousness that turns into revenge in their drive for getting justice. Both Nagas and Kukis churn their memory in order to situate the events of brutalities and, without being able to reconcile, fall into the trap of violence and, counter violence. In case of Nagas too, the formation called

Chakesang comprising of Chakri, Keza and Sangtang is also an emergence from below. Such emergences portray a bottom-up expropriation of a national identity achieved through decisive solidarity between small ethnic and often clan groups based on inter-clan and inter-group relationship. Such pattern of solidarity is a reciprocation of a larger group solidarity that tries to appropriate the small and distinct identities, and at the same time empowers itself with a value of sharing certain traces of the symbolic life-world. They remain in the interstices between national identities and ethnic identities without featuring a collective clamour for rights such as their bigger counterparts, by merely resisting appropriation at the institutional level. They creatively re-invent their traditions for the purpose of resistance, while larger national groups keep referring to their past in a palimpsest mode.

What the state aims at in such situations of assertion by larger nationalities versus small group collectives is to settle its score against certain communities that question its authority and enforce peace through its penal apparatus. This is how the state reacts to violence in the civic sphere, stemming out of the conflict in the native sphere. In its avowed objective of maintaining law and order, the state intervenes to discipline the warring communities and capitalizes the sense of loss to forge some sort of reconciliation. This reconciliation remains as a loose and fragile embrace. The role of an interventionist state in neutralizing and quieting the clamour for identity that voices counterposing rights for itself goes beyond the civic statist-nationalist limits. It sponsors a kind of nationalism that suits the dominance created by the state. The accords signed by the Indian state during the 1980s with All Assam Students' Union (AASU), Tripura National Volunteers (TNV) or Mizo National Front (MNF) were all intended to strike a reconciliation with conflicting identities in order to subsume them under the state. This will of the state presents a figure of dominance through its game of power that seeks to normalize the cultural politics of identities from below. The normalization takes place by co-optation of the advanced section of these identities, and this is how dominance re-enacts itself against resistance from below.

What remains unrealizable under dominance is the independent and sovereign status of various identities, clamouring for their community aspirations. The state-sponsored nationhood thrust from above dominates over the claims of nationhood from the communities below. As a result, the radical state supplants a kind of accommodation for these claimants, while radical nationality movements incorporate a demand for secession from the Indian state. The NSCN (I-M) demand for sovereignty and the ULFA demand for an independent Assam are all but a manifestation of the reaction to the statist approach to the nationality question. Their struggle to sustain the emergence from below gives rise to nations-from-below posed against a state-nation that imposes a nationhood from above by way of granting subsidiary position to ethnic and cultural self-definitions.

DOMINANCE THROUGH DIFFERENCE

The crucial question that arises in any such emergence from below is: can the unitary Indian state-nation allow a transgression of defined limits of the statist sphere of politics without any coercion? Streamlining and adding smaller identities into a larger whole constitute the statist agenda of national integration, while smaller identities as actors in the sphere of state politics reproduce themselves in their distinctness. Democratization as part of statist agenda merely means the possibility of tying together such distinctive identities, while it excludes the possibility of contestation between such identities. As democratization through a process of contestation between the identities assumes a greater possibility of a critique of statist politics, it is often disbanded by the state. Contestation is encountered with a strategy of containment that shifts the balance of power towards the dominance of larger identities.

Nations-from-below is a metaphor for the emergence of smaller identities. The case of Bodo emergence marks such a contest against the 'dominance' of the Assamese nation and a clash with other peripheral and dominant identities such as Santhals, Bengalis or the Koch. While the contest necessarily flows out of an appropriation of the dominant, the clash emanates out of refusal to tolerate other non-dominant identities. Thus, nations-from-below, based upon socially rooted dominance, act as smaller identities, which do not appropriate each other in the manner the dominant identities do. The clash between Bodos and Santhals brings forth the issue of 'who came first' or 'who is an encroacher' only to strengthen negativelsy the cultivated 'politics of difference' while refusing to appropriate each other's cultural and political positions. There is no contest over jobs, property or land but a question of setting 'who is first', which is a relapse into a primordialist position. Such clashes therefore, produce losses on both sides of Bodos and Santhals without a contest over definite 'areas of interests'. Further, the absence of cultural appropriation between Bodos and Santhals spills over onto issues of ethnic, racial and religious differences creating fixations of the paranoid kind, an ethno-pathology.

Such an ethno-pathology is the most disconcerting failure of statist politics of culture that results in incoherent behavioural responses. Ethno-pathology perceives other communities to be the source of suffering in political, psychological and cultural terms, against which an emergence becomes necessary. The emergence is un-mediated; it is the assumption of an agonized self-empowerment over others. Looked at from another angle, it is a way of defining 'Others'. One case in point is the definition of 'immigrant Bengali Muslims' who were perceived as a potent factor that would change the balance of demography, land and community resources, and a discourse of exclusion emanates from such an imposing definition. An ethno-pathological sensitivity perceives the other in fearful terms: immigrant Muslim community as an UFO community. Such an analogy points to an omnipresence of immigrant Muslims and the ensuing danger. This ethno-pathological construction of an enemy is from a position of dominance and the victim turns into a subaltern who can't speak from his/her excluded position. The resistance of victimized communities likes Santhals, Bengalis and Kochs against such exclusion by the Bodos goes into re-defining themselves as legitimate settlers of the place. The wrath of Bodos upon them as a majority community fixes them as subalterns, as they are treated as outsiders in the Bodo areas. Again, within Bodos, the separation of Dimasas as a separate identity marks an emergence from the inclusivity ascribed to them.

Nations-from-below figure out an articulation from an excluded position in order to recuperate the self lost in alien definitions. Immigrant Bengali Muslims of the char areas of Lower Assam experienced a loss of self-definition. Their experiences of being washed away in floods, rampant governmental corruption and complete neglect from various agencies of development make them speak without an organization that can represent them. They remain as an inarticulate community known at large as migrants from Bangladesh. The Santhal, Koch and many such ethnic communities of North-East India, who began to affirm themselves through their native organizations, present a case for themselves and articulate a position of difference from the dominant. The contrast between such 'inarticulate' and 'articulate' communities looms large when inarticulate communities get defined in terms given by dominant Others, while an 'articulate' community evolves a politically correct discourse about itself. For example, immigrant Bengali Muslims, Santhals and other smaller tribal communities like Tiwa, Mishing or Moran are defined as 'immigrant', 'tribals' or 'labourers', connoting 'lower' social positions'. Thus, they experience a simultaneous inclusion as being dominated and lost in the greater articulated identities, and also an exclusion from these legitimately constituted spaces because of their self-identity. The politics of domination revolves around the assignment of a place or value within an articulated space of culture. An exclusion of Hmars, Brus or Chakmas from the articulated cultural and political space of Mizos, or an exclusion of Muslims and smaller tribal communities from an articulated space of Assamese identity, simultaneously represents their exclusion from the dominant and also their appropriation within the dominant. Rather, exclusion signifies the arrogance of the dominant from yielding a democratic space to these communities and their appropriation commands them to follow a legitimate and legitimized path of politics and culture. Exclusion further signifies the possibility of emergence of smaller identities as distinct identities, and political appropriation signifies a norm-governed situation within legitimate forms of dominant politics.

The inarticulate identities are made the subject of state discourses, such as development of Char areas or improvement of conditions of peasant folk. The state always situates these identities in an excluded space and marks them as the subject of discourse. Statist discourses then go for elimination of such excluded identities as 'references' and the exclusion is complete when they are categorized in quantitative and objective terms. Therefore, one can say that the state assumes the agency for structuring such identities into some translatable, rational and development oriented messages or public 'packages' meant for them which are diversified to accommodate 'all' into a conglomerate nation space. Such a conglomerate space is marked by mechanical reproduction of social identities and it tends to encode them in terms of statist quota and norms. For example, the statist definition of a Scheduled Tribe in India or more specifically an agency like the North-Eastern Council aiming to perpetuate the idea of a 'region', almost of a colonial type, safeguards the dependency relationship between the Indian state and the region called 'the North-East'.

As a consequence, there are two levels of discursive production: firstly, identities are aroused to organize resistance; and secondly, alternative positions are explored, an articulation of which is simultaneously ethnocentric and resistant to the state. Also within ethnocentricity, a weak response to the Other makes it feebly selfish, while a stronger and articulate response produces a sense of fidelity to the ways in which the self evolves in the community. Resistance remains as the prime motivating force for a community to turn inward and ethnocentric. Ethnocentricity of larger nation-alities tries to create an agenda for smaller groups within, but the smaller groups articulate a more authentic and rooted position. So within ethnocentricity, the choices vary. For example, while a national group like Meitieis or Assamese use the trope of 'moth-erland' and 'home of Brahmaputra', a smaller group like Chakesang uses 'cave of khezakano'. Or, for a formation like Komhrem, sharing the same route of migration becomes more important. In a certain sense, nations-from-below remain more authentic in their sense-making enterprise that draws a boundary between the real and the symbolic, while larger national groups attempt to make their symbolic a substitute for the real. The symbolic articulation of the nations-from-below draw on a layer of memory, that is, prior to being appropriated, and rediscover it in a discourse of self-identity without necessarily reproducing it as something that is their very own; while larger groups own these symbols as inherited from the past. A distinction between sense and inheritance makes the point clear in order to distinguish two distinct style of making them subjects of the larger dominant national spaces.

INSURGENCY AS A METAPHOR

'Insurgency', as it is called, signifies a subversion of the statist strategies and policies of dominance. In the sphere of culture, as we have seen, it means a rejection of the 'national' in favour of the 'native', a celebration of the indigenous and ethnic over the civic popular culture. In the case of the North-East, a greater acceptance of Western popular and media culture is also subversive of the dominant Hindi-Hindu national culture, which at the same time means consumption of modern culture by the 'natives' with their own ethnic mode of life. Insurgency establishes a naturalized affinity of the masses with those media images that present triumph of masculine and macho forces over media, systemic and governmental agencies. It induces a regime of supermen, gangsters, terrorists, spy and spy catcher flowing from Americanized industries of film and media.[4] The instant popularity of such images perpetuates the already seething discontent against the non-indigenous populace and the Indian state. The non-indigenous populace are those who have come from other parts of the country and settled in the North-East for various purposes. They are not considered as the sons and daughters of the soil. The cultural resistance also assumes a guerrilla war image against dominant cultural figures having its ready similarity with urban guerrilla figures in the media. What this pattern of cultural preference indicates is a sharp distinction drawn between one's own cultural roots and dominant cultural images. In ethnic terms, this distinction is actualized by clearly demarcating the cultural boundary of an ethnic group from others. This is demonstrated in the distinctions that exist between self-enclosed ethnic communities from others. One can observe examples of how smaller communities such as Paite, Baite, Phom, and so on, distinguished themselves from their brethren communities like Hmar, Lushei and Kuki and claim themselves as separate tribes. Similarly, distinctions of a generic inter-tribal nature such as a sense of difference existing between Khasis and Mizos presents a picture of ethnic consciousness that assumes the content of nationhood in spirit. The consciousness is based upon drawing a distinction between 'inside' and 'outside', while the 'inside' fashions itself in relation to the 'outside'.

The positioning of the self and the community requires an 'inside' to sustain its identity by way of counter position to the process of abstraction of generic markers out of their localized existence. This 'positioning' is very relevant in grasping the resistance to dominance, as it operates as a network of power that fixes dominance of an identity to a definite position within the network. The 'state', acting as an 'outside' with its national network of power, forces a community of the North-East to position itself inside the network by way of distinguishing itself from an 'outside'. This is how a community places itself in the signifiers of domination and sees itself different from others. In the context of cultural reproduction of the community, the ethnic signified plays the role of retaining a mark of self-identify and difference simultaneously without merging itself with a generalized reproduction of the nation. Often it clashes with the dominant Others without diluting its self-identity.[5]

This positioning of the self in various indigenous communities takes a metaphoric meaning in designating the 'outside'. In the context of the North-East, the metaphor 'outsider' assumes a crucial importance in relating itself to the state. 'Outsider' becomes the code for settling scores with other communities in which the state is dragged in to address the unfulfilled aspirations of a community. Often, 'outsider' becomes the synonym for identifying an alien state machinery in tandem with the business establishment, all of whom stand together in depriving the region of many essential developments. The coding of 'outsider' on the issues of granting citizenship to Chakmas, Nepalis and Bengalis acts as a legal camouflage to manoeuvre the state and reclaim the indigenous authority. The conflict over citizenship sharpens as the claim of indigenous rights is posited to be greater and wider than the universalizing field of citizen rights that treat everyone on the same footing. 'Outsider' encodes the apprehension of the native communities on the unreserved extension of citizenship rights in the ethnic habitats of the North-East, producing many encroachments. The sense of being an 'Indian' is constructed by the citizenship acquired from the state to enter the ethnic domain of communities in the most intriguing ways. 'Outsider' as a metaphor signifies the internalization of citizenship among the ethnic communities of the North-East.[6] Pointing at the 'outsider' further signifies occupation of a space within the space of the nation. This further makes it possible to enunciate the relationship of dominance between state and people articulated at the level of common sense. The imagination of indigenous nationalism articulates both an inside and an outside (Mignolo, 2000: 5–7).

The resistance of the ethnic communities expresses itself into something legitimate from the perspective of the state. This legitimate camouflage is utilized in demanding certain rights that have been hitherto denied to it. Through such encoding of legitimate rights, the communities articulate their sovereignty. For example, the demand of the Bodoland Autonomous Council for inclusion of many villages of the controversial kind in the proposed 'Bodoland' shows the legal battle that a surging ethnic group can fight with the state.

This kind of legitimate demand often occasions a tirade against others from extremist factions. The state aims at resolving such demands through both deliberative and coercive means. The legitimate demands of ethnic community gain legitimacy by way of questioning certain principles and acts of the state that supposedly go against the genuine rights and aspirations of the indigenous people. This critical legitimacy of the ethnic movements earns legitimacy in the consideration of the community, which often questions the authority of the state in the sphere of norms. This requires an agenda of counter-legitimacy that is attained by way of rejection of norms and laws framed by the state and by way of affirming the specific ethnic standpoint. Such counter-affirmations often clash with inviolable essentials laid down by the state. The logic of insurgency is such that in distinguishing an inside from an outside and in encoding its message in a legitimate demand it aims at subverting the essentials of the state like 'sovereignty' and 'territoriality'. In the context of the North-East, it occurs by way of affirmation of national rights and a separate homeland for an ethnic community, which produces the condition of displacement of the ideological and ethnic basis of the state. It primarily counterposes the concept of a unified civil society and unitary civic sphere of rights, which by implication induces an independent claim of national right with sovereignty unto an ethnic group (Nag, 1993: 1521–32).[7] The response of the state is counter-insurgency violence aimed at curbing the struggle of smaller ethnic groups.

THE RESPONSES OF THE STATE

The consequence of this struggle between legitimacy and counter-legitimacy is the struggle between an ethnic community and the state. The mobilization of insurgency is counteracted by the state by way of de-recognizing the claims of nations-from-below. There have been allegations of atrocities and counter atrocities from both the battling sides. The cases of torture and atrocities produce a sense of warfare between the state and the communities: the centre of the struggle remains a lasting and continuous process of violence and counter-violence that takes turns to events of state sponsored atrocity as well as atrocities on ethnic minorities. The state attributes militant violence as 'terrorism', while it does not recognize the demand for recognition of ethnic communities in its operation for peace. One of the Amnesty International reports entitled *India 'Operation Bluebird': A Case Study of Torture and Extrajudicial Executions in Manipur* (October 1990) stated:

> The testimonies cited...demonstrate that witnesses giving evidence in court face a real risk of repercussions. This is one of the reasons why victims have only rarely complained to the civilian courts, even though reports of human rights violation in the North East have been frequent. Another reason is that the victims live in inaccessible regions with poor communications; the only contact many have with outsiders is the Army. Many are illiterate, and they often do not know how to approach the courts, and do not have funds to bring legal action and believe that petitions would not be accepted. Although villagers have complained to the civilian authorities such as the local police or deputy commissioner, these authorities have often said that they felt powerless to do anything about matters concerning security forces that are controlled by the central government. Finally,...section 6 of the Armed Forces Special Powers Act prevents citizens from bringing a case against the security forces without prior permission from the central government (cited in Hazarika, 1994: 373).

Such 'subjects' of state violence heighten the already embedded structural lacks such as illiteracy, poverty and backwardness on the one hand, and legal blockage on the other, accentuating the refusal to recognize collective aspirations and widening the base for collective struggle for redemption from state repression (Bhuyan, 1991).[8]

Ethnic cleansing by targeting an ethnic minority is also a surrogate of this dominance and its corresponding surge for liberation of an ethnic community. The cases at Nellie and Kokrajhar in Assam and Bilonia in Tripura present the misplaced anger of ethnic communities on minorities, who are neither properly protected by the state nor secure socio-economically. The persecution of such minorities could be taken as a displacement of ethnic aspirations in annihilation of fellow human beings, who as settlers never enjoy privileges that are unattainable by an indigenous community.

Is there a way to re-describe this situation? One can notice the reactivity against dominance expressed in terms of encroachment of a community's rights and also in terms of blaming other communities vis-à-vis the state. In all its expressions, it assumes a subaltern position in articulating a position of difference and subordination where the primary target remains the state, while a different cultural group and its dominant image produces a reaction at the secondary level. These two simultaneous struggles to resist totalization within the 'nation' and an affirmation of difference by creating an inside invert the dominant discourse (Avineri, 1968: 32–33).[9]

This inversion of the dominant discourse prioritizes nation-from-below as a possible alternative position that is subordinated from a position of nation-from-above. The nation-from-below expresses itself not through the state conduits but by striking against an established harmony by way of extreme means. The affirmation of a subaltern ethnic group negates the state and designs an expression for itself in order to make it visible. It seems that the selective struggle with the state, claim of national identity by an ethnic community and its politics of difference have to be filled with events of violence.

THE OLIGARCHY OF VIOLENCE

Violence plays an important role in instilling ethnic markers in terms of difference. But a politics of difference puts into play the limits of the already evolved and legitimized social identities to generate a contest over those already settled markers and norms. This whole process signifies the possibilities of violation or violability of a so far sacrosanct national self-definition and a way of overcoming strictly defined identities by certain interpretation and re-interpretation of boundaries. A definite amount of sensitization accompanies this process of reconfiguration of ethnic boundaries. The felicity of being reconsidered as a distinct entity through a performative re-appropriation and demonstration of one's own heritage is like recasting/re-embodying oneself with a gesture of identity, something new and yet so passionately drawn from 'a source of collective identification'. Within the nation-space, such an emergence means tangible re-drawing of physical and political boundaries, with which the state should come to terms. The coming to terms of the state flags off a politics of consolidation in echelons of power by various identities. This becomes a moment of internal and external contest for various identities. But what the state peremptorily does is to stabilize the fuzziness of ethnic and cultural boundaries, that is, fuse them into categories of power/authority. This logic of the state runs counter to the logic of identity politics (Connoly, 1991: 64–65).[10]

For the Indian state, accommodation of emergent identities is directed to strengthen and widen the space of national identity. The state reinforces a national identity over contesting identities without addressing the issues of contestation, offering politics of piecemeal redressal for singular communities that increase separatist tendencies (Datta, 1993).[11] The Indian state projects the dominant identity as the only legitimate identity that can resolve contestation between identities. We can call it 'identity-given-by-the-state'. Culture-specific identities contest the state because of the latter's partial and preferential inclination to some dominant identities, interests of which are protected under the universalistic identity given by the state. The state, in fact, gets identified with such dominant social identities and it can no longer protect the interests of smaller identities. Therefore, smaller identities need to negotiate from a subaltern position as imposed on them by the state. Other identities are delegitimized even though they are recognized as Others. Such delegitimized identities are forced to articulate a case from a marginalized and excluded position. The dominant discourse that pushes them outside the legitimized sphere of culture and politics is contested by these delegitimized identities from an excluded subaltern position. Their position of being excluded creates a space for interrogating the legitimized identities, and their exclusivity.

The dominant identities created by the Indian state cobble together as the markers of a unified, singular state-community and fuse it into a well-formed entity. Such markers are chosen selectively in order to reduce distinctiveness of various segments within a community and give it a common colour. This process of muting of identities by the rationale of domination from the state makes it a state-nation or nation-from-above. The naming of an Assamese identity and acceptance of its demands by the Indian state, which is a result of the six-year long Assam movement (1979–85), strengthened both the Indian national identity as well as appropriation of smaller identities within a conglomerate Assamese identity. In the case of a state like Tripura, recognition of tribal and non-tribal identities by the Indian state is a continuation of the same process of strengthening the national identity as well as the dominant identity. But such state-sponsored dominant identities involve a picture of contestation. Cases like Assamese, Mizo and Naga identities refusing to be just included within Indian identity without due recognition of their aspirations are the still contesting ones. Therefore, the successful and unsuccessful attempts of the Indian state to incorporate such identities within a conglomerate national identity remained a mere statist appropriation, while the identities resisted such appropriationist tactics. Therefore, statist appropriation merely produced state national identities, while distinct national identities of such communities remained as nations-from-below retaining a distinct indigenous form of their own.

THE CRITICAL POLITICAL CONTEXT

Against the appropriation by the state of various social identities in the network of nationalizing them, various such identities register their emergence. The United Liberation Front of Assam asserts that Assamese nationality is formed by the united struggle of various smaller communities of Assam against the landlord-bourgeois-imperialist forces (see Chapter 5). ULFA further cites the case of the 1962 Indo-China War to point out Nehru's disowning of Assam in his All India Radio address to the nation where he famously pronounced good-bye to Assam, as the Chinese army entered areas near Tezpur (Hazarika, 1994). This was more shocking to the people of Assam than being under Chinese control. The supreme sacrifice of Maniram Dewan, Piyali Phukan, Kanaklata, Kushal Konwar and scores of martyrs did not matter as Assam was denied its rightful place in the scheme of federal and independent India (Misra, 2000: 62–153). The nationalist leadership from the mainland looked upon Assam as an appendage. Even the sacrifice of a large number of people during the Non-cooperation and Quit India movements, according to ULFA, could not convince the mainland's leaders of Assam's contribution to India (AIPRF, 1996: 151–55); Hobswam, 1992: 12).[12] Further, the role of the central government in turning a blind eye to Assam's problems like underdevelopment and exploitation of Assam's resources by various central agencies have only compounded the alienation of masses, who suffered this plight to sustain the continuation of Assam within India. This distinction from pan-Indian history and economy provides the objective conditions for assertion of Assamese national identity as distinct from that of Indian. Regarding the Naga assertion, a similar politics of statist appropriation of national right is countered and resisted. Nagas strike a different note against statist appropriation. The chief of the NSCN (I-M) army stated:

> We are committed to peace and we'll not go back on it. But we have repeatedly made our mind known to the Indian leaders that we'll not buy peace at the expense of our rights...if we are betrayed, will not hesitate to betray (Atem, 1998).[13]

In the context of the Naga struggle, with the experience of being dispersed in many terrains, Naga leaders especially refer to the occupation of the southern part of Nagaland by the Indian army and the Indo-Burmese joint offensive against Nagas as examples of systematic statist appropriation. From these experiences the struggle derives its political content of unification of Naga inhabited territories and building up of a joint front with organizations of other dominated tribes. This whole attempt overcomes the limits posed by statist boundaries and it opens up the possibility of attaining freedom for all Nagas in their own homeland. It also produces a counter discourse to the dominant state discourse, which negates the possibility of a solution in terms of the Naga struggle. The current negotiations between the emissaries of the Indian government and NSCN (I-M) centres around the unification of Naga-dominated areas under one administrative unit, which is a reverse appropriation of the statist agenda of creating Nagaland. It simultaneously highlights the tenuous logic of territorial integrity of Naga dominated areas, to which the state of Nagaland proved to be a mere anathema. It also demonstrates the possibility of removing the strict political boundaries that Indian state has erected. The long struggle in Manipur against the NSCN (I-M) claim of the unification of the Naga-inhabited territories of Manipur brought out another interesting issue of inclusion of Manipur hills and plains within one single state vis-à-vis integration of Manipur within Indian territory. One of the fundamental flaws of integration of the North-Eastern Indian states gets exposed on such an occasion as the linguistic basis of making a state comes under question. Apart from the reference to political consensus during inclusion within India, there is no other justifiable basis of either making a state or its inclusion within the Indian Union.

In the case of the Mizo struggle, the peace accord signed between the Mizo National Front and the Government of India still serves to legitimize the Mizo struggle for independence and its subsequent settlement within the framework of the Constitution. But in the absence of proper devolution of state power and representation of smaller identities within the fold of the Mizo accord, the accord seems to have failed to reign in Hmars and Brus in Mizoram.

In all such cases, the feature of appropriation of an ethnic community by the Indian state through formation of a defined identity was contested by affirming ethnically specific ways of life by identities like Assamese, Naga and Mizo. The need for affirmation arose from contesting the culturally dominant identity that came to be imposed upon them through a statist mechanism. The statist concept of Indian nationhood did not have any legitimate grounding within these communities except by the wielding of state power. The percolation of influence of other dominant ethnic communities in the civic sphere also became a contestable terrain for native communities. So, there was a three-fold mediation from above by the state:

(*i*) Construction of a defined ethnic identity in and through state power.

(*ii*) Legitimizing such a state-defined identity by including it within an Indian identity.

(*iii*) Percolating dominance of other communities in the ethnic sphere and thereby trying to merge the line between the ethnic and the civic.

All the three mediatory moves by the Indian state came from above, as none of these could grow from within. These produced a spectre of domination upon the native, haunting him/her by the apprehension of being submerged by other dominated communities. This created an effect of being dominated and disempowered among various native communities of the North-East. Correspondingly, they responded by way of contesting the mechanism and the effect of such a statist-nationalist process from above. The attempt of the state to construct a defined identity was contested by constructing a self-definition with greater latitude. 'Nationalism' in the case of various North-East communities assumed a sovereign and independent homeland, undercutting the threads of Indian statist-nationalist definition. So far as legitimization of such well-defined identities within the state was concerned, the identities interrogated the legitimacy of the Indian state itself. Further, they questioned the formation and structuration of their community within an arbitrary political unit through their own political bodies. The dominance of others in the civic sphere became an immediate bone of contention for all such communities.

The construction of nations-from-below produced an autonomous sphere of dominance that got enmeshed with the statist mechanisms from above. The case of Bodo uprising against the dominance of Assamese community from within and the case of Hmars from within Mizos, portray that dominance of a particular section of the unified identity produces resistance from within. The politics of statist appropriation extends through dominance of the elites within an identity against which its own internal others fight. The Bodos, Kochs and tribes like Mishing, Rabha, Tiwa, etc., within Assamese identity, found themselves unrepresented and neglected. Similar is the case with Hmars of Mizoram. We have to make a distinction between cases of Bodos or Hmars with the cases of those who are excluded and delegitimized—Santhals, Bengali Muslims, Chakmas and Brus—in the process of constructing the dominant identity. The contiguous native communities became the subjects of ethnic violence precisely because the dominant communities intended to register the strength of their movement by ostracizing and cleansing them. These subjects of violence were made defenceless victims as the dominant communities debunked the legitimacy of their existence.

In the context of Bodo movement, the rage against the Santhals was paradoxical as Bodos as an ethnic minority were fighting against Assamese hegemony. Then, how could they riot against the Santhals, who are another ethnic minority? The logic of violence could be explained in terms of displaced anger. The subjects of such displaced anger are the 'new subalterns' who did not even have a language to articulate their pain. The Bengali Muslims similarly are 'soft targets' of ethnicized 'displaced anger'. One can explain it in terms of a revenge motive against the state and the dominant community, who are seen as the cause of presence of Others in one's own land. A kind of Lebensraum motif of cleansing the space from communities who are different operates in the action programme of ethnic organizations. The rage against Brus or Chakmas is also a product of a supposedly incommensurable presence of these communities in someone else's home. The case of expatriation of large number of Brus from Mizoram or Paites from Manipur presents a picture of an increasingly hostile inter-ethnic coexistence. Further, ethnic violence produces a ruptured interior of the violator's own symbolic that can never reconcile with its own existential state of being. Even if others are not there, violence is not going to cease in the process of ethnocentric identification and deepening of self, as it would produce internal differences within one's own self (Biswas, 2007). The case of self-inflicted violence in the silence of the collective in moments of critical self-reflection is a negation that is produced by the violent self (Akoijam, 2006).

A state-nation never allows various ethnic formations to grow independently in their own ethnos and so it constantly interrupts them from various sources such as economy and politics, producing clashes between communities. When issues become troubles, contestation over symbols, myths and authority remains unresolved within the parameters of civil society. The state once again comes down heavily from above to clear out the whole terrain of contest, resulting in many inter-ethnic clashes and blatant human rights violations.[14] In these melees of conflicts, what stems out is an ontological ground for clash between the mainstream dominant discourse and the marginal narratives. The recent clash (2003) between struggling ethnicities in Southern Assam Hill District of North Cachar presents a picture of the breakdown of strategic alliances between struggling communities. A clash over which outfit would own which area has been written in the blood of the innocent. There is a kind of critical isolation and difference between struggling outfits that would dampen even any state-sponsored peace process. The reason being that today or tomorrow the state has to face the mutually warring groups, a part of whose war with each other would be attributed to its discriminatory and divisive policies that would, thereby, weaken any lasting solution to clashes between the state versus the identities.

The voices of the nations-from-below are muffled by a number of factors. The most important is the dichotomy between cultural politics and democratic politics. Cultural politics seeks a space of nativity that merely accommodates constitutional values, while the civic space singularly embodying those formal-legal-juridical values exhort facelessness or rather 'the face of the other'. It is a conflict between the voice and the body, the voice being free and the body being surrounded and controlled. While the body is that of liberal democratic politics, the voice of authenticity in speaking to oneself is not responded to by the other, while the body demands a necessary response to the other. The body politic or the space of articulation denies alterity to the natives and the natives try to move away from the determinate predicates of democratic politics to a sense of identity that delivers them a promise of alterity. This promise is the new form of sovereignty based on identity with a difference to itself, a being-for-itself that is not determined by the look of the other.

Notes

1. Frantz Fanon coined the term neo-colonialism in his *Wretched of the Earth* (New York: Grove Weidenfield, 1963) to describe the strategy of national rulers to facilitate the educated elites among the natives to take over after the departure of initial colonizers. In case of North-East India, other elites from the already advanced communities of mainstream India also engaged themselves in competing with local elites. The process and its consequences are described in Apurba Kumar Baruah, *Social Tensions in Assam: Middle Class Politics*, Guwahati: Purbanchal Prakash, 1991, pp. 4–9.

2. Customary rights specify places of significance by custom for ethnic communities of North-East India. It also specifies conventions by which such rights are endowed. See Verrier Elwin, *A Philosophy of NEFA*, Shillong: North East Frontier Agency, 1959, p. 145.

3. The lack of such inter-cultural contact could be understood from national anthems by Mizos, Nagas and Assamese communities. Sanjoy Hazarika, *Strangers of the Mist: Tales of War and Peace from India's North East*, New Delhi: Penguin, 1994, p. 354. He cites the example of an Assamese teacher who instructs students to sing the Assamese National Anthem instead of the National Anthem.

4. Various pulp fiction written in vernacular such as Mizo, Khasi, and so on, are already available along with a high demand for various films and images from the West.

5. Refer to P.S. Datta (ed.), *Ethnic Movements in Poly-Cultural Assam*, New Delhi: Vikas, 1990, p. 19. Datta gives an example,

> We are yet to have a definition of Assamese which is stable over time and place and people. With the changing circumstances the definition too changes. On some people an Assamese identity is imposed while some others are allowed to accept an Assamese identity. At another point of time the allured neo-Assamese are identified as non-Assamese and hence non-Indian.

> One can read here how self-identity is never diluted, but constantly rehearsed as a process of struggling against Others.

6. Prasenjit Biswas and Sukalpa Bhattacharjee, 'The Outsider, the State and Nations from Below: North East India as a Subject of Exclusion', in Kousar Azam (ed.) *Ethnicity, Identity and the State in South Asia*, New Delhi: South Asian Publishers, 2001, pp. 237–39.

7. The demand for sovereignty is a common theme among most of the prominent nationalist groups of the North-East. See Sajal Nag, 'Multiplication of Nations: Political Economy of Sub-Nationalism' in *Economic and Political Weekly*, Vol. 28, Nos. 29 and 30, 1993, pp. 1521–32.

8. This kind of struggle against state repression mobilizes the democratic section of the masses and, also by bringing into light the atrocities committed, puts the state in the spot. See Ajit Kumar Bhuyan, A *Report on Human Rights Violation and State Terrorism in Assam*, Guwahati: Manab Adhikar Suraksha Samiti, 1991.

9. This is a strategy of democratization of politics in which politics is derived from the primacy of constituent processes than achievements of rights. Inversion of the dominant unfolds as a constituent process of assertion of subaltern identities. Further, this inversion carries out an investment in its own subjection. See Sholmo Avineri, *The Social and Political Thought of Karl Marx*, Cambridge: Cambridge University Press, 1968, pp. 32–33.

10. One can refer to demands like Bodoland, unification of Naga inhabited areas, and so on. For a theoretical understanding, see William Connoly, *Identity/Difference: Democratic Negotiations of Political Paradox*, Ithaca, NY: Cornell University Press, 1991, pp. 64–65.

11. Various Accords such as Mizo Accord, Assam Accord, etc., have taken care of demands of the dominant communities. In the Mizo Accord, the demand for Hmar Autonomous Council was not incorporated. In the Assam Accord, the other linguistic and religious minorities were also not given a fair deal. The Accords remained ethnocentric and exclusive in character. See P.S. Datta, *Autonomy Movements in Assam* (Documents), New Delhi: Omsons Publications, 1993.

12. ULFA's critique of such a non-recognition is presented in 'National Question In Assam' in AIPRF, *Symphony of Freedom: Papers on Nationality Question*, New Delhi: All India People's Resistance Forum, 1996, pp. 151–55. One could also remember Ernst Renan's statement, 'getting history wrong is a part of being a nation', quoted in Eric Hobswam, *Nation and Nationalism Since 1780* (Cambridge: Cambridge University Press, 1992: 12).

13. Interview with V.S. Atem in *The N-E Sun*, 1–14 March 1998.

14. How such violations of human rights are taking place is evident from the mass scale deaths due to lack of supplies to the camps inhabited by victims of riots. The total number of such riot-refugees reached a few lakh. There has been rampant child mortality, sickness and death prevalent in such camps. There are cases when camp dwellers have been attacked by killer gangs during day and night time. One can refer to *Sadin* (in Assamese) vol.10, No. 18, 17 July 1998, for a deft reporting of such events.

7

Rethinking India's North-East

Within and Beyond Life-Worlds

An apparent examination of the conglomerate concept 'North-East India' reveals a deep psychology of affirmation and ambivalence. Affirmation, in the sense that as India's own North-East it affirms a rightful place within India and hence resists exclusion or domination. What is ambivalent in this affirmation is the resistance to mainstreaming which the numerous nations-from-below of the North-East articulate with a clear stream of reason and express their freedom to voice a difference with the rest of India. But such ambivalence is often reduced to narrow games of polity management, the Focauldian notion of governmentality. 'Governmentality' as an expression of supervision, suspicion and subjection combines both strategic assimilation and politico-ideological dominance by the state-nation without any room for manoeuvring. Such a process of state-building in the North-East gets instituted by regimes of development and procedural democracy. Both these instruments of the state find local allies in the 'eager to gain elites' from within the societies of the North-East. As far as 'regimes' are concerned, these intervene in the very structure of the life-world(s) of the communities of the region by way of altering the given meanings and by way of creating divisions therein. Regimes, thus, are identifiable in cultural and political terms. Terms such as 'homeland', 'indigeneity' and 'tribal identity', etc., produce a sense of well-defined 'self' opposed to Others. Notwithstanding the attributions of these terms of self-identity, the very idea of being a part of the ruling apparatus of colonial and post-colonial periods has given rise to a discourse of erasure that conflates the identity-constructs with cartographic structuring of the region. With the stepping in of what is known as Globalization, the image of the 'self' has become prosthetic, as it necessarily involves looking at oneself the way the Other looks—a 'self' haunted by the look of the Other. This 'look of the Other' has been narratively constructed, even when the Other is absent from the perception. Most of the times, the Other is construed as 'outsider', 'immigrant' and 'oppressor', and thereby generating ceaseless conflicts that pits one against the Other—a prolegomena to meet the other with weapons of defence and offence, calling for the blood of the other. This brings us to the question, does identity politics in India's North-East thrive on construction of a hostile Other?

As Anthony Giddens has shown that within modernity, the self-identity of people became reflexive (1991: 15–6), that is, a claim of identity that reciprocates both to the given as well as to other claims of belonging; there is a simultaneous possibility of being what one is and being what one is not, without necessarily negating each other. Therefore, it is possible to become multiple within the singular notion of unified self-identity; unified as long as one requires to relate oneself with the world and share with the Other—a Kantian apperceptive self (Kant, 1956: 171–2). Multiplicity arises out of possibilities of belonging to different categories of identity—tribal, communal, national, post-national diasporic without a nec-essary objective and empirical correspondence, but with an always-already-constituted deductive and analytic content that can be put to use for pragmatic purposes. This situation could be best understood in terms of what Manuel Castells (1996–98) calls reconstructed defensive identity communities that arise after a shift from the sense of place/belonging to circumscribing oneself within a territory and cultural bonding. The situation gets complicated when claims of necessity are advanced within a fixed frame of history, for example, ethnic Assamese claim that Axom belongs to Assamese, Meitei claim that hills of Manipur cannot be given away to Nagalim, etc.[1] Such fixed frames of place/belonging, on the one hand, ensures the continuity of boundaries as historically determined facts and, on the other, settles for a procedurally better frame of governance of identity claims in terms of institutional and economic good. But boundaries are a part of reproductive imagination of spatial and temporal distinctions already in place, such as hills and plains, sacred and profane, etc., marked by limits of lived experience that often desists from universal expressions of languages beyond the senses. This determination of not moving beyond the senses carves out an *outside* as opposed to an *inside*. As an example from contemporary North-East India, while the mainstream Assamese culture speaks of 'Assam: Home of the Brahmaputra' and carves out an inside of northern and southern banks of the river to be called 'Axom', there remains an outside at the periphery, the western bank of Brahmaputra, N.C. Hills and Barak valley. Seemingly, the sense of the self does not stretch beyond the cultural-linguistic domain, giving rise to others who live at the possibility of being assimilated involuntarily. Contrast is the case of Manipur: the five hill districts are claimed to be a part and parcel of an integrated Manipur even though it has vast difference with the culture of the valley (Phanjoubam, 2006: 275–87).[2] Such contrasts deepen the cleavages that separate the self from the politics of power by rendering it only 'capillary' that makes ethnic solidarity possible—a negative dialectic between development of cross-cultural civil society and solidarity along axis of self-identity. But this axis is not unipolar as one can see inter-sectional conflicts within communities like Assamese and Manipuri, such as caste-Hindu Assamese versus Ahoms (popularly called Ahom-Bamun conflict), and Vaishnavite Hindu versus Sanamahi cults. It is also interesting to note that such inter-sectional conflicts are attempted to be overcome by way of a strategic exteriorization of conflicts with the Other. In a sense, such an attempted exteriorization develops into a conflict between the self and the other in order to overcome the crisis within. This is a duality of sorts, between being and becoming, between belonging and the longing to belong, that calls for the inclusion of some and exclusion of others. Ironically enough, such dualities aim at a singular goal of maintenance of boundaries (Favell, 1999: 229) that reinforce the presence of the community as a hegemonic entity in the ideological sense. This is also a construction of a political community that can respond to other local, ethnic, religious and cultural communities.

MODULARITY VERSUS SEGMENTALISM

As Gellner (1995: 41–2) argues about the modular character of modern identities that design a way of being with others and transcend 'ascriptive features' through institutional and other associational means, some of the dominant ethnic identities of North-East India practice a modularity of political and cultural association. As opposed to such modularity, what Gellner conceived as 'segmentalism', as a marker of the traditional societies, operates right within the heart of a discourse and politics of ethnic othering, which by and large defines an identity in the context of the North-East. In a sense, segmentalism often challenges any possible inter-ethnic engagement and thereby curtails modularity that is supposed to work in a modern civic space. What ethnic exclusivism does in the context of the North-East is to violate modularity and thereby generate conflicts that undermine norms of civil society and rule of law (Barbora, 2006: 3805-812). Segmentalism and inter-sectional conflicts are concomitant upon each other by altering the discourse of ascriptions in such a way that the ascriptions become historically conflicting, blurring all possibilities of inter-ethnic engagement. Intra-ethnic conflicts are the paradigm cases of segmentalism. Such conflicts arise out of representations that undermine the presence of the other and also from practices that discriminate against the other. In the case of North-East India, segmentalism places a heavy burden on the identity of the dominant. For example, in Assam, the definition of being an Assamese is still under threat from segments within, such as Tai-Ahom, Tiwa, Mishing, Rabha and other tribal groups, apart from neo-Assamese communities. Such segments are claiming their separate cultural, linguistic and political recognition. The very modularity of Assamese nationalism in terms of an assumed unity within and in terms of its difference from 'immigrants' gets threatened by internal differences that are playing a significant role of downplaying the ideological role of Assamese nationalism.

The main plank of linguistic nationalism with its attendant cultural pluralism as advocated by Assamese nationalism has always remained weak from within because of variegated linguistic formations and plural cultural life-worlds. This resulted into a centre versus periphery kind of distinction between mainstream neo-Vaishnavite culture versus indigenous cultures and faiths that plagued even the Ahoms, supposed to be the originators of Assamese society of today. Such a culture clash generates inter-sectional differences and segmentalism as reflected in Tiwa, Mishing, Rabha and Tai-Ahom struggles, each deriving its strength from cultural and historical distinctness. One can say that each of these particularist segments open up the possibility of other new segments, an ironical internalization of difference with Others that come as a consequence of the supposedly 'principal contradiction' between Assamese nationalism with foreigners/outsiders/aliens, which is a consequence of late linguistic nationalism of 'middle classes' that a thinker like Hiren Gohain (1995: 1–9) could foresee during the height of Assam movement. Even the Bodo movement for autonomy could also realize the sense of hegemonic Assamese nationalism, as All Bodo Students' Union (ABSU) proclaimed:

> One of the most responsible factors as to why the tribals have become alienated from the mainstream of Assam is the attitude of the Assamese people. The Assamese people have never accepted the tribals as a part and parcel of Assamese community and society in a real sense, though they give a motivated slogan of greater Assamese nationality (ABSU, 1987).

The sense and purpose of linguistic and cultural nationalism and its middle class leadership has asserted its ideological dominance, which is not necessarily hegemonic. As 'hegemony' depends on the capability to mobilize the symbolic realm of culture in the service of dominance, such mobilizations have been absent in nationalist movements of Assamese nationality. This absence is felt by the radical nationalists such as United Liberation Front of Assam (ULFA) when they asserted:

> The factor that united the various communities like the Ahom, Moran, Matak, Koch, Deuri, Chutia etc., of non-Aryan origin and

the Brahmins and Kalitas of the Aryan origin was the emergence of the Assamese (Asomiya) as the lingua-franca. The lingua-franca essentially becomes the mother tongue of a new cultural community called the Assamese (ULFA, 1996: 153).

This is a limited description of the formation of Assamese linguistic and cultural identity that is supposed to achieve national self-determination, according to ULFA, through its struggle against the colonial domination of the Indian state. As long as this is not achieved, the sovereign status of Assamese nationality is not fulfilled. This is precisely hitting the 'limits' of linguistic and cultural nationalism within the framework of statist nationalism but, politically speaking, this is also the limit of a hegemonic negotiation of the self-identity that mobilizes the pre-political cultural past in the service of the new entity. But this equivalence between cultural aspiration and the political sovereignty becomes indefensible within the framework of liberal democracy, as liberalism in its final adjudication shelves culture into other normative principles that are applied to other political and institutional issues. Therefore, claims of cultural identity become claims about autonomy, much less than claims of sovereignty. What these amount to is a modularity of becoming free under the condition of living together within a liberal democracy, the compulsions of which are felt by an ethnic majority more than the minorities within. This is the contemporary dilemma of Assamese nationalism that becomes a part of mainstream Indian statist nationalism without forgiving the Indian state for the experiences of discrimination. But minorities within Assamese formation do not share the same anguish, as they would also like to get the share of the cake by constituting them as minorities.

MINORITY DISCOURSE AND THE TOWER OF BABEL

Every generic identity comprises of minorities within that proclaim cultural and social differences in an ethnically diverse region like India's North-East. They speak in different voices and ask for a culture or group specific liberation. The goal of political liberation, therefore, most often turns into a claim of recognition and redistribution. But within the logic of liberal democracy's subsumption of culture, within broader institutional issues, such claims are negotiated within the context of cultural, social and political formations. In sharp difference to a Kymlica kind of liberal multiculturalism and pluralism, such claims of identity in the context of North-East play a different politics of recognition by way of a negative dialectic that is not based on reciprocity, but based on counterfactual responses (Biswas, 2005: 93–96). Such responses assume the conceptual-semantic role of being an Other within one's own generic identity that is simultaneously directed to the self as well as the Other. A few examples will demonstrate the rich variety of minority discourses in the identity struggles of North-East India.

The immigrant Muslim communities of Assam attempt to establish an identity with the mainstream Assamese linguistic and cultural formation by way of drawing narrative parallels. Such parallels reveal a distinct life-world of transition, a way of becoming rather than being. This also becomes an attempt to situate oneself in the other. An example of cultural appropriation between the immigrants and the native could be found on the occasion of Bihu, the most significant cultural festival of Assam that is celebrated thrice a year corresponding to harvesting cycles. During Bihu, native Assamese people visit the immigrant households for *Huchori*, while immigrant Bihu performers visit native Assamese households with troops of singers who sing songs called *Magon Geet*. Both Huchori and Magon Geet share similar rites and rituals celebrating a good harvest. During the post-harvest *Bhogali Bihu*, while the native Assamese people enjoy various rice delicacies, immigrant societies organize a festival of gaiety called *Sokhipota* that celebrates the bond of personal friendship between immigrant youth and native youth. This is a kind of mutual cultural appropriation that also finds its literary expressions in many a writings centring the lives of Sankardeva and Ajan Fakir (Ahmed, 2002: 16–20). The purported message is the foundational cultural unity between the immigrant Muslims and the Assamese society. The construction of such a unity is theorized in terms of mutual appropriation of river-based life-worlds. In the famous *naokhel* or boat races prevalent in the riverine belts of lower Assam, the song sung in Assamese addresses the immigrant peasantry as *Maluwa* (meaning both riverine people and Muslims) which is responded in their song by addressing Assamese as *Mahuwa* (meaning a valued fruit, keeper of animals, etc.). This is an exchange of emotions of owning each other in an act of recognizing each other's mental worlds and cultural roots, where the other is given a larger than life image. In another sense, it is an exercise of building up a hybrid, participatory and intermingled sense of belonging to the discourses of the life-world.

The conception of Assamese linguistic and cultural identity in terms of 'assimilation' has its ambivalent moment of making a distinction between indigenity and Otherness. Such a moment is often called in the discourses of Assamese nationalism that overrules the possibilities of greater assimilation. The irony is that such overruling results in a binary opposition between the desire to rule and the idea of an unmixed linguistic and cultural identity. In other words, an ambivalence between conceptions of self-identity and the hegemonic desire to rule has often been the driving force behind deconstruction of minority assimilation within the dominant Assamese society. The dominant discourse of Assamese nationalism runs thus:

> (...) the Assamese construct of the historical threat from the perceived outsider/foreigner is not a new one. The concept of *bidekhi* too is different to that of mainland India where many communities have accepted 'outsiders' and settlers as part of their own land. In Assam, anyone who is not an Assamese speaker or one who does not speak any of the original aboriginal languages, whether Bodo and its numerous dialects, or Ahom, Tiwa, Rabha and Mishing to name a few, is viewed as an outsider, no matter how long he has lived in the region (Hazarika, 200: 27–28).

The concept of 'foreigner' is invented to make a claim of distinctiveness and assert a difference with mainland Indian culture, which prioritizes Assamese as the first language over other smaller linguistic identities, which is self-subversive as proven by the history of claims of difference, both within the Assamese community and outside the community. But the crucial question here is: does not being bidekhi ensure a common belonging to an imagined homeland? Rather, bidekhi is a cultural stereotype that gains much currency precisely because the cultural and linguistic hegemony needs to be perpetuated within the social space that does not yield any space to the other. In terms of the discourse of group rights such a position is doubly defeasible—on account of its inner debility to manage internal differences that replicate the external and also on account of its preferential denial of equality to others on this plea or that. Both these conditions of defeasibility are manifest in the hegemonic construction of the community that tries to appropriate the disused rights of the Other and in the process fails to withstand its own internal Others. The more a hegemonic voice speaks of its Other, the greater the chance of creation of its own Others to an extent that the 'self' loses its original relationality. If Assamese as a language has emerged out of many a creative and transformative syntheses with aboriginal languages like Bodo and Ahom, notwithstanding its extremely close connections with Bengali, Oriya and Hindi, the dominant discourse of Assamese nationalism discounts these historical linkages only to achieve a deconstruction of its constituent cultural and linguistic segments. Probably this reminds one of what Benedict Anderson had commented about the significance of vernacular languages: 'Language is not an instrument of exclusion: in principle, anyone can learn any language. On the contrary it is fundamentally inclusive, limited only by the fatality of the Babel: no one lives long enough to learn *all* languages' (1991: 134).

Is it the law of Babel that fails in the case of immigrant Muslims who accepted Assamese to be their mother tongue or is it the Assamese nationalists who are creating a Tower of Babel in Assam? Is it also the collapse of cultural nationalism of an assimilative kind into an ethnic and religious nationalism that pivots around a clientele of 'middle classes'?

Although the minorities seek to assimilate themselves the ideology of Assamese nationalism keeps them apart, and, thereby, constantly creating one or another bogey. The ideological debunking of Bangladeshis is supported by the legal questions about citizenship, which amounts to acceptance of certain groups of people by the dominant majority. This severely undermines the normative adjudication of the labeling of someone being a foreigner instead of following procedures to establish the rights of the citizen. This also deals a body blow to the foundational principles of democratic citizenship as skullduggery of antecedents in Bangladesh deprives the contemporary social and political space of granting voice to the voiceless. As democratic citizenship is based on non-discriminatory practices even towards the alien, and withdrawal of certain rights from the alien, only amounts to securing the country from intrusion, the attribution of the term 'foreigner' to a section of the populace (Hazarika, 2000: 30)[3] on the rationality of being settlers or competitors that calls for catching and deporting the foreigners. Invariably this has resulted into physical harassments of Bengali- speaking Muslims of the lower Assam that included even those who claimed to have assimilated themselves within the Assamese mainstream. Very recently, it involved strictures on the movement of Bengali-speaking Muslim labourers across various parts of North-East. There have been larger number of victims of anti-foreigners drive by the state as well as several vigilante organizations since the repeal of the Illegal Migrants (Determination by Tribunals) Act, 1983 in the Supreme Court of India. As no legal procedures need to be followed in giving the 'right to defense' to a suspected Bangladeshi, it has been the heyday of vigilante groups to speak a language of exclusion and raise a hullabaloo about the possible demographic swamping of the indigenous and the natives by the Bangladeshis. All kinds of figures are being dished out liberally to identify the foreigners. This has all the potential of going the 1979 way that visited the politics of the North-East in ethnic terms and resulted into ethnic cleansing of the immigrants and non-ethnic Others. The problem is further compounded by non-fulfill-ment of constitutional rights of various tribal and other smaller groups, as they keep demanding their autonomy. Until that point of time of accomplishment of rights by these smaller groups, there will exist a material ground for harassment of genuine Indian citizens just because they have settled in an area where they are in a minority. Going by such a fragmented logic of autonomy and human rights, there will only be a lot of scampering on who trespasses whose domain. For example, the rights of an ethnic Assamese speaker or a Bodo in a tribal state like Meghalaya or Arunachal Pradesh will always remain susceptible to ethnic dis-crimination. The question of being an outsider will not only effectively constrain the indigenous communities from being at home in the larger national and international space, but it will erect many walls between the native and the outsider to an extent that intra-regional movement and settlement of various groups of people will remain badly affected for a long time. Further, this will create internal minorities and their human rights will be stumped by the majority or the dominant community with the logic that they 'had no business to be there' (Hazarika, 2000: 53).[4] This logic can be applied to justify all forms of racial and ethnic hatred, and it can be conveniently used against the minorities well within one's imagined territory. That citizenship rights have a universal basis is often conflated with context-based specific rights of priority of native groups only to establish a case for denial to non-native Others, which is a kind of ethnic victory on matters of conflict without resolving issues of entitlements that such victory is supposed to accrue to the natives.

Apart from this situation of conflict between the majority and the minority in terms of native versus outsiders, minority discourse in the context of India's North-East has evolved into a discourse of loss, deprivation and displacement. Owing to the market forces and the land grabbers from among nouveau-riche, the tribal communities are losing land to business and developmental projects leading to 'secondary primitivization' of smaller tribal and ethnic groups. The case of Bodo-Kacharis selling away land to nouveau-riche in various localities of the city of Guwahati, eviction of indigenous communities from the Doyang reserve forests, Lalungs losing their cultivated land for the East-West corridor on the outskirts of Guwahati, and too many other such instances from various parts of North-East India give rise to a discourse of loss and its attendant claims to justice. But such discourses are marginalized within the mainstream discourses of linguistic nationalism and they are subjected to manipulation by the ruling elite to divert the whimpers of protest. In case of Assam, the discourse of marginalization that followed from the eviction of indigenous ethnic tribes from the Doyang reserve forest by the Government of Assam does not really find many takers within the discourse of Assamese nationalism. The displacement of Bodos and Rabhas due to the *Pagladiya* dam and the resultant misery similarly does not find much footing within the discourse of Bodo nationalism. Could we now bring forth the logic that 'they simply have no business to be there', an existential irony that could be best described in Heideggerian metaphor of 'being thrown', a metaphor of helplessness that marked the Auschwitz victims. What is deemed to be genocide or ethnocide finds its repugnant justifications in ethnic Othering, which is the main strategic plank of the ethno-nationalist discourse of dominant Assamese nationalism. Peoples thrown out from their land and livelihood are also 'thrown out' of their ethnicity, defined by the so called 'elite/middle-class nationalism/sub-nationalism'. Is the fate of such thrown out people any different from their ethnic others who are thrown out just because 'they simply have no business to be there'? In a liberal democratic poly-ethnic state, the social and political space can never be homogeneous, howsoever correct be the claim of belonging or the claim of authenticity, whose real facet gets exposed in its sui generis tendencies of lebensraum. Just as Auschwitz gave rise to an ideology of anti-Semitism, the brutal and barbaric holocaust of minorities in Nellie gave rise to the ideology of ethnic cleansing and ethnic othering. The metaphysical experience of extermination in the killing fields of Nellie had actually sounded the death knell to the claims of assimilation as put forth by minority discourses of 'belonging', or rather it had inaugurated a moment of sundering ethnic solidarity from citizenship, as the latter requires a non-ethnic and contractarian national identity. The impossibility of a trans-ethnic, if not a non-ethnic basis of citizenship, that would have ensured an unfaltering minority, discourse vis-à-vis the dominant majority, finds its labyrinth in the contradiction between assimilative practices and ethnic Othering. This found its ideological expression in the politics of demography that reduces the majority Assamese, Manipuri or Naga nationalism to the threat of being swamped by the outsiders. There is an ideologically generated 'fear of the Other' that acts as the core of negation of the very basis of a consocial-contractarian citizenship. This fear finds its conditions of boundary fixation in an uninterrupted notion of ethnic exclusivism, as 'interruption' in an ethical sense (Cohen, 2003). The whole idea of re-building Assam after the Assam movement fell apart as it is a contradiction in terms, reminscient of what Adorno had said after Auschwitz about rebuilding culture, which is 'its negation by itself' (1974).

Both the majority construction of the political and cultural myth of assimilation and the minority myth of 'belonging' got negated in the aftermath of ethnically exclusivist upsurges one after another, giving rise to a Tower of Babel for the national unity of India.

'THE FEAR OF SMALL NUMBERS': POLITICS OF DEMOGRAPHY

Slogans such as 'Withdraw Indian Army as they are anti-Assamese' or 'Bangladeshi Mian go Back' apparently has an explicit target, but behind it remains the perceived threat of the Other. The Other is perceived everywhere, even in a struggle against the 'dominant state'. A recent ULFA circular (2007) imposing taxes on 'Indians' is reminiscent of many an ethnic movements of the region, for example, All Manipur Students' Union banning Hindi or any cultural symbol of India in the early 1990s. What these prorogations voice is apparently a resistance to Indian, but, ironically enough, when such gestures are perceived as anti-Indian in the mainstream media, these movements also identify what all in public life are anti-Assamese or anti-Meitei or anti-local. The question that is pertinent here is: Is there a deeper basis for semantics of 'anti' kind, be it anti-Indian or anti-Assamese? Is there a semantic equivalence that is established on the basis of mutual reciprocity in identifying the 'opposite'? Being anti-Assamese is being pro-Indian, while being anti-Indian is being pro-Assamese. Such simplistic antinomies of an ethnic struggle share a deeper metaphysical stereotyping of the enemy outside the Cartesian self. In identifying the enemy, such stereotypes makes one also the enemy being anti-Assamese, which by implication also means that Assamese cannot be pro-Indian, and thereby leaving the scope for treating the Assamese as enemies of India by other Indians. This is a scheme of construing the Indian identity in the discursive frame of reclusive regional identity, which does not stand on sufficiently multicultural and poly-ethnic bases, it can merely see the other as enmeshed within. The moot question is: does ethno-nationalism need an exterior enemy who is bigger than itself? Does it need to project itself as an enemy at the margins? Should Assamese nationalism be necessarily anti-Indian? Also, should we consider Indian identity as necessarily anti-X or Y in the context of North-East India?

The question of recognizing the other either as different or as enmeshed within oneself often becomes the question of number based majority/minority. Claims of identity based on numbers justify the fear of the Other. Political demographers have long conceived such fears based on numbers as 'racist' and such politics is aimed at re-creating the justification for the dominant ethnic power without any predictable or intended outcome (Teitelbaum and Winter, 1998: 61, 75). The fear of being swamped by the 'foreigners' (read Bangladeshis) goes with the perceived interests of the dominant communities that try to secure their homelands. Sanjoy Hazarika's (2000: 232–34) interpretative correlations between loss of population in Bangladesh during the period 1971–91 and corresponding rise of Muslim population in Assam, Tripura and Bengal is a fine statistical exercise that go into the discourse of the anti-foreigners drive. This is what Teitelbaum and Winters think of such demographic rendering of fear of the Other:

> Ethnic conflict always entails counting the size of groups whose growth rates are low or negative and who are threatened by assimilation. These groups, feeling besieged, respond by cultivating a collective consciousness, and this frequently includes pro-natalist campaigns—nonviolent conflicts fought over the long term. This kind of demographic ethnic conflict—a culture war about numbers—harms no one, but as soon as cynical politicians and their followers try to take a shortcut and redress the imbalance by forcible eviction of another ethnic group, demography becomes lethal (1998: 81).

In the context of Assam and the North-East, it is not the counting of the groups threatened by assimilation, but those who are besieged by the fear of minorities migrating from across the border who have turned demography into a means of resistance and preservation of group interests. Pro-natality campaigns, of course, are rarely resorted to as political campaigns can provide the solace to losing on account of numbers. In case of the Bodo movement too, identification of villages based on Bodo majority has resulted into ethnic cleansing of the Adivasis and others. Any other movement by smaller ethnic groups posit their minority status as the cause of their claims of difference and distinctness: for example, Tiwa, Matak, Rabha, Moran, Ahom and other smaller groups assert their identity in order to protect themselves from assimilation within the larger cultural and linguistic group. The fear of being lost as part of a larger group develops into a fear of the Other that justifies one's in-group preservationism, which also takes the form of being wary of one's small number of members. Such fears become the basis of new forms of primordialism that are 'secondary' and based on a perception of how the other is entrenched in the system. Within a multi-ethnic state, the fear of losing out because of one's small numbers makes one look for promoting one's interests at the cost of the Other.

The secondary primordialism is often reflected in terming others with a 'non' participate, something like non-tribal, non-Assamese etc., that gives priority to the self over the Other and the very Otherness is defined as a negation of the prioritized notion of the self as applied to oneself. The Others are reduced to non-self, which is a negation of their otherness as well. Within this negation of Otherness, the fear of being outnumbered grows into a habit of the mind. Such a fear has its direct link with inventing a common enemy, who now disappears into a rationality of claims of distinctness. In effect, the big numbered enemy is no longer there in its place, it is rather culled up into one's sovereign domain of control, outside which the presence of enemy does not matter. Enemies, as Carl Schmitt would explain, are always beyond the line that is drawn up. The line is drawn up against anyone who is existentially different and with whom conflict is possible; and as long as such a possibility exists, anyone can become an enemy (Schmitt, 1996: 27). In the context of identities with internal fissures, the search for an external enemy is an antidote to the enemy within. The external enemy could be found out in 'vertebrate form' that can present challenges to the 'cellular form' of indigenous majorities (Appadurai, 2006: 15–6).[5] Claims of indigeneity as an envelope for sovereignty and authenticity can be effectively challenged by cellular migrant identities, who occupy an excluded space and yet pose an 'existential difference' to the majority, is looked upon as a threat through prototypes of numbers and hence the fear. For an internally fissured majority, the fear in the diminution of their size is existentially complemented by the fear of small others, who are seen as a part of global majorities elsewhere. This is how indigenous tyrannies sustain themselves as against majoritarian state structures.

'Fear of small numbers' in such a situation of extreme suspicion of the other in the context of North-East India finds it abyss in rampant inter-ethnic conflicts as well. The prolonged conflict and ethnic cleansing between Dimasas and Karbis since 2003 has been a case in point. What culminates into prolonged ethnic conflict and cleansing at its roots assumes that ethnic identity itself is the site of political and cultural othering instead of claims over concrete resources and entitlements. These battle lines are drawn without borders and are not controlled by territories, resources and contests over symbols. Communities living together side by side across imaginary borderlines and often overlapping those borders entered into violent conflicts as violence served the purpose of asserting superiority. In the words of Dima Halam Daoga, the overriding rationale for such a conflict lay in establishing legitimacy in the Karbi territory as their designated camp was situated in Hamren sub-division of Karbi Anglong. In the alleged role of Karbi militant outfits in disturbing the settlements of Khasi-Pnars, the question is whether the Khasis have the right to live within Karbi territory. Such a sense of territoriality went along with the politics of Othering and thereby undercutting the very right to live in one's territory, as denial of such rights to others would only jeopardize the fabric of mutually lived civic space that a nation-state warrants. It is an idea of 're-territorialization' within the lived space as well as in politics that rigidly created the idea of territorial identities that does not allow any overlap. As long as the territorial identity of an ethnic group can sustain its prioritized rights, it will be upheld as the basis for those rights, strangely undercutting an extension of these rights across the political and social spaces of the nation-state as a whole.

In the case of Arunachal Pradesh, the right of Chakma and Hajong refugees to enjoy citizenship is questioned on the ground that refugees can't be a part of the citizenry. A rigid and unbreakable barrier, which is, of course, not valid in the adjudication of constitutional rights in India, has been raised to treat them as non-citizens. The logic here again is if refugees are allowed to stay put in Arunachal Pradesh, the rights of indigenous people will be affected. Ethnic mobilization on the basis of local and indigenous identity had created the fear of being outnumbered by the refugees. The story is slightly thicker in the case of Mizoram. The rights of smaller ethnic groups like Brus, Hmars, Paites, etc., are not yet recognized for the reason that they should become a part of larger Mizo identity. In the case of Tripura, ethnic minorities like Tripuri tribes and others are seemingly overpowered by the Bengali linguistic identity, as the re-constituion of Tripura resulted in the inclusion of areas in the plains inhabited by a sizeable Bengali population. One of the most significant denial of rights happened in the case of the tea tribes of Assam, who had been brought by the colonial masters as indentured labourers in the Bodo context. When the Bodos were demanding the right of autonomy, a parallel ethnic cleansing of many of these tea tribes went on for a while in order to establish Bodo majority in certain pockets of mixed populace.

The crucial theoretical issue is: how does one ensure the rights of internal minorities in situations when majorities become exclusivist and pursue a violent method of Othering? What should be the constitutional mechanism in place? The claims of exclusive citizenship rights on the basis of ethnicity within one's demarcated territory has the potential of being inadequate in the face of the logic of the market as well as in the political calculus of a large representative democracy. Therefore, a mechanism of representation of the internal minorities should be in place along with the representation of indigenous majorities, and whatever constitutional protection applies to such indigenous communities must also be extended to internal minorities. This requires a practice of recognition of cultural, linguistic and ethnic identities without an emphasis on their numbers, but with an emphasis on their relative aspirations. Politics of recognition played on numerical basis has often resulted into paranoia and exclusion.

The greater ramification of the politics of (mis)recognition lies in seeking revenge for supposedly 'historical wrongs' and attempting to convince the powers that be about the implausible other. Interestingly, the patrons of exclusivist politics at the national level are often those forces that are hegemonic and yet who seek legitimacy by supporting the local majorities. The Constitution of India, of course, upholds a different sense of justice for the marginalized and the minoritized groups.

POLITICS OF RECOGNITION AND LEGITIMATION

Ethnic insurgencies of the region seek recognition in terms of legitimizing their claims and rights. The legitimacy comes not from the popular support but from the recognition by the state or by the powers that be. Such recognition often results in a political and economic patronage by the central government that is utilized by the leadership of a group in mustering greater power. The interesting question to ask at this point is: to what extent the members of a community get empowered by such politics of recognition and its resultant redistributive policies? Or, is it just that an armed group acquires democratic legitimacy and gets appropriated in the mechanism of centralized power without deliverance to members of their in-group community? Does insurgent mobilization coincide with the empowerment of the in-group marginalized people when it acquires legitimacy? Or does the entire process move in an iterable circular trajectory of *recognition → legitimation → disenchantment*? Does this trajectory also determine the outcome of ethnic movements in the region?

Insurgent outfits like NSCN (I-M) and ULFA who want to change the map of India by seceding from it also get caught in this circle, as they emerge as both winners and losers in this circle of outcomes. Draconian provisions, such as the Armed Forces Special Powers Act 1958, empower the army and the paramilitary forces to let loose a reign of terror during the course of counter-insurgency operations. Such a reign of potentially offensive military power makes a devious entry into the scene only to lengthen the list of casualties, but the politics of recognition gets the necessary immunity from such acts of the state. Parleys between the state and the insurgent outfits keep dotting the headlines and every act from both the sides receives greater attention in an unqualified manner. The outcome of such parleys is determined by apparent agreement and disagreement on issues that do not go into the larger social and political context of such issues. What prevents the secessionist groups to understand that the communities outside their own group are also clamouring for sovereign rights, and what prevents the Indian state from understanding that struggling ethnicities need to be given greater dignity, empathy and respect does not become clear immediately. Only after the talks fail, some of the inside political wrangling come to fore. Assuming that the talks are successful, what equations have played a role can only be known post-facto. For example, why did the Shillong Accord, signed between A.Z. Phizo's NNC and the Government of India, fail in 1975, and if it failed, why did NNC accept the accord is a question that still needs to be answered? The ongoing peace talks between NSCN (I-M) and the Government of India seems to be breaking down off and on. The resolve that dialogue will result into a mutually acceptable solution lapses into a game of scoring over each other. The losers in the dialogue talk of 'lack of will' or 'unresolvability', which is overcome somehow by a renewed attempt of return to another dialogue. A true dialogue cannot be abandoned half way as it has to always remain committed to address what has been left unresolved for the other side.

For identities in conflict such as Naga and Meitei or Assamese and Bodo, outstanding issues related to sharing of territory and power take a non-negotiable turn. What is non-negotiable is settled in terms of the winners of an ethnic conflict. Most of the times, the majority loses out in such conflicts that are directed at their hegemony and superiority. When the Other is defeated and disengaged, ironically enough, the very goal of achieving superiority is surprisingly over. For example, for argument sake, if the Meiteis give up their attachment to the hill districts of Manipur, what would be left for the NSCN (I-M) to negotiate with the Indian state? If Bodos are given a separate state, what would the National Democratic Front of Bodoland have to negotiate with the big brother? Such possibilities of disengagement are restricted by the acts of negotiations as the expected outcome is deferred in the course of such a process. Resorting to an armed conflict often strengthens the counter-insurgency mechanism of the state, a dilemma from which the outfits breaking away from dialogues suffer. Militant groups that enter into a ceasefire with the state try to ensure a fair deal for themselves, but interestingly such deals are fraught with the possibility of a return to factional armed conflicts. The ULFA is currently undergoing this dilemma of relapse into a armed conflict all over again, which is reducing its striking capability to a significant extent. It is to be remembered that the state is only interested in bringing an end to insurgency without addressing the substantial issues.

The interesting question in such transitional state is: to what extent will conflicting parties reciprocate? Do they merely calculate each other's strengths and weaknesses? The claims of authenticity from the conflicting parties give rise to a contest over legitimacy that cannot be negotiated in terms of concessions and consents. As far as the Indian state is concerned, it finds it difficult to reciprocate to many demands that are made by the insurgent outfits. In the course of negotiations with NSCN (I-M), the Indian state has delved into the issue of self-determination in terms of constitutional provisions that emphasized more on fulfillment of opportunities and representation than on secession from the Indian Union. The NSCN (I-M) could reciprocate to such an approach by way of agreeing to read and understand the Indian Constitution before embarking on an enactment of a separate constitution for Nagalim. The art and politics of constitutional interpretation and writing of a constitution is a mutual engagement in speaking out the possible normative positions of their respective sides, a liberal dèmocratic tool called into the service of making peace. If secession is not permissible within the ambit of Indian Constitution, the question is, how does the NSCN (I-M) pursue the cause of self-determination? Does not having a separate constitution help in gaining legitimacy for the project of self-determination? This is an alternative to the constructivist and groupist politics pursued by many an insurgent movement from North-East India that tends to define 'self-determination' on the basis of such identity constructs and not on the basis of 'validity' of such constructs. Constructs embedded in identity schemes and cultural idioms tend to become totalistic and irresponsive to the necessity of arriving at a valid normative argument about one's rights and thereby it turns the very enterprise of struggle into another such group-specific construct (Burbaker, 2004).[6] The cognitive practice of structuring group identity around what is familiarized and naturalized gives rise to the basic structure of life-world of group identity that needs a normative resolution. The art of constitution-making and the process of normativizing make the still underground Nagas think of coming to terms with a constitutional state that is non-coercive. This means that early attempts at normativization of the Naga struggle within the constitutional state which recognizes them as a legitimate social formation can possibly resolve the outstanding issues.

In the case of the ULFA struggle for self-determination, normativity plays an essential role in determining the role of identity in the process of making certain political claims. Different from the Naga struggle, such claims made by ULFA arose only after the normativizing processes failed to meet their demands. Identity, which ULFA calls the 'national identity', becomes important only in case where attempts of resolution through means of mediation come to an end. Such an end meets ULFA's teleological discourse of emancipation of the national identity. In a sense, identity is the last resort for ULFA, as the Assamese national identity is undergoing a fast transition. At the same time, the legitimacy of ULFA claims are often in conflict with what the constitutional state proclaims and, therefore, a significant amount of legitimation can be the only source for a successful negotiation between the ULFA and the Indian state.

Politics of recognition based on mutual reciprocity tries to expand the notions of legitimation beyond the circle of disenchantment by way of separating the worlds of claims and norms. This gives rise to local determinism of identity—speaking in terms of community, faith and territory without its global counterparts. The absence of the global in the local determinism of claims of identity and authenticity go well with an already globalized world of capitalism that merely throws up floating signifiers, vanishing histories and deterritorialized communities. This meeting of the local and the global, in a regime of power that makes claims unrepresentable, goes into a politics of self-determination at the cost of the other. Such politics also weighs heavily on a contextual mimicry of the global in the form of fratricide and ethnicide, a paradoxically self-defeating game against dominance. Given the ethnic plurality of the North-Eastern region as a whole, the relapse into numerous inter-ethnic conflicts over claims of territoriality serves as a fratricidal moment of history. The moment is also self-defeating as the Other has already been dispersed and, hence, the move gets directed to self-inflicted tortures and cruelties. Finally, cruelties committed to others to satisfy one's claims turns fratricidal, sooner or later.

SHARMILA'S FAST AND THE THEATRE OF THE OPPRESSOR

What arises out of this politics of claims-making is a reverse moment of legitimacy of the oppressor. The oppressor legitimizes itself in the name of the nation and its territorial integrity. Sharmila's fast in New Delhi hasn't scaled down the Armed Forces Special Powers' Act, 1958, as the Army bosses feel insecure about it. This is a theater in which the lawmakers and the judge are one and the same in their intent as they see Sharmila and the insurgents as two sides of the same coin. The victims of the Act are permanently slain like the victims of Auschwitz—Manorama and Ajit Barua cannot speak any more. The slain among the army are on the defensive, as the army can still speak for its slain. But when the civil society voices for the slain, the gun can silence that, which is much more than slaying a person in a democratic state. This explains why the Indian state is still trying to delay the repeal of the Act as it faces the paradox of being democratic: the more democratic a state, the greater is the strength of its coercive agencies. In fact, the strength of Indian state lies in the strength of its army. Strength of law also lies in its punitive capacity. Strength of civil society and resistance movement lie in pursuing an agenda of change by going against the tide.

In this jinx, the North-Eastern states are caught in the vortex of the legitimacy and the illegitimacy of their 'self-other' relationship. In the meantime, political movements in the region suffer from the dilemma of resolution versus continuation, and they bear witness to that act of irresolvable dilemma for which they do not yet have a language. Phrases like 'self-determination' or 'liberation from the colonial rule of India' fall short of addressing the question of justice in its full sense. The idea of justice gets contrasted with justifiability of a political programme and most often the purpose of resistance gets decided on the basis of actor's advantages. The politics of insurgent outfits such as United National Liberation Front (UNLF) of Manipur in resisting the idea of Manipur's incorporation within India as well as in opposing the Armed Forces Special Powers' Act bring out a kind of alignment with the civil society bodies. This strengthens the movement against the Act, but at the same time, it attempts at recovering the main plank of their politics of secession from India. When the Indian Army claims that removal of the Act would mean tying the hands of army at the back, they mean that this would be an augmentation of secessionist capability in a narrow and limited sense. This is a contest of positions that blunts the edge of the democratic sensibility of living in a free country. The precession of politics over the agenda of creating a democratic environment perpetually defers resolution of the issues like curtailment and suppression of the right to voice protest.

The spectre of blasts and killings of the ordinary mortals in the context of insurgency makes the target simultaneously anonymous and spelt out. ULFA's pronounced opposition to resource extraction results in many a blast on pipelines carrying crude oil from the oil refineries of Assam, while blasts on railway tracks is directed at creating a scare within the state machinery as well as among the public. An argument from the position of being a target makes the possibility of such attacks more and more ominous as the language of victimhood assumes for itself an always ready state of being persecuted. Enthusiasm about the drive against terrorists by the state uses a language of being caught in the crossfire that justifies acts of state terrorism in its conceit. When targets get spelt out by the state and the insurgent outfits, there is no other way of distracting the targets who are now really caught in between. The language game of terror remains incommensurable with that of the victim, but it is entirely fashioned to suit the perpetrator or the saviour. The victimhood of the internally displaced in the conflict zones of North-East India is a case of victims not being able to establish the referent of genocides and ethnicides. At the same time, the risible suffering in the refugee camps and the successful glee of perpetrators at their bases stand as the two faces of the representations of the brute fact of terror.

Smaller ethnic groups of the region are made to follow this logic of perpetration and victimhood. The very process of 'being aware of' one's ethnic identity that apparently coincides with the emergence of 'values conducive to such assertions' is a process of participation in the theater of oppression and facing the oppressor. Ethnic identity assertions over and against the dominant result into coalescence of an equivalent cultural and national identity that fixes its referents in the nations-from-above'. When it attempts to delimit these referents by picking out the dominant forces within itself, such forces posit themselves as the sole representative of the ethnic group or community. But such positing tries to grant an agency to the very group identity, which acts as a symbolic domain of mobilization of an identity. As noted earlier (in Chapter 3 and

Chapter 6), such mobilizations are a process of politico-cultural constructionism which necessarily runs against the governmentality of representational democracy. Two contradictory consequences follow from such a state of affairs: one, it does not compete the dominant notion of well-being that is given; and two, it wages a narrow conflict over its own relative place within a polity. These consequences are contradictory because the first one depends on a tacit acceptance of dominance, while the second one tries to assert autonomy; but combining the two, one comes close to an ongoing conflict between ends. This turns out to be an assertion of autonomy within the frame of dominance.

Autonomy of ethnic identity sustains itself by the subjectivity of instituting a place for itself within the given frame of history and memory. In a sense it resists transformation of those boundary conditions that give rise to a closure of identity, but by doing so it constructs a contradictory and yet mutually inclusive space for itself. What it includes becomes a source of its negation. This setting of identity construction is an internal site of resistance that faces an oppressor. In case of North-East India, the conscious attempts at distancing oneself from perceived Others in terms of a duality between identity/non-identity is a strategy of introducing a discursive mark of difference that refuses any alterity. Such a duality is sustained by the presence granted to an omnipresent oppressor, who often also becomes non-present in the thrust for an enclosed notion of self. In a paradoxical way, boundaries drawn around a construction of identity not only shelter an identity, but also become a site of protection from oppression. But this diminished frame of identity in a defined boundary results into a forced resistance to the Indian nationhood, often relapsing into exclusivist politics. As a contrast to the dominant and the mainstream nationalist discourse, exclusivist identities narrow down the lived space to a reified notion of the self and the Other in order to practice exclusivist nationalism that often fails to deliver the goods. Other-bashing chauvinism sometimes emerges as the counterpart of the mainstream sense of the dominant nationalist-patriotic definition of who is an 'Indian'. This is also an inverted use of nationalist discourse of citizenship and nationality in the cause of exclusivist nationalism, often construed as a middle class nationalism within the bounds of regional identity struggles.

Interestingly, such a discourse of inverted nationalism against an Other becomes a hobby horse for the regional rulers as well as for the national rulers. The talk of a 'Look East Policy' or the talk of a regional discourse for the entire North-East India that exploits cultural homogeneity as its basis for a pan-Asian economic corridor is an example of how the hobby horse of globalization is braided. This is structuring of a patrimony in North-East in the service of a US-doctored vision of a 'bridge' between Central and South and South-East Asia (The Telegraph, 2006). The current criticism of the Government of India by the World Bank (WB) for pursuing large developmental projects by massive destruction of forest and environment as detrimental to the livelihood of the indigenous populations belonging to the tribal states of the North-East is also akin to 'David mouthing Jesus' name'. The WB itself along with its partner, the Japanese Bank for International Co-operation, has already funded $1,050 million in North-East India for projects of reform and restructuring of production and infrastructural facilities that have a major environmental impact. What is in the pipeline is the plan of river linking and damming and commercialization of water resources that the WB is envisioning, which will form a part of NE Vision Document 2020. Another major international financial institution, the Asian Development Bank (ADB), moots the idea that 'all export opportunities and trade promotion in the North-East should be seen in view of WTO [World Trade Organization] standards and norms that have come, or will come into force with the completion of India's WTO accession' (ADB, 2003). This framework of development envisages no role for indigenous local communities, except that they should follow the diktats, which in all proportions is much lesser than the role envisaged by the Indian nation-state. At least the constitutional state provides certain safeguards to Scheduled Tribes and does not throw them into the merciless hands of global players.

Can this assure an idea of bargaining on one's own that guarantees the choice of opportunities for the indigenous communities of the North-East? Or, is it a litany of appropriated agency and space? The absence of agency role for the communities as actors has resulted in competitive ethnic mobilizations that fail to secure 'rights' within the decision-making processes. For example, demands such as setting up of Special Economic Zones (SEZs) in the North-East still await the trickle down effect instead of securing places within the broader democratic decision-making processes. As it is known, SEZs are meant for export processing in the private sector, and with a 'hire and fire' policy that will apply therein, it could only compound problems of an already existing extractive economy. The moot question is, to what extent shall the opening of primary and productive sectors of the economy have the desired trickle down effect of development? Seemingly, issues for political mobilization of the youth in the North-East boils down to the Centre's discrimination towards the North-East even in setting up SEZs.

It is at this point, Sharmila's fast again brings out the crucial significance of articulation of rights that are right instead of promotion of 'wrong rights' that aim at suppressing rights that are politically correct. If North-East needs to voice the right to SEZs as the legitimate right of communities of North-East, it suppresses the lack of support for products that emanate from the very life-world. Typical handicraft, agricultural and horticultural products of the region meet their nemesis in the SEZs, which will process exportable electronic goods and exploit the North-East as a back-yard of the global market. The question of cultural identity and the right to struggle against dominance of the Centre can similarly be suppressed by demanding economic packages from the Centre. Demand for special constitutional status for the development of North-East can include projects that would spin money, but result in alienation of local masses from the decision-making processes that form economic activity. The material conditions for seeking only those rights that empower the agency of communities shall still exist, but without its proper utility in the discourses of our times. Especially, at a moment when the terms of discourse are set by powerful global financial agencies complemented by organs of the state such as army and judiciary, what follows is a suspension of sovereignty of communities and peoples themselves. Sharmila's fast in New Delhi symbolizes this suspension of sovereignty that seems to be a never-ending moment in contemporary North-East.

AGENCY AND IDENTITY

The category of 'national identity' as used by various large and small communities of the region states the everyday experience of the life-world and it remains immanent as a token of identity in context of the nation-state. The emergence of smaller identities from within larger ones brings out the unresolved tensions within larger 'national' identities such as Assamese, Mizo or Naga. When the larger identities posit themselves as sovereign and united, smaller groups within them become marginalized and isolated. This shows why mere emergence of a self-conscious elite, who act as moral leaders of the community cannot alone explain the rise of difference within an identity. It is rather a contest over the meaning of what it means to belong to a certain identity that creates the historical and material conditions for asserting a difference. Such assertion of difference centres upon the appropriation of tradition and the symbolic realm that appears in the very discursive frame that defines an identity. The discursive frame of defining Assamese identity in terms of the lineage of Ahom kingdom and later in terms of a syncretic movement did leave out certain segments such as Bodos and other plain tribes. Apart from this sense of being at the exterior, the very assertion of a unified Assamese identity based on linguistic nationalism and rootedness widened the already existing gulf. This background of internally differentiated life-worlds en-courages further division and fractures that result into a radical deconstruction of the commonness between various factions within an identity. Such a process only multiplies the difference of the sense of belonging with various segments getting divided in terms of remembered pasts and contemporary differences. The celebra-tion of coronation of the Tiwa king in lower Assam and the revival of various Ahom rituals produce a simultaneous moment of revival and assertion of difference, which is more cultural than political and economic.

In the case of Naga unity too, the difference between Nagas of Manipur and Nagas of Nagaland is not just geographic, it assumes contests over history. The close links between Ahoms and Aos do not really cover other sections of Nagas to share a unified history. The battle of Khonoma (mentioned in Chapter 2) and the Second

World War, two landmark moments of Naga encounter with the colonial modernity, do not present shareable and common memory between the eastern and western Nagas within Nagaland. The claim of a unified Naga national identity, therefore, remains internally fractured. The irreconciliable factionalism between NSCN (K) and NSCN (I-M) does not smooth out the situation for the cause of Naga unity. It is rather the derivative discourse of unified nationalism that acts as the urge behind setting one's true identity against an imposed identity, which again becomes the motive force of deriving a territorial entity called Nagalim. Nationalism, despite being heterogeneous produces a canopy of unity and a mosaic of multiple fragments. Naga nationalism is no exception to this process of interior differences combined with exterior unity.

Post-insurgency Mizoram also portrays significant cultural and linguistic differences between various groups within and the divide assumes horizontal differences between Pawis, Lakhers, Maras and Lusheis. Interestingly, post-insurgency Mizoram speaks in terms of a greater Zo diaspora that widens their social boundary beyond the precincts of Manipur and Mizoram. Further, a section of Mizos have established their connection with the Jews of Israel. Ideologically speaking, diasporaization of local Mizo identity in terms of a larger group migration and settlement is the other side of the politics of difference practiced in case of Naga and Assamese nationalism.

Yet another interesting manifestation of the assertion of difference is through a process of ethnic re-negotiation. Cases such as Khasis and Garos demanding separate states for themselves, of course by important politicians of both the communities, show a moment of renegotiation of their identities through a renewed sense of difference. The renegotiation between Brahmaputra valley and Barak valley in Assam in terms of mutual interdependence and appreciation is also an interesting case of renegotiation carried out by All Assam Students' Union (AASU), notably on the occasion of supporting the singer Debojit Saha who hails from Barak valley. Similarly, renegotiation between Apatanis and Nyshis, Galongs and Apatanis, Chakmas and Arunachalese tribes is noteworthy. The ethnic contest between Nagas and Noctes and Shingpos of Changlang district is also an example of defining ethnic boundaries without vertical conflicts. The presence of Nagas in Changlang district of

Arunachal Pradesh is viewed as both a source of strength as well as difference.

Within these contrary moments of renegotiation, there are temporal disjunctions between the past and present that appear as playing out the politics of difference. Post Assam election of 2006, there is a rant of ethnic Othering of the so-called immigrants. But with a significant difference from the politics of 1980s that we discussed in the foregoing, there is a simultaneous attempt at recovering a plank of internal unity as well as a move to bring greater political correctness on the question of illegal immigrants. The demand for border fencing and the suggestion for work permits for the Bengali-speaking Muslims dominate the agenda of such a drive. Also, this is a result of what analysts called a political response to the politically correct stance of the religious minorities in Assam. The articulation of a constitutional safeguard for the religious minorities of Assam was worked out in the form of Illegal Migrants Determination Tribunal (IMDT) Act 1983, that was deemed to be an outcome of minority pressure politics. With the repeal of the IMDT and with the rise of Assam United Democratic Front (AUDF), it is once again the turn of the majoritarian assertion by (AASU) for deportation of the so called 'illegal migrants' identified with the Muslims at large. This time mere suspicion is good enough to deport, albeit with the provision for 'work permits' in the hill states of the region. Given the financial dependence of the hill states on the grants from the Centre, the internal vulnerability also gets reflected in the participation of the state machinery in the anti-foreigners chorus that results in top-heavy political action against the internal minorities of the state. These suspected individuals and communities are deprived of the right to defend themselves and most often the criterion of inclusion in voters' list is put in place, although the list deletes in many a case the names of genuine Indian citizens who do not belong to the majority linguistic group.

This form of identity assertion by the majority groups is responded in many ways by their own constituents. Their participation in an agenda of fighting the Other remains limited. The call given by United Committee of Manipur to deport all outsiders from the state did not find many takers given the vertical rift between the Meteis and tribals. Similarly, AASU's all out campaign against the so-called foreigners did not find many takers. The tribes and other segments within the generic notion of Assamese identity have so far remained only alert but did not close their ranks with AASU, as it happened in 1980s. This is a moment of becoming reclusive, an inversion of the promised assimilation to various neo-Asomiya communities. In the case of Mizos, the government of Mizoram had a knee-jerk reaction in tightening the inner line permit system by asking sufficient proof of being an Indian citizen from the inhabitants of only Barak Valley, a case of ethnic Othering. Mizoram's border with Myanmar never comes into question, although it cannot be said that there is no so-called illegal immigration from Myanmar.

In a critical sense, the articulation of an identity over and against an Other as a common enemy demonizes and projects the concerns of the self in a xenophobic mode. This brings out the facile construction of an agency on one's own strength, and it gets diverted to the strategy of mobilization of the community. This diversion from defining oneself to a strategy of othering is borrowed and inherited from the politics of the nation-state that attempted to control the communities. But the limit of such a strategy lies in majoritarian ethnic assertions that does not only disarticulate the community of its historical memory and cross-cultural links, rather it borrows the perspective of the Other (be it the state, power or policy makers) that reduces the self-identity to an artifact of Othering. The agreement between the Indian state and an ethnic organization on matters of legality of citizenship decontextualizes the identity from its own roots to a certain extent. Overemphasis on land alienation and settlement by others reduces the historical and cultural context of indigeneity to a tool of governance that short-circuits the issues of agency to successful acquisition of power. In effect, the choice of self-definition and drawing of the boundary against an Other get blurred into an agenda of revenge, reconciliation and retribution, a vicious cycle that keeps rolling in every aspect of the world. Can one live with perpetual conflict with the Other? There is a reification of the community and the self, the very notions with which one describes one's identity in such antagonism towards the other. This is also a fractured space of identity that invariably fragments the concepts, institutions and values located within it.

LOOKING BEYOND LIFE-WORLDS

A significant moment in the history of the region is constituted by recalling the past that lies in distant terrains. For example, remembering that *Pusa*[7] had been a form of blackmailing that resembled taxes paid to the underground, or that there had been intimate connections between black magic and mother goddesses as a cultural form, are re-stated in order to establish a parallel between the contemporary insurgency and the existing socio-cultural practices. This is a textual overlapping between the present and the past, which also had been a canon of colonial ethnography that finds an honourable place in the contemporary historiography of the region. Modern forms of control and repression through the rituals of surrender of the militants often conducted by the army echoes the surrender of the defeated before the victor with the only difference that the surrendered are normalized in terms of mainstreaming. The clamour for peace as an instrument of good governance is often turned into a battle cry by the state.

Ethnic positioning of the self in an uneven field of struggle results into a saga of loss and victory. In the process, acts of cruelty are often justified in the name of valor and pride in one's pedigree, almost into a resounding pleasure in killing the enemy. The voyeur of such struggles does not find an easy sublimation in the events themselves, it looks for an opportunity of re-telling and reconstructing the experience. In one of the poignant pieces written on early Naga struggle against the Indian army, Kaka D. Iralu wrote:

> (…) the elderly foreign minister Isak Swu who was near death was able to escape to China while he, the young vibrant soldier, was captured by the enemies. Perhaps, it was true of soldiers when they spoke amongst themselves that there was a grey area beyond the areas of human limits into which only the most experienced of the soldiers are allowed to tread (2000: 323).

Such was the description of Naga army's sojourn to China that is recounted in this heroic and yet adventurous vein. Without any loss of its meaning, ethno-national struggles of the Nagas keep producing such narratives of battle that sublimates the voyeur into grandeur, that too in a fight against the mighty Indian state. What goes beyond the immediacy of the senses is the reconstructed landscape of the past into the vanishing present. I.M. Simon, recounting his visit to Arunachal Pradesh in the early 1950s writes:

> Although the tribesmen of Subansiri appeared to a superficial observer to be dressed and accoutred alike, there were obvious differences in the way they dressed their hair. (...) While the Nishis used to go for the thick roll tied in place with cloth or cane thongs and the Apatanis preferred a plain hair-do, the Hill Miris (who also called themselves Nishis) were one better and plaited their hair even more elaborately and seemed to feel undressed if this crown of glory was not further adorned with bear-skin! As an ultra-conservative I mourn the passing of the old ways of life, but who am I to grumble when the local people prefer what the world has to offer them today! (2006: 45)

Such a description once again speaks of a connotation of the 'hair-do' as a marker of identity, but it has undergone changes beyond recognition by the forces of modernity. Although there is a positivist cognizance of the present, it is juxtaposed against a past. This surpasses the life-world of the present in presenting a picture of the lost horizon. In quite a similar vein, Moji Riba, a young filmmaker and cultural activist of Arunachal Pradesh can be a source of concluding this piece. He cites a piece of poetry to discuss change in the context of Arunachal Pradesh:

> The rainbow is a ladder by which a god climbs from earth to meet his wife in the land of the moon. The earth and sky are lovers and all living beings are born from the union of them. Lightning is a star-maiden running across the sky (Sen, 2006: 113).

He further says, 'The poetic vibrancy of the images like these, forming an intricate part of the folklore and myths in abundance in Arunachal Pradesh, hides much of the transformations occurring at the very core of traditional society today' (Ibid.). One tends to generalize in coming to conclude that such is the way in which folklores are appropriated within the contemporary in the form of 'hiding', and probably better as a form of cultural capital that is hidden within the transformations wrought in by globalization.

Such hidden resources reappear as simulacra in the cultural logic of late capital as mere 'form' that plays the role of substitution of real by signs. The 'signifieds' as Riba says remains hidden within the new meanings of cultural artifacts and act as the source of hiding the change. Such hidden signifieds become a part of the politics of representation that goes beyond the life-world by assuming a transcendental reference outside the domain of the sensible. For example, The Mizo god Pathien in representational terms 'resides above the clouds in heaven' and He is the 'provider of rain and daily needs of man' (Miri, 2005: 30). Such a representation goes into enacting oneself as 'daughter of nature' such as the one in the Mizo tale of 'Ramenhawii' (Ibid: 51). The story goes like this:

> There was a beautiful girl called Ramenhawii who was famous for her very long hair. All the young men in the village desired her but none could win her favour. One day she was washing her hair in the river, a fish swallowed her hair. A strand of the hair found its way to the plate of the king of the valley as he was being served dinner by the palace cook. Filled with curiosity at the sight of the beautiful hair the king ordered his guards to look for the owner of the hair as he wished to make her his queen. After a long search, the guards at last found the place where the girl lived but they were unable to approach her as she lived protected by barricades around her.
> Oh! Please tell us at least your name implored the king's guards. She replied:
> 'No name, no name have I,
> I live on pure water, I live on pure vegetables'.

What the story tells us is how Ramenhawii performs a notion of 'self' different from the notion of 'self' prevalent in the society by identifying herself with pure water and pure air. In a sense, she assumes the form of the sensible as opposed to corporeal. This is a representational substitution of the real by the imaginary and the self of Ramenhawii gets substituted by way of decentring that makes it an artifact of representation. This artifact does not serve any prevalent social norm as she does not agree to the King's proposal, but merely shows up as a dream object which she confirms by way of enacting a different definition of self, that is, 'no name' to refer to herself and yet 'living' on nature. Such artifacts evolve from imaginary to symbolic when the self is enacted in a narrative of artifactuality. Discovery of such artifactual meaning of the self-identity in the case of ethnic and tribal identities of the region often ventures into a politics of representation that is not merely formal and constitutional, but it is also a reverse appropriation of the dominant, within which it can posit a different notion of performance of an agency. Such an agency takes them beyond the life-world that sustains itself from within the very life-world by way of transforming, juxtaposing and redescribing the given and the past. This is also a naturalized description of the self that encounters the other and qualifies to become an actor beyond the life-world.

Notes

1. For an articulation of such claims see Sanjoy Hazarika, 'Bangaladesh and North-East: Facing Migration, Ending Rhetoric and Embracing a Realistic Strategy for Change', in C.J. Thomas (ed.), *Engagement and Development: India's North-East and Neighbouring Countries*, New Delhi: Akansha, 2006, pp. 122–23. Also see Jairam Ramesh's statement covered in a report entitled, 'Manipur reassured on Naga Fall Out' in *The Telegraph*, Guwahati edition,1 October, 2006, wherein Ramesh says, 'What is negotiable is new political institutions and new initiatives for better economic opportunities', implying that boundaries between states of India are non-negotiable.

2. For details see, Pradip Phanjoubam, 'Manipur: fractured land', in Geeti Sen (ed.), *Where the Sun Rises When Shadows Fall: The North-East*, New Delhi: Oxford University Press, 2006, pp. 275–87.

3. Sanjoy Hazarika writes that the Bengali speakers have been resented by various linguistic and ethnic groups in Brahmaputra valley and Bengali speaking Muslims are the prime suspects. Therefore, the attribution of 'foreigner' is justifiable. Also he argues that the pressure of immigrants on land based economy as well as in the job market results in conflict between the indigenous and the settlers. He paints a larger discourse on 'the rejected peoples', 'unwanted migrants' and legal strictures on labour. See Sanjoy Hazarika, *Rites of Passage*, New Delhi: Penguin, 2000.

4. Sanjoy Hazarika writes on the Nellie massacre, '... the immigrants and every single non-tribal sitting on Tiwa land had no business to be there'. See Hazarika op.cit., p. 53.

5. We are twisting Arjun Appadurai's arguments to explain the clash between two forms like 'cellular' and 'vertebrate' as Appadurai talks of in the clash between Globalized world systems and nation-states. For details of his

290 ETHNIC LIFE-WORLDS IN NORTH-EAST INDIA

arguments, see, Arjun Appadurai, *Fear of Small Numbers: An Essay on the Geography of Anger*, Duckworth: Duke University Press, 2006.

6. We are closely following the arguments given by Rogers Burbaker in his book, *Ethnicity Without Groups*, Cambridge MA: Harvard University Press, 2004.

7. Pusa had been a form of tax in kind that used to be paid to the hill tribes during the Ahom rule in order to prevent them from raiding the foothill localities under their kingdom.

Conclusion

The exclusionary status of North-East India as a field of struggle has gone into the social, scientific and philosophical formulations about the region. The language game that is played by nationalist constructions of 'hostile' and 'alien' terrain of North-East India finds its echo in the response from the North-East as well. Such dominant constructions are matched by ethnic boundaries that are historically and culturally formed by communities themselves, as if mimicking the nationalist distancing of the East and the North-East. This hermeneutic strategy applies to the discursive representation of the self, a marker of state-society relations in the context of the North-East. One can account for this hermeneutic shift of subjectivity of the social identities by taking into account how the North-East is treated as an Other of India.

Life-worlds of various communities present a dialectic between the self and the Other. The dialectic is concretized in a few foundational binary oppositions such as native and nation, civic and ethnic, underground and overground, and so on. Such oppositions are sustained by a structure of correspondence between the self and the Other without presenting a possibility of transformation. As an example of embeddedness of such a dialectic, one could locate in the language (*i*) the pre-ontic murmur, (*ii*) prior contact with the Other, and (*iii*) transformation of the natural world in interpretative uses of language. But such a combined functioning of what we call embeddedness in language is based on the condition of operation of practices, in terms of how language accesses these practices. Access to these practices does not happen as something prior to language that lies out there in the world but as an available representation of a concept, which is accessed in language to exhibit the original intentional experiences that present the referent instantiating the concept. This assumes the knowledge of conditions of assertibility by which the application of a concept would either be true or false. Such knowledge occurs in the specific context of a community that anthropologists establish through an intuitive knowledge of the Other. The radical alterity of the Other, which is the subject without alterity, appears with differentiating, non-relational and non-universal generality that produces discrete notions and concepts within culture, the value of which is contingent and undecidable. Embeddedness within language as a global notion becomes effective here without decidable and determinable value content, which makes the anthropologists' ascription of 'Otherness' possible. It is this ascribed Otherness, from the point of view of ethnography's bare particulars, to a Khasi or an Apatani that a simultaneous assumption of stability of the subject in language and iterability of subject of language is constituted. Nevertheless this anthropological rationality cannot answer the question: whose product is language? The question makes possible an internal realism about their belief, while making it open to an externalist interpretation, thus shedding the position of the anthropological-ethnographic subject. Our attempt here is to recuperate the lost subjects in their own narrative that access their world. These are descriptions about the world that fit their linguistically-embedded world to provide them access to that world, that which further instantiates for the whole set of anthropologists and ethnographers the 'reality' of their world. But this world is the discrete, non-relational world that only provides a non-universal generality of constitution of the subject. The ethnographic-anthropological bias lies in a juridical autonomy to construct their discursive subjects, as if such subjects are constituted by and in rules guiding their practices. Such subjects remain open to deconstruction of their assumed stability, rather they do not represent the truth of their lives by presenting them as mere candidates in a story of life. In case of assertion by smaller ethnic identities, it is not just repositioning themselves as ethnic elites, but it is also re-articulation against the dominant. Moving beyond affiliation, it sets a domain of articulation, a way to meet demands of democratization. Those who lose their non-representative power see it as an attempt of the 'Others' to reposition themselves. Therefore, they respond from a carefully designed strategy of ensuring their own power. The fear is that, if once given in, there will be other such occasions of those who had hitherto remained away from such assertions raising their voices. There is an expressed helplessness on such occasions from the rulers that be. It is at this moment that re-invoking old faultlines is blended and blurred by new alignments and break-offs become a strategy of maintaining a potentially collapsing ideological hegemony.

The dominant social group 'satisfies' its political access and power at the cost of other social groups by playing a politics of marginalizing them and keeping them out of equal access to power and resources. As a result, the dissatisfied social groups are frustrated and feel (more and more) marginalized and excluded from social, economic and political participation. In the context of a peace process, such dissatisfied groups clamour for their specific rights, but such clamours are delegitimized as suspects as they question the dominant distribution of power and resources. In other words, clamour against political and economic inequality could be ideologically suppressed by the dominant and this is what acts as the counterproductive mechanism in disarticulating the very peace process that is initiated in a given situation. Apart from such 'peace regime' types, the knowledge of peace assumes a distinct historical and cultural form. The knowledge is constituted phenomenologically by way of bracketing the non-textual connections with ground reality, which almost borders on an unrecognized ethnography of peoples of the region. Knowledge from such an ethnographic context holds the secrets of many an ethnic conflict, which peace regimes overlook. This produces a paradox: the more democratic a state is and the more accommodative to specific claims of communities and ethnicities, the more belligerent it is in establishing a peace regime. Another paradox is that the more a state has a history of inflicting trauma on dissenters and the more it practices norms of democracy, it is more likely that it is more aggressive in peacekeeping. The crux of such paradoxes lies in the identity of the actors in double playing the internal dichotomies of a regime type such that one side of the dichotomy invariably calls for the other side. Cases from North-East India present a host of such peace regimes with associated support structures. Dialogues with the Naga underground suggest a peace regime based on 'suspect strategy', where key issues of political sovereignty and territorial integration are treated as suspect grounds for the sole purpose of suspension of troublesome contexts. On issues like rights of the migrants and refugees in Assam, Arunachal and Tripura, the peace regimes advocated by the dominant communities and the state assume the character of 'deligitimization of suspects'. Within the larger democratic and liberal set up of the Indian state, such a deligitimization of suspects ironically gives rise to a legitimating legal principle that contradicts the normative aspects of justice and fairness. Regimes of this type construe embodiment of illegality on others and legality on the self. In the case of territorial autonomy, the peace regime becomes appropriationist as it necessarily subsumes the Other. Further insurgencies grow out of a historical consciousness of questioning the appropriationist discourse of subordination and subsumption under the political, cultural and legal framework of the state and the capital that attempts to introduce legitimate forms of structural relations of appropriation. The questioning takes the form of resistance and counter appropriation. It builds up a logic of critique of the structure: the way structure develops into a mechanism of extraction of surplus by way of negating the role of the sovereign, as the 'subject' is reversed into a field of struggle that either tries to change it or appropriate it. To put it formally, governance in North-East India does not depend upon civil society alone, but it needs the consent of the underground in some form or the other. Two questions are imminent here: one, does the subjugated nationality or people somehow become the collaborator to subjugation? two, do the insurgents themselves become another consensus building hegemony in their own strength? In both cases, insurgents come to a parity of strength with the state, but such insurgencies see themselves as contingent only in advancing and achieving the end. The ends of insurgencies are constituted by a combination of ideological and political components: ideological, in so far as it resists the dominant ideology; and political, in so far as it aspires for self-determination. The ideological component expresses itself in the form of an alternative nationalism, a kind of 'non-state nationalism', while political aspirations for self-determination not only mean state power but full decision-making capacities in social, economic and cultural aspects of life. The political component derives its strength by countering the interventionist strategies of the state and devising a path of 'development' open to the needs of the community. Such positions of insurgency draw the communities of the region into their fold as there is not much of a democratic space between state and the civil/political society to negotiate the claims of redistribution and recognition. In the absence of such a space, what happens is that state tries to mediate between contesting claims of identity and demand for share of resources without strengthening the communities. Put in another way, the actors of various movements are looked upon as people to be won over, without placing them in the context of decision-making, as also the political achievement of such movements are either benumbed or capitalized by the state machinery for its own ends.

References

Adorno, Theodor W. 1974. *Minima Moralia: Reflection from Damaged Life* (translated by E.F.N. Jephcott). London: New Left Books.

Ahmed, Fazal Ali. 2002. *Asomor Jatiya Sanghatit Ajan Fakir* (Assamese). Guwahati: Nandan Prakashan.

Ahmed, Rafiul and Prasenjit Biswas. 2004. *Political Economy of Underdevelopment of North-East India.* Delhi: Akansha.

Akoijam, A. Bimol. 2006. 'Towards A Wholesome Holistic Self: On Silence, Identity and Coloniality of the Postcolonial', First Arambam Somorendra Memorial Lecture. Imphal: Arambam Somorendra Trust: ix

ABSU. 1987. *Why Separate State.* Pamphlet Kokrajhar: All Bodo Students' Union.

ADB. 2003. *Assam Governance and Public Resource management Programme, India.* Manila: Country Strategy and Programme 2003–06, Asian Development Bank.

AIPRF. 1996. *Symphony of Freedom: Papers on Nationality Question.* New Delhi: All India People's Resistance Forum.

Allen, B.C., F.A. Gait, C.G.H. Allen and H.F. Howard. 1889. *The Provinicial Gazetteer of Eastern Bengal and Assam.* Calcutta: Government of India.

Anderson, Benedict. 1983. *Imagined Communities.* London: Verso, Duke University Press.

———. 1991. *Imagined Communities: Reflections on the Origin and Spread of Nationalism,* (revised edition). London: Verso.

Anonymous. n.d. *Mizo Inchei Dan.*

Appadurai, Arjun. 2006. *Fear of Small Numbers: An Essay on the Geography of Anger.* Duckworth: Duke University Press.

Atem, V.S. 1998. Interview, *The N-E Sun,* 1–14 March.

Avineri, Sholmo. 1968. *The Social and Political Thought of Karl Marx.* Cambridge: Cambridge University Press.

Balibar, Etienne. 1990. 'The Nation Form: History and Ideology', *Review,* 13 (3: Summer): 329–61.

Barbora, Sanjay. 2006 'Rethinking India's Counter-Insurgency Campaign in North-East', *Economic and Political Weekly,* 11 (35): 3805–812.

Baruah, Apurba Kumar. 1985. 'Regionalism and Student Power in Assam', in K.M. Deka (ed.), *Nationalism and Regionalism in North-East India.* Dibrugarh: Dibrugarh University.

Baruah, Apurba Kumar. 1991. *Social Tensions in Assam: Middle Class Politics*. Guwahati: Purbanchal Prakash.

Berger, Peter L. and Thomas Luckmann. 1966. *The Social Construction of Reality: A Treatise on the Sociology of Knowledge*. Garden City, NY: Doubleday.

Bhuyan, Ajit Kumar. 1991. *A Report on Human Rights Violation and State Terrorism in Assam*. Guwahati: Manab Adhikar Suraksha Samiti.

———. 1996. 'Flames of Freedom Still Burning: A probe into the National Question in India', in All India Peoples Resistance Forum, *Symphony of Freedom: Papers on Nationality Question*.

Biswas, Prasenjit. 1996. 'Ethnophilosophy: Politics of Culture in North-East India', in M.M. Agrawal (ed.), *Ethnicity, Culture and Nationalism in North-East India*. New Delhi: Indus.

———. 2005. 'Politics of Recognition in North East India', *North East India Studies*, 1(1): 93–96.

———. 2007. 'Between State and Ethnography: A Paradigm for Everyday', *Man and Society: A Journal of North East Studies*, iv (Spring): 112–13.

Biswas, Prasenjit and Sukalpa Bhattacharjee. 2001. 'The Outsider, the State and Nations from Below: North East India as a Subject of Exclusion', in Kousar Azam (ed.) *Ethnicity, Identity and the State in South Asia*. New Delhi: South Asian Publishers.

Bordoloi, Lachit. 2001. *Atmaniyantran aru Ganobhotor Prastab* (Assamese). Guwahati: Uttaran Prakashan.

Brown, Wendy. 1993 'Wounded Attachment', *Political Theory*, 21(3): 390–410.

Burbaker, Rogers. 2004. *Ethnicity Without Groups*. Cambridge MA: Harvard University Press.

Butola, B.S. 1996. 'Sublimation of Identities in the North-Eastern Region of India', *Proceedings of North East India History Association*, Sixteenth Session, 3–5 December 1995. Shillong: North East India History Association.

Cabral, Amilcar. 1970. *National Liberation and Culture*, Occasional Paper no. 57. New York: Maxwell Graduate School, University of Syracuse.

Campbell, Aidan. 1997. 'Ethical Ethnicity: A Critique', *Journal of Modern African Studies*, 35(1): 53–79.

Caroll, John B. and Benjamin Lee Whorf (ed.). 1964. *Language, Thought and Reality: Selected Writings*. Cambridge, MA: MIT Press.

Castells, Manuel. 1996–1998. *The Information Age: Economy, Society, Culture*. 3 Vols. Oxford: Basil Blackwell.

Chandra, Sudhir. 1992. 'Defining the Nation', in *The Oppressive Present: Literature and Social Consciousness in Colonial India*. Delhi: Oxford University Press.

Chatterjee, Partha. 1994. 'Claims on the Past: The Genealogy of Modern Historiography in Bengal', in David Arnold and David Hardiman (ed.), *Subaltern Studies*. Vol. 8. Delhi: Oxford University Press.

Chattaopadhaya, Partha and Gautam Bhadra (ed.). 2001. *Nimnabarger Itihas* (Bengali). Kolkata: Ananda Publishers.

Cohen, Josh. 2003. *Interrupting Auschwitz: Art, Religion, Philosophy*. London: Continuum.

Connoly, William. 1991. *Identity/Difference: Democratic Negotiations of Political Paradox*. Ithaca, NY: Cornell University Press.

Connor, Walker. 1994. *Ethnonationalism: The Quest for Understanding*. New Jersy: Princeton University Press.

Das, Parag Kumar. 1993. *Swadhinatar Prastab* (Pamphlet in Assamese). Guwahati: Seuj Sathirtha Prakashan.

Datta P.S., (ed.). 1990. *Ethnic Movements in Poly-Cultural Assam*. New Delhi: Vikas.

———. 1993. *Autonomy Movements in Assam* (Documents). New Delhi: Omsons Publications.

Davidson, Donald. 1984. 'The Inscrutability of Reference', in *Inquiries into Truth and Interpretation*. Oxford: Clarendon Press.

Deleuze, Giles and F. Gauttari. 1986. *Kafka: Toward a Minor Literature*. Minneapolis: Minnesota University Press.

Elwin, Verrier. 1958. *Myths of the North-East Frontier of India*. Shillong: Directorate of Research, North East Frontier Agency.

———. 1959. *A Philosophy for NEFA, North-East Frontier Agency*. Shillong: North East Frontier Agency, Research Department.

———. 1961. *Nagaland*. Shillong: Government of Assam, Research Department Publications.

———. 1965. *Democracy in NEFA*. Shillong: North-East Frontier Agency.

———. 1970. *A New Book of Tribal Fiction*. Shillong: North East Frontier Agency, Research Department.

———. 1986. *The Arts and Crafts of Nagaland*. Kohima: Naga Institute of Culture.

———. 1991. *A New Book of Tribal Fiction*. (Reprint). Itanagar: Government of Arunachal Pradesh, Directorate of Research.

Fanon, Frantz. 1963. *Wrteched of the Earth*. New York: Grove Weidenfield.

Favell, Adrian. 1999. 'To Belong or not to Belong: the Transnational Question', in Andrew Geddes and Adrian Favell (eds), *The Politics of Belonging: Migrants and Minorities in Contemporary Europe*. Aldershot: Ashgate/ICCR.

Foucault, Michel. 1982. Afterword', in Paul Rabinow and Hubert Dreyfus (eds), *Beyond Structuralism and Hermeneutics*. Chicago: University of Chicago Press.

Geertz, Clifford. 1993. *The Interpretation of Culture*. (Reprint). New York: Fontana Press.

Gellner, Ernest. 1995. 'The Importance of Being Modular', in John Hall (ed.), *Civil Society: Theory, History, Comparison*. Cambridge: Basil Blackwell.

Giddens, Anthony. 1991. *Modernity and Self-Identity*. London: Polity Press.

Gohain, Hiren. 1995. 'Deshodrohi Kon?' in *Tejor Akhore Likha*. (Assamese) Guwahati: Lawyers.

Goodman, Nelson. 1978. *Ways of Worldmaking*. Indianapolis IN: Hackett.

Goodman, Nelson and Catherine Z. Elgin. 1988. *Reconceptions in Philosophy and Other Arts and Sciences*. Indianapolis IN: Hackett.

Gopal, S. (ed.). 1983. *Jawaharlal Nehru: An Anthology*. Delhi: Oxford University Press.

Habermas, Jürgen. 1987. *Theory of Communicative Action*. Vol. 2. London: Polity Press.

Haimendorf, Christophe von Furer. 1974. *Return to the Naked Nagas: An Anthropologist's View of Nagaland 1936–70*. Delhi: Vikas.

Hazarika, Sanjoy. 1994. *Strangers of the Mist: Tales of War and Peace from India's North East*. New Delhi: Penguin.

———. Hazarika, Sanjoy. 2000. *Rites of Passage*. New Delhi: Penguin India.

———. 2006. 'Bangaladesh and North-East: Facing Migration, Ending Rhetoric and Embracing a Realistic Strategy for Change', in C.J. Thomas (ed.) *Engagement and Development: India's North-East and Neighbouring Countries*. New Delhi: Akansha.

Hobswam, Eric. 1992. *Nation and Nationalism Since 1780*. Cambridge: Cambridge University Press.

Horowitz, Donald. 1983. *Ethnic Groups in Conflict*. Berkeley, CA: University of California Press.

Hooghe, Liesbbet. 1997. 'Nationalist Movements and Social Factors: A Theoretical Perspective', in John Coakley (ed.), *The Social Origins of Nationalim*. London: Sage Publications.

Hutton, J. H. 1921. *The Angami Nagas*. London: Macmillan and Co. limited.

———. 1986. *Report on Naga Hills*. Delhi: Mittal Publications. (Originally published in 1932 as *Notes on two Unadministered Districts of Naga Hills*, Calcutta Home Department).

Imchen, Lima. 1996. 'Politics of Tribal Identity and Interpretative Monopolies', Paper presented in a seminar on Dynamics of Identity and Intergroup in North-East India from 12–14 November Shimla: IIAS.

International Working Group on Indigenous Peoples Yearbook, 1998. Copenhagen: United Nations Publications.

Iralu, Kaka D. 2000. *Nagaland and India: The Blood and the Tears*. Kohima: N.V. Press.

Jacobs, Julian (ed.). 1990. *The Nagas: Society, Culture and Colonial Encounter*. Cambridge: Cambridge University Press.

Jameson, Fredric. 1992. *The Novel as the Political Unconscious*. New York: Routledge.

Kamuf, Peggy. 1991. 'Reading between the Blinds', in Peggy Kamuf (ed.), *A Derrida Reader: Between the Blinds*. New York: Columbia University Press.

Kani, Takhe. 1996. *Socio-Religious Ceremonies of the Apatanis of Arunachal Pradesh*. Itanagar: Frontier Publication.

Kant, Immanuel. 1956. *Critique of Pure Reason* (2nd edition; trnaslated by Norman K.Smith). New York: St. Martin's Press.

Kaviraj, Sudipta. 1994. 'Crisis of the Nation State in India', *Political Studies*, 42 (Special issue).

Lefort, Claude. 1988. 'The Question of Democracy', in *Democracy and Political Theory*. Cambridge, MA: MIT Press.

Lentricchiaa, Frank. 1982. *Reading Foucault (Punishment, Labour, Resistance)* Part Two, *Raritan*, 2:1

Lewis, David. 1973. *Counterfacturals*. Cambridge, MA: Harvard University Press.

Loyd, J. Meirion. 1991. *History of the Church in Mizoram*. Aizawl: Synod Publication Board.

Lyngdoh, Morning. 1991. *The Concept of Virtue in the Khasi World View*. Unpublished Ph.D. Dissertation. Shillong: North Eastern Hill University.

Mackenzie, Alexander. 1979. *The North-East Frontier of India* (Reprint). Delhi: Mittal Publishing House. Originally published in 1884 as *A History of the Relationship of the Government with the Hill tribes of North East Frontier of Bengal*. Calcutta: Department of Home.

Mahanta, Harin. 1994a. *Amar Hiyat Kiyo Jwaliche Jui?* (Pamphlet in Assamese). Jorhat: Seuj Satirtha Prakashan.

———. 1994b. 'Chhabishe January Akal Natun Delhir Babe Sristhi' (Assamese), in *Sadin*, 28 January.

Manifesto of the National Socialist Council of Nagaland. 1987. Oking: NSCN.

Meetei, M.C. Birla. 1996 'Anti-Merger Movement', *N-E Sun,* 14 November.

Mignolo, Walter. 2000. *Local Histories/Global Designs: Coloniality, Subaltern Knowledges and Border Thinking*. New Jersy: Princeton University Press.

Mills, J.P. 1926. *The Ao Nagas*. London: Macmillan and Co.

Miri, Mrinal. 1997. 'Of Fusions, Alliances and Isolation', in *Grassroot Options*, bi-monthly published from Shillong, June–July: 49–51.

———. 2003. 'Identity, Tribesman and Development', in *Identity and Moral Life*. New Delhi: Oxford University Press.

Miri, Sujata. 1988. *Khasi World View: A Conceptual Exploration*. Chandigarh: Centre for Regional and Rural Development.

———. 2005. *A Book of Paintings: Themes from the Hills of North-East India*. New Delhi: Mittal Publications.

Mishra, P.K. 2003. 'J.H. Hutton and the North-East', in T.B. Subba and G.C. Ghosh (eds), *The Anthropology of North-East India*. Hyderabad: Orient Longman.

Misra, Udayon. 1983 .'Naga Nationalism and the Role of Middle Class', in B. Datta Ray (ed.), *The Emergence and the Role of Middle Class in North East India*. Delhi: Uppal Publishing House.

———. 2000. 'The Quest for Swadhin Asom' in *The Periphery Strikes Back* Shimla: Indian Institute of Advanced Study.

———. 2001. *The Transformation of Assamese Identity: A Historical Survey*. Shillong: North East India History Association.

Mukhim, Patricia. 1996. 'Conflict and its Resolution: A Case Study of a Modern Tribal Situation', in M.M. Agrawal (ed.), *Ethnicity, Culture and Nationalism in North-East India*. Delhi: Indus.

Nag, Sajal. 1993. 'Multiplication of Nations: Political Economy of Sub-Nationalism', *Economic and Political Weekly,* 28(29 and 30): 1521–32.

Nehru, Jawaharlal. 1946. *The Discovery of India*. Calcutta: Signet Press.

———. 1957. 'Foreword', in Verrier Elwin's *A Philosophy for NEFA*. Shillong: North East Frontier Agency.

———. 1973. 'The Tribal Folk', Speech Delivered at the Opening Session of the Scheduled Tribes and Scheduled Areas Conference in New Delhi, 1952, published in *The Tribal People of India*. Delhi: Government of India, Publications' Division.

————. 1986. *Letters to Chief Ministers*, Vol.1. Delhi: Government of India, Publications Division.

————. 1989. 'The Tribal People: Need for Love and Protection', in *Nehru and the North East*. Aizwal: North Eastern Hill University Publications.

Nora, Pierre (ed.). *Realms of Memory: The Construction of the French Past*, Vol. 1, *Conflicts and Divisions*, (translated by A. Goldhammer). New York: Columbia University Press.

Omvedt, Gail. 1993. 'Social Movement and the Demand for Autonomy' (mimeo). NERC Special Lecture Series 3. Shillong: ICSSR, North Eastern Regional Centre.

Pakem, B. 1995. 'Politics of Identity, Conflict and Nation-Building in North-East India'. Unpublished paper. Dibrugarh University: Department of Political Science.

————. 1996. 'Inaugural Address', in M.M. Agrawal (ed.), *Ethnicity, Culture and Nationalism in North-East India*. Delhi: Indus.

Phanjoubam, Pradip. 2006. 'Manipur: Fractured Land', in Geeti Sen (ed.), *Where the Sun Rises When Shadows Fall: The North-East*. New Delhi: Oxford University Press.

Phukon, Girin. 1985. 'Ethnic Nationalism in North-East India: Overview of its Legacy', in K.M. Deka (ed.), *Nationalism and Regionalism in North-East India*. Dibrugarh: Dibrugarh University.

Puthenpurakal, J. (ed.) 1996. *Impact of Christianity on North East India*. Shillong: Vendrame Institute Publications.

Rev. Lalsawma, 1994. *Four Decades of Revivals: The Mizo Way*. Aizwal: Self-published.

Roy Burman, B.K. 'Land and Forest Rights', *Seminar*, 366: pp. 25–29.

Reid, Robert. 1983. *History of the Frontier Areas Bordering on Assam* (Reprint). Delhi: Eastern Publishing House. (Originally published in 1942 as *History of Frontier Areas Bordering on Assam*, Shillong: Government Press.)

Rupacahandra,Yumnam. 1997. 'Kuki-Paite Clash', *NE-Sun*, 15–31 July.

Sachdeva, Gulsan. 2000. *Economy of the North East: Policy, Present Conditions and Future Possibilities*. Delhi: Konark Press.

Sadin (Assamese). 1998. 10 (18): 1, 22, 17 July.

Satirth, Sachetan. 1996. 'The Nationality Question in the North-East', in AIPRF, *Symphony of Freedom: Papers on Nationality Question*, pp. 163–70 Delhi: All India People's Resistance Forum.

Schmitt, Carl. 1996. *The Concept of the Political* (translated by George D. Schwab). Chicago: University of Chicago Press.

Schutz, Alfred.1989. *The Structures of Life-World*. 2 Vols. Evanston: North Western University Press.

Sen, Geeti (ed.). 2006 . *Where the Sun Rises When the Shadows Fall: The North East*. New Delhi: Oxford University Press.

Shepoumaramth Regional Church Bulletin. 1995. Reprinted in *The Shepoumaramth in the Naga National Movement*. Shepoumaramth: Government of the People's Republic of Nagaland.

Simon, I.M. 2006. 'Arunachal Reminiscences', in *Reminiscence: Lest We Forget*. Shillong: Arunachal Pradesh Pensioners' Welfare Association.

Singh, B.P. 1987. *The Problem of Change: A Study of North-East India*. Delhi: Oxford University Press.

Smith, Anthony D. 1993. 'The Ethnic Sources of Nationalism', *Survival*, 35(1): 48–52.

Swain, Nirmal Kumar. 1996. 'The Post-Colonial Indian State: A Paradigm for Identities', in M.M. Agrawal (ed.), *Ethnicity, Culture and Nationalism in North-East India*. Delhi: Indus.

Teitelbaum, Michael S. and Jay Winter. 1998. *A Question of Numbers: High Migration, Low Fertility, and the Politics of National Identity*. New York: Hill and Wang.

The N-E Sun. 1997. 'Isak Chisi Swu's Speech', 1–14 April.

———. 1997. 'We Discourage Communal Violence: Interview with Meiraba Luwang', 1–14 July.

The Telegraph. 2006. 'US Plans Asian Power Pipeline', 28 April (Guwahati, edition).

———. 2006. 'Manipur Reassured on Naga Fall Out', 1 October (Guwahati edition).

Thiong'o, Ngugi wa. 1993. *Moving the Centre: The Struggle for Cultural Freedoms*. Oxford: James Currey.

Ugresic, Dubravka. 1998. *The Culture of Lies*. London: Phoenix House.

ULFA. 1991. Press Release on the Eve of 1991 Parliament and Assembly Elections in Assam. *The Assam Tribune* (Guwahati), 25 April.

ULFA. 1996a. Statement at the All India Peoples' Resistance Forum's International Seminar, New Delhi, 16–19 February.

ULFA. 1996b. 'National Question In Assam', in AIPRF, *Symphony of Freedom: Papers on Nationality Question*, pp. 151–55. New Delhi: All India People's Resistance Forum.

ULFA. n.d. *History of Assam* (pamphlet).

Williams, Bernard. 1990. 'Politics and Moral Character', in *Moral Luck*. Cambridge: Cambridge University Press.

Index

About the Authors

Prasenjit Biswas is Reader in the Department of Philosophy at the North Eastern Hill University, Shillong, Meghalaya. A Ph.D. in Philosophy from the North Eastern Hill University, he has been Reader, Assam University, Silchar (2004–05); Assistant Professor in the Department of Philosophy at the Indian Institute of Guwahati, Guwahati (2003–04); Senior Lecturer in Philosophy at the Indian Institute of Technology, Mumbai (2001–03); and Lecturer at the Indian School of Mines, Dhanbad (1998–2001).

He has authored *The Post-modern Controversy: Understanding Richard Rorty, Jacques Derrida and Jürgen Habermas* (Rawat, 2004) and co-authored *Political Economy of Underdevelopment in North-East India* (Akansha, 2004). He has co-edited *Peace in India's Northeast: Meaning, Metaphor and Method* (ICSSR-NERC and Regency, 2006). He has also published a number of papers in journals and contributed chapters to edited books.

Chandan Suklabaidya is Assistant Teacher of Biology at the Town High School in Silchar, Assam. He has conducted extensive fieldwork studies on Hmar, Ao and Ahom villages and on the tea garden diaspora of Assam. He is currently in the process of collating these field notes into two manuscripts entitled *Autobiography of Hmarkhawlien: A First Person Essay* and *Ahom Death Rituals: Observations on Select Villages of Upper Assam.* He has presented papers on the subjects in national and international conferences.

A Dalit activist, he has written a volume of poems and collected oral literature from the untouchables in Assam's southern districts. A nature lover, he has also discovered tree fossils in Lakhipur and the North Cachar Hills.